MW00399768

THE ESSENTIAL GREEK HANDBOOK

An A–Z Phrasal Guide to Almost Everything
You Might Want to Know About Greece

BY

TOM STONE

HIPPOCRENE BOOKS
New York

To
Samantha and Oliver
from their father,
with love

For information, address:
HIPPOCRENE BOOKS, INC.
171 Madison Avenue
New York, NY 10016

Cataloging-in-Publication Data available from the Library of
Congress.

ISBN 0-7818-0668-2

Printed in the United States of America.

CONTENTS

AUTHOR'S NOTE

The basic form of this book is alphabetical: one finds the word, phrase or information one wants by looking it up as in a dictionary.

However, there are certain words and phrases which seem to be more conveniently listed together under categories rather than in their separate alphabetical order. In the ENGLISH-GREEK DICTIONARY, verbs and their tenses, for instance, are listed under the infinitive, and, in the SPECIAL CATEGORIES section, medical and pharmaceutical terms, as well as parts of the body are to be found under DOCTOR while terms of endearment, as well as advice on their consequences, under LOVE.

Greek words spelled in Greek script have not, for the most part, been included—first because the space saved allows for the inclusion of many more words in English and phonetic Greek, and second, because it is the author's belief that people not familiar with Greek will only be intimidated, not helped, by the strangeness of its script.

However, in PART 1, there is a brief and easy outline of Greek sentence patterns to help you to construct your own phrases, although it should be pointed out that no matter what you do, you are going to make mistakes. This is unimportant. No one, least of all the Greeks, expects people on a brief visit to the country to be able to speak perfect Greek, and it is not the intention of this book to go into the intricacies of the language. Pidgin Greek would be more like it. And the Greeks will like it. Any effort on your part to speak even a few words will be as cherished by them as if pearls had dropped from your mouth. So, go to it.

PREFACE TO THE SECOND EDITION

In the spring of 1976, when my wife and I were living and painting and writing in splendid isolation in a farming valley on the remote island of Patmos, we were astonished one warm March afternoon to see a tourist floating towards us on the road leading down to the beach from the village above. She was dressed in a blue-and-lavender sari which wafted behind her in the breeze, was deeply tanned, with a head of curly blond hair and a smile as bright as a Pepsodent advertisement. Her name, we learned, was Bettina. She was German, in her early forties, and spoke perfect English. With her she was carrying two of the best phrasebooks then available, one German-Greek and the other English-Greek. Well-prepared, she was there to rent an inexpensive house, preferably in our valley, and enjoy the island and its natives for the month that remained before Easter, Greek and Western, when the first of the season's holiday hordes would descend upon us.

She did find a house in the valley and we became good friends, but for the most part she left us considerately alone. Eventually (and some might say "inevitably") she began an affair with a handsome Greek fisherman, a lovely boy named Andonis, who was about half her age and spoke not a word of any foreign language. For a while we saw even less of Bettina than before as she went out fishing with Andonis during the day and dancing with him at night. But then one morning she came trekking across the half-mile of rock-strewn fields and low stone walls that separated our houses, apologized profusely for bothering us and then took out a notebook in which she had written a number of English phrases that she needed translated into Greek, phrases that were not even approximated or apparently considered important in either of the books she had brought with her.

During the weeks that followed, as the love affair between her and Adonis waxed and waned, she came for more and more phrases, and by the time two of them parted just after Easter, she had quite a supply in her notebook. As she was leaving, I asked her to photocopy these for me when she returned to Germany. I promised her that one day I would use them as the basis for a phrasebook I would write for

9

people like her who might come to Greece and, if they didn't fall in love, at least want to communicate something more than when they'd like their clothing dry cleaned.

When Bettina sent me the photocopied pages and I spread them out before me in chronological order, they were almost a love story in themselves:

"Isn't the moon beautiful?" went one of the first phrases.

"Why are you late?" came another somewhere just past the middle.

And, at the end: "I'm free, you're free."

So this book is dedicated to Bettina and people like her. To all of us, in fact.

PART 1
INSTANT GREEK GRAMMAR

I n order for the examples in the following section to be clearly understood, it is necessary to first explain the phonetic system developed for this book.

PHONETICS

One of the most important aspects of the Greek language is the placing of stress on the correct syllable. Placed on the wrong syllable, it can possibly change the entire meaning of the word, sometimes with disastrous results, as in the following (where **the accented syllable is in bold-face type**):

line or queue	oo**ra**
urine	**oo**ra

That aside, the pronunciation of Greek is relatively easy for an English-speaking person since all of the vowel and most of the consonant sounds are to be found in English.

As in English, there are two "th" sounds, and these are transliterated phonetically in this book as follows:

"th" as in "theater": "th" (i.e. "**theh**-atro)
"th" as in "those": "dh" (i.e. "**dhee**eta"—"diet")

The latter is used when the letter δ (capital Δ) is employed, while the former substitutes for the letter θ (capital Θ).

There are some consonant sounds which are virtually impossible to adequately transliterate phonetically. They are as follows:

g (γ)	When followed by an "a" or "o" it is pronounced as in "ghost" but with the "h" clearly aspirated.
ps (ψ)	As in "lips" with the "p" clearly pronounced, even at the beginning of a word.
h (η)	Heavily aspirated, as in "hew" as opposed to "how."

11

Key to Pronunciation: dh = then; **th** = thin; **a** = father; **e** = end; **ee** = meet; **i** = kiwi; **o** = go; **oo** = moon; **ou** = you; **oy** = boy; **ay** = say; **y** = yes.

STRESS ITALICIZED SYLLABLES.

WORD ORDER

With a few exceptions, the basic pattern of Greek phrases and sentences is much the same as in English and can be relatively easy to manage, as the following example will indicate:

Mary drinks coffee with milk and sugar. Ee Mar*ee*a pee*nee* ka*feh* meh *ga*la kay *za*haree.

The three major exceptions are as follows:

1) Pronouns that are the subjects of sentences are rarely used, as the form of the verb indicates what the subject is: **I want coffee. The**lo ka**feh.**
2) Pronouns that are objects of verbs precede the verb: **I want it.** Toh **the**lo.
3) Possessive pronouns follow the noun they possess: **my coffee** toh ka**feh** mou (lit. "the coffee my").

NOUNS

All nouns have three genders: masculine, feminine, and neuter. Articles and adjectives precede the noun and must conform to its gender. Personal names are also preceded by articles, but only when the person is being spoken about, not when he or she is being spoken to:

Where is Mary?	Poo *ee*nay ee Mar*ee*a?
Hello, Mary!	Ya*soo*, Mar*ee*a!

PERSONAL PRONOUNS

As noted above, since the form of the verb indicates its person, personal pronouns are rarely used as subjects except for emphasis:

Mary's hungry.	Ee Mar*ee*a pee*naee*.
She's hungry.	Pee*naee*.
She's hungry again?!	Af*tee* pee*naee* pah*lee*?!

There are two **verb forms** for "**you**": one is singular and familiar, being usually used only with friends and close acquaintances; the second is plural (for a number of people) or singular formal (used when speaking to someone you don't know very well or as sign of respect to special or older people).

What do you want?   Tee **thele**es? (singular, familiar)

                                Tee **thele**teh? (plural or formal)

VERBS

These change their forms according to which person (1st, 2nd, 3rd) they are in. The **negative** is formed by putting "dhen" (i.e "not") before the verb:

Mary isn't hungry.   Ee Mare**e**a dhen peena**ee**.

The **future tense** is formed by putting "tha" before the infinitive tense of the verb:

She will be hungry.   Tha peena**ee**.

I will not be hungry.   Dhen tha peena**o**.

ADVERBS

These follow the verb and are often formed by substituting an "a" ending in an adjective, as we often add "ly":

complete   o**lok**lero

completely   o**lok**lera

INFINITIVES

Often, but not always, formed by adding "na" to the indefinite tense of the verb according to its person:

I want to eat.   **Thel**o na f**a**o.

She wants to eat.   **Thel**ee na f**a**ee.

Certain verbs, however, change their forms when put into the infinitive and future tenses, others do not. Don't worry about it. You will be understood.

DIRECT & INDIRECT OBJECTS

As nouns, these follow the verb:

Peter gave Mary a lamb.	Oh **Pet**ros **eh**doseh stee Ma**ree**a **en**a ar**nee.**

As pronouns, they precede the verb:

Peter gave it to her.	Oh **Pet**ros tees (*her*) toh (*it*) **eh**dooseh.

POSSESSIVES

These follow the object possessed, the object being preceded by its definite article "the":

Peter's lamb	Toh ar**nee** tou **Pet**rou
His lamb	Toh ar**nee** tou
Mary's lamb	Toh ar**nee** tees Ma**ree**as
Her lamb	Toh ar**nee** tees

But:

It was his, now it's hers.	**Ee**tahn dhee**ko** tou, to**rah** **ee**nay dhee**ko** tees.

Finally, most (but not all) nouns have an extra stress added to the last syllable when put into the possessive with a pronoun:

the car	toh afto**kee**ni**toh**
my car	toh afto**kee**ni**toh** mou

CONJUNCTIONS

Used exactly as in English:

Mary bought peas and potatoes.	Ee Ma**ree**a ah**go**raseh beeze**li**a kay pata**tess.**

PREPOSITIONS

Certain prepositions, such as "with" (**meh**) and "like" (**sahn**) are used exactly as in English; others, such as "to," "at" and "in" change their form according to the gender and number of their objects. Consequently these are impossible for a beginner to even bother about learning.

PAST TENSES, GERUNDS, GENITIVES, ACCUSATIVE CASES, ETC.

See a real book of Greek grammar, or forget it.

SUMMARY

Aside from the above-mentioned exceptions (genders, possessives following their objects, pronoun objects preceding the verb), the basic pattern of Greek phrases and sentences is much the same as in English and can be relatively easy to manage, as the following example will indicate:

Mary had a little lamb and ate it with peas and potatoes —
Ee Mar**ee**a **ee**-heh **en**a mee**kro** ar**nee** kay toh **ef**ageh meh bee**sel**ia kay pata**te**ss.

THE GREEK ALPHABET

Greek letter		Greek name of letter
A	α	**al**fa
B	β	**vee**ta
Γ	γ	**gah**ma
Δ	δ	**dhel**ta
E	ε	**ep**silon
Z	ζ	**zee**ta
H	η	eeta
Θ	θ	theeta
I	ι	eeohta
K	κ	**kah**pa
Λ	λ	**lahm**dha
M	μ	mee
N	ν	nee
Ξ	ξ	ksee
O	o	**oh**meekron
Π	π	pee
P	ρ	roh
Σ	σ, ς	**see**gma
T	τ	tahf
Y	υ	**ee**psilon
Φ	φ	fee
X	χ	hee
Ψ	ψ	psee
Ω	ω	**omeh**ga

Part 2
ENGLISH-GREEK DICTIONARY
AND PHRASEBOOK

A

a—**en**as (m), **mia** (f), **ena** (n)

abortion, an—**mia** ektrosee

    Perfectly legal in Greece as long as they are deemed necessary and performed by a qualified physician or gynecologist.

about—yeero; **about seven o'clock**—yeero stees eftah ee ora

above—epahno

abroad (out of the country)—sto eksoteriko

accident, an—**en**a dhisteeheema

acquaintance, an—**en**as gnostos (m), **mia** gnostee (f); **Pleased to make your acquaintance**—Hayro pohlee

actor, an (the)—**en**as (oh) eethopiohs

actress, an (the)—**mia** (ee) eethopiohs

adapter, an (the)—**en**as (oh) prosarmostees

addition, the—ee prosthesi; **The addition is wrong**—Ee prosthesi eenay lathos

address, the—ee dhee-efthinsee; **my (your) address**—ee dhiefthinsee mou (sou)

adultry—meekheeah

Aeschylus—Oh Ayskheelos

affair, an (love)—**mia** (erotikee) skhessee; **I'm having a (love) affair with...**—Eh-ho (erotikess) skhessees meh...

afford (I can't)—Dhen eh-ho ta mehsa

afraid (I'm)—Fovahmeh; **He (she) is afraid**—Fovahteh; **Are you afraid?**— Fovahseh?; **I was afraid**—Fovohmoon

after—metah; **after lunch**—metah toh yevma; **after tomorrow**—methahvrio; **after a while**—seh leego; **after** (later)—argotera

afternoon, the—toh apoyevma; **this afternoon**—seemera toh apoyevma; **tomorrow afternoon**—ahvrio toh apoyevma; **Sunday afternoon**—Kiriakee toh apoyevma; **Good afternoon!**—Hayreteh!

again—pahlee or ksanah; **again and again**—ksanah kay ksanah

Agamemnon—Oh Ahgamemnon

agency, a (the)—**en**a (toh) praktor**ee**o; **travel**—praktor**ee**o taksi-**dhee**on

agent, an (the)—**en**as (oh) **prak**tor

ago—preen; **a week ago**—preen mia ev-dhoma-dha

agree (I)—Seem**fan**o; **Do you agree?**—Seemfan**ees**?

aid—vo**ee**thia; **First Aid**—**Pro**tess Voeethi**ess**—kathar**os** ah-**ehr**as

air conditioner, a (the)—**mi**a (ee) meekhan**ee** climatis**moo**; **air conditioning, the**—oh climatis**mos**

airline, an (the)—**mi**a (ee) ah-eroporik**ee** gram**ee**

Names, addresses and telephone numbers of all foreign airlines can be found in English in the Blue Pages of the local Greek telephone directory.

air mail (by)—ah-eropori**kos**

air mattress, a (the)—**en**a (toh) ah-ero**stro**ma

airport, a (the)—**en**a (toh) ah-ero-**dhro**mio

alarm clock, an (the)—**en**a (toh) ksipni**teer**ee

alcohol—eenop**nev**ma

Means both wood and ethyl (grain) alcohol. There are two kinds of wood alcohol sold in Greece: the more expensive, white (**ahs**pro eenop**nev**ma) for medical uses, and the less expensive blue (bl**eh** eenop**nev**ma) for use as use as a cleanser, solvent, etc. Both can usually be found in groceries, although in some areas the white is available only in pharmacies.

Alien's Bureau, the—ee Eepires**ee**a Allo-dha**pon** (written on signs as: ΥΠΗΡΕΣΙΑ ΑΛΛΟΔΑΠΩΝ).

The Athens Alien's Bureau is located at 9 Halkokondili St. In other cities and towns, usually a section of the local police handles these functions. See also VISA.

all—**oh**lee (m & f), **oh**la (n)

allowed—epitrep**et**eh; **Is it (am I) allowed?**—Epitrep**et**eh?

almonds—ahmeeg-dhala

alone—**moh**nos (m), **moh**nee (f); **I'm alone**—**Ee**may **moh**nos (**moh**nee) mou; **Are you alone?**—**Ee**say **moh**nee (**moh**nos) sou?; **Leave me alone!**—**Ah**seh meh!

also—ehpee**sees**

alteration (of clothes)—metatro**pee**; **Can you alter this?**—Bor**ees** na toh metat**rep**sees?

alternating current—enalasomeno revma; **alternating days**—mehra para mehra

always—pahnda *or* pahndoteh

ambassador, a (the)—enas (oh) presveftees

American (adj.)—Amerikahnikoh; **person**—Amerikahnos (m), Amerikahneedha (f)
On the other hand a Greek born in America is called an "Amerikahnos."

amperes—ahmbehr; **How many amps?**—Posa ahmbehr?

amphitheatre, a (the)—ena (toh) amfitheh-atro

amphora, an (the)—enas (oh) amforeh-ahs

amusement park, an (the)—ena (toh) Luna Park

ancient—arhayos (m), arhayah (f), arhayo (n); **the Ancient Greeks**—ee arhayee Eliness

anchor, a (the)—mia (ee) ahn-ghira

and—kay

angry (adj.)—thimomenos (m), thimomenee (f)

angry: I'm angry (with)—Thimohno (meh); **I was angry**—Theemohsa; **Are you angry?** Eesay thimomenos (thimomenee)?

animal, an (the)—ena (toh) zooh; **animals**—ta zoah

annoying—enoklitikos (m), enoklitikee (f), enoklitikoh (n); **You are annoying me**—M'enokleeteh

another—ahlo *or* akoma; **another one**—ahlo (akoma) ena; **another time**—ahlee fora; **one more time**—akoma mia fora

ant, a—toh mirmeeghee; **ants**—ta mirmeeghia

antenna, an (the)—mia (ee) keraya

antique, an—mia anteeka; (pl.) anteekess; **antique** (adj.)—arkhayo

antiquities—arhay-ohtitess

anxiety—ahn-eesiheea

anxious—ahn-eesihos (m); ahn-eesihee (f); ahn-eesiho (n)

anybody, anyone—kanees *or* kanenas; **Is anybody here?**—Eenay kanees ehdhoh?; **Is anyone coming?**—Tharthee kanees?; **I don't know anyone**—Dhen ksehro kanena

anything—teepota (also means "nothing"); **Do you want anything?**—Thelees teepota ahlo?; **Nothing else, thank you**—Teepota ahlo, efharistoh

anywhere—pouthena *or* opoo-dheepoteh

apartment, a (the)—ena (toh) dhiamerisma; **furnished**—epiplomeno; **for rent**—ya eneekio

apiece—toh komahtee; **How much apiece?**—Poso toh komahtee?

Apollo—Oh Ahpohlon

apologize (I)—seegnomee or meh seekhorees

appetite—oreksi; **Good appetite!**—Kahlee oreksi!

appetizers—mezeh or meze-dhakia

appointment, an (the)—ena (toh) rahndehvou ("rendezvous"); **Shall we make an appointment?**—Na kleesomay rahndehvou?

Aquarius—oh Ee-dhroho-os; **The Age of Aquarius**—Ee epohee tou Ee-dhroho-ou

archaeologist, an—enas arhayologos; **arcbaeology**—arhayologyeeah

archbishop, an (the)—enas (oh) arhee-epeeskopos

Aristophanes—Oh Ahreestofahnees

Aristotle—Oh Ahreestotelees

army, the—oh strahtohs; **army** (*adj.*) strahtiotikoh

arrange (to)—na kanoneeso; **I'll arrange it**—Tha toh kanoneeso; **I've arranged**—Eh-ho kanoneesee; **Will you arrange it?**—Tha toh kanoneeseteh?; **We'll come to an arrangement**—Tha kanoneesoumeh

arrest (under)—eepo krahteeseen

arrive (I will)—Tha fthaso; **We will arrive**—Tha fthasoomeh; **It (she/be) will arrive**—Tha fthasee; **It (she/he) has arrived**—Eh-hee fthasee; **I arrived yesterday**—Efthasa ekthess.

art—ee tekhnee; **a work of art**—ena ehrgo tekhnees; **art gallery, a (the)**—mia (ee) pinakotheekee; **art supplies**—ee-dhee zografikees

artist, a (the)—enas (oh) kahlitekhnees; **artistic**—kahlitekhnikoh

as far as (a place)—meh-hree; **as soon as possible**—ohso toh dhinaton greegorotera

ashtray, an (the)—ena (toh) tasahkee or ena (toh) stakto-dhoheeo

ask (to)—na'roteeso; **I want to ask**—Thelo na'roteeso; **Did you ask?**—Erotisess?; **She (he) asked**—Erotiseh; **I will ask**—Tha'roteeso; **Will you ask?**—Tha'roteesees?

asleep (He/She is)—Keemahteh; **I was asleep**—Keemohmoona

aspirin—ahspireeni; **for children**—dheeah pay-dheeah

assistant, an (the)—enas (oh) vo-eethos

astrology—ee ahstrolog-**yee**a

at—sto (n), steen (f), ston (m), stees (f), toh (n), ta (pl), etc.

Its form depends on the gender and spellling of the object:

I will be at the hotel—Tha ee**may** sto ksenodhok**hee**o; **at home**—sto **spee**tee; **at the beach**—steen plahz; **at the restaurant**—sto estiatorio; **at the taverna**—steen ta**veh**rna; **at the corner**—steen go**nee**ah; **at church**—steen ekli**see**ah; **at six o'clock**—stees **ek**see ee **o**ra; **at noon**—toh mesi**meh**ree; **at midnight**—ta mee**sah**nikta; **at Christmas**—ta Hrees**too**yena; **at Easter**—toh **Pah**ska

at all—ka**tho**lou; **at first**—steen ar**hee**; **at last**—epi**te**loos; **at least**—tou **lah**heeston; **at once**—ah**meh**sos

attaché case, a (the)—**en**as (oh) harto**fee**lakas

Attention!—Pro**so**hee!; **Pay attention (be careful)**—**Pro**sekheh

attractive—elkisti**kos** (m), elkisti**kee** (f), elkisti**koh** (n)

aunt, an (the)—**mia** (ee) **thee**ah

au pair girl, an—**mia** eeki**a**ki vo-**ee**thos

(lit. "a house helper," but basically the Greeks have no real word for or concept of "au pair.")

au revoir—kah**lee** ahn**da**mosi

authentic—ahfthenti**kos** (m), ahfthenti**kee** (f), ahfthenti**koh** (n)

author, an (the)—**en**as (oh) singrafa**yas** (m), **mia** (ee) singrafa**yas** (f)

authorities, the (the police, etc.)—ee ark**hess**

automatic—ahfto**matohs** (m), ahfto**hmatee** (f), ahf**toh**matoh (n)

automobile, an (the)—**en**a (toh) aftokee**ni**toh

autumn, the—toh f**thee**noporo

avenue, an (the)—**mia** (ee) leh-oh**fo**ros

awake (adj.)—ksee**pni**os (m); ksee**pni**a (f); **He (she) is awake**—Ee**nay** ksee**pni**os (ksee**pni**a)

awake (to)—na ksee**pnee**so; **When I awake**—**Oh**tan ksee**pnee**so; **Awake me**—Ksee**pna**meh (**at nine o'clock**—Stees **en**aya ee **o**rah); **I awoke**—Ksee**pnee**sa; **He (she) awoke**—Ksee**pnee**seh.

away (far)—mah**kri**ah; **He (she) is away**—**Lee**pee *or* E**fee**geh.

B

baby, a (the)—**en**a (toh) mo**roh** *or* **en**as (oh) **beh**bis (m), **mia** (ee) **beh**ba (f)

Bacchus—Oh **Bah**khos

bachelor, a—**en**as **ah**gamos

back (I'll be)—Tha yi**ree**so

backgammon—**tah**vlee

>The national pastime of Greece. Most cafés have sets which are available free of charge to their customers; just buy a coffee or soft drink and you can sit there playing as long as you want.

backpack, a (the)—**en**a (toh) sakee-**dhi**o

bad—**kak**os (m), ka**kee** (f), ka**koh** (n)

bag, a (the)—**mi**a (ee) **tsahn**da; **paper bag**—harto-sa**kou**la; **plastic bag**—**mi**a plasti**kee tsahn**da; **suitcase**—**mi**a va**leet**sa

baggage—ee aposke**vess**

bait—**doh**loma

baker, a (the)—**en**as (oh) four**nar**ees

bakery, a (the)—**en**as (oh) **four**nos (lit. "the oven")

>However, the sign above the bakery, derived from the ancient Greek word for bread (**art**os) is ΑΡΤΟΠΟΙΕΙΟΝ. It is never used when speaking about the bakery.

ball, a (the)—**mi**a (ee) **bah**la; **rubber ball**—**mi**a elasti**kee bah**la; **tennis ball**—**mi**a **bah**la tou **ten**nees

balls, the (testicles)—ee **ork**hees; **slang**—ta ark**hee**-dhia

balcony, a (the)—**en**a (toh) bal**kon**i

ballpoint pen, a—**en**a **steel**oh

bank, a (the)—**mi**a (ee) **trah**peza

bar, a (the)—**en**a (toh) **bah**r (written as: ΜΠΑΡ).

>Bars, as we think of them, are a relatively new phenomenon in Greece and are usually patronized only by foreigners and upper-class, internationalized Greeks. True Greek bars are usually cafés and some confectionary stores. They serve a variety of alcoholic beverages (but not mixed drinks) at any hour of the day they happen to be open, the liquor laws of Greece being very elastic.

bartender—**bar**mahn

barbeque, a—**mi**a ska**ra**

barber, a (the)—**en**as (oh) **koureh**-ahs

bargain, a (good price)—**mi**a efka**yree**a; **agreement**—**mi**a seemfo**nee**a

bargain (to)—na paza**rep**so; **I don't want to bargain**—Dhen **thel**o na paza**rep**so

bargaining—toh pazahree

barrel, a (the)—ena (toh) varelee (pl. varelia); **barreled wine**—heema krasee

base, a (the)—mia (ee) vahsee

bath, a—ena bahnio; **hot/cold**—zestoh/kreeoh; **I want to take a bath**—Thelo na kahno bahnio (also means "take a swim"); **bathrobe**—rohba; **bath room, a (the)**—ena (toh) lootroh *or* bahnio; **Where is the bathroom?**—Poo eenay toh lootroh (bahnio)?; **Is there a bathroom? Eh-**hee lootroh (bahnio)?; **bath-towel, a (the)**—mia (ee) petseta tou bahniou; **bathtub, a (the)**—mia (ee) bahnyehra; **with a shower**—meh doos.

Note: In Greece, a bathroom is a room where is a bathtub or shower; it is not a euphemism for "toilet" (too-ahleta), although the British euphemism "loo" may be derived from the ancient Greek word for toilet, loo**troh**. The Greek euphemism for "toilet" is "toh **meh**ros," lit. "the place".

battery, a (the)—mia (ee) bahtereea (pl. bahteree-ess); **transistor**—trahnseestor; **flashlight**—fahkoh.

bay, a (the)—enas (oh) kolpos

B.C.—Pro Hreestoo (written as: π.χ.)

be (to)—na eemay; **I want to be**—Thelo na eemay; **She (he) wants to be**—Thelee na eenay; **We want to be**—Theloumeh na eemasteh.

Present	Past	Infinitive
I am—Eemay	I was—Eemoonah	na eemay
You are—Eesay	You were—Eesoonah	na eesay
He (she/it) is—Eenay	He (she/it) was—Eetan	na eenay
We are—Eemasteh	We were—Eemasteh	na eemasteh
You are—Eesteh	You were—Eesasteh	na eesteh
They are—Eenay	They were—Eetahn	na eenay

Future—put "tha" before present tense: **I will be**—**Tha** eemay. **Negative**—put "dhen" before the verb: **I am not**—**Dhen** eemay; **I won't be**—Dhen tha eemay.

beach, a (the)—mia (ee) plahz

bead, a (the)—mia (ee) hahndra; (pl. hahndress); **worry beads**—kombolo-ee

beard, a (the)—ena (toh) moosee

Beaufort Scale, the—ee klee**maks** Bofor

beautiful—orayos (m), oraya (f), orayoh (n)

beauty parlor, a (the) na (toh) **komoteerio** or **mia** (ee) komosees

because—yahtee (also means "why"; used exactly as in English.)

become (to)—na yeeno; **I will become**—Tha yeeno; **You will become**—Tha yeenees; **He (she, it) will become**—Tha yeenee; **They will become**—Tha yeenoon; **I am becoming**—Yeenomay; **You are becoming**—Yeenesay; **He (she, it) is becoming**—Yeenetay; **I became**—Egyeena; **You became**—Egyeeness; **He (she, it) became**—Egyeeneh

bed, a (the)—ena (toh) krevahtee (pl. krevahtia); **double bed**—dheeploh krevahtee; **single bed**—monoh krevahtee; **I'm going to bed**—Pao ya eepno; **Shall we go to bed?**—Pahmeh ya eepno?

bedbugs—koriee

bedclothes—ta klino-ske**pahs**mata (**blankets**—couvehrtess; **pillow**—mahksilahree; **sheets**—sendohnia)

bedroom, a (the)—mia (ee) krevahtoh**kah**mara or ena (toh) eepno-dhomatio

bee, a (the)—mia (ee) melisa (pl. melisess); **honey**—meli

beehive, a—mia keepselee

before (in time)—preen; **Before I leave**—Preen feego; **an hour before**—Preen mia ora

before (in front of)—embrohs or brostah

begin (I)—Arheeso; **When does it begin?**—Poteh arheesee?; **Shall we begin?**—Tha arheesomeh?; **to begin with**—Prota-prota; **I began**—Arheesa; **You began**—Arheesess; **She (he, it) began**—Arheeseh

beginning, the—ee arhee; **in the beginning**—steen arhee

behind—peeso; **behind the door**—peeso apo tee porta

behind, the (slang)—oh peesinohs

believe (I)—Peestevo; **I believe so**—Peestevo; **I believe you**—Seh peestevo; **I believe it**—Toh peestevo; **I don't believe you (it)**—Dhen seh (toh) peestevo; **Do you believe me?**—Meh peestevees?; **She (he) believes**—Peestevee

bell, a (the) church—mia (ee) kampahna (pl. ee kampahness); **doorbell, goat's bell, etc.**—ena (toh) koudhoonee (pl. koudhoonia)

belly, the—ee keeliah; **bellyache**—enas keeloponos; **belly**

button—oh afa**lohs; belly dance, a**—ho**rohs** tees kee**liahs** (Native to Turkey and the Middle East and doesn't really belong to Greece. However, see **"tsifteteli"**, under Greek Dances in **Part 4**.)

below—**kaht**oh

belt, a (the)—**mia** (ee) **zon**ee

beside (next to)—**dheep**la

best, the—oh pioh **kal**os (m), ee pioh **kal**ee (f), toh pioh **kal**oh (n)

bicycle, a (the)—**en**a (toh) po-**dhee**latoh

For rent almost everywhere. If there are not rental shops around, then look for enterpnsing individuals.

I want to rent a bicycle—**Thel**o na enee**kiah**so ena pod**hee**latoh.
For one day (3 hours)—Ya **mia mehr**a (treess oress)

big—me**gah**los (m), me**gah**lee (f), me**gah**loh (n); **bigger**—mega-**lee**tero; **bigger than**—mega**lee**tero ah**po**

bill, the—oh logarias**mohs; The bill, please**—Ton logarias**moh,** paraka**loh; separate bills**—hori**stee** logarias**mee; all together**—**ohlee mahz**ee; **There's a mistake**—**Eh-hee lath**os

birth (I give)—**Yenn**o; **I will give birth**—Tha yen**ee**so; **When will you give birth?**—**Pot**eh tha yen**ee**seteh?; **She will give birth**—Tha yen**ee**see; **I gave birth**—**Yenn**eesa; **She gave birth**—**Yenn**eeseh

birth, the—ee **yenn**isee ("Genesis"); **birth certificate, a (the)**—**en**a (toh) pistopee-**ee**ti**koh** yen**ee**seh-os; **birth control**—**el**eghos yen**ee**seh-on; **birth control pills**—andisi**lip**ti**ka**

birthday, a (the)—ta yen**eth**lia; **my birthday**—ta yen**eth**liah mou; **your birthday**—ta yen**eth**liah sou; **her (his) birthday**—ta yen**eth**liah tees (tou); **birthday party, a (the)**—**en**a par**tee** yen**eth**lee**on**

Rarely celebrated in Greece as a person's Name Day is considered much more important.

biscuit, a—**en**a bees**ko**toh (pl. bees**ko**ta)

bite, a (the) animal—**en**a dhah**go**ma; **Does it bite?** Dhah**go**nee?; **It doesn't bite**—Dhen dhah**go**nee; **A dog (snake) bit me**—Meh dhah**go**seh oh **skee**los (toh **feed**hee); **a bite to eat**—**mia** bouki**ah**

bitter—**peek**ro; **bittersweet**—gliko**peek**ro

black—**mahv**ros (m), **mahv**ree (f), **mahv**ro (n); **a black man (woman)**—**en**as **mahv**ros (**mia mahv**ree)

blanket, a (the)—mia (ee) couvehrta (pl. couvehrtess)

blonde—ksanthos (m), ksanthee (f), ksantho (n)

blood—ayma (See DOCTOR.)

boat, a (the)—mia (ee) varka (pl. varkess); **fishing boat**—ena kaeekee; **motor boat**—mia venzeenakatos; **rowboat**—mia varka meh koupiah; **sailboat**—mia varka meh pahnee

A varka is the name for virtually any type of small boat.

body, the (human, animal)—toh sohma

boil (to)—na vrahso; **Should I boil it?**—Prepi na toh vrahso?; **Will you boil it?**—Tha toh vrahsees?; **boiled**—vrahstoh

bolt, a (the)—enas (oh) seertees

bone, a (the)—ena (toh) kokalo (pl. kokala); **without the bone**—horees kokalo; **Can I have the bones for my dog (cat)?**—Boroh na eh-ho ta kokala ya ton skeelo (teen gahta) mou?

book, a (the)—ena (toh) vivleeoh (pl. vivleeah); **foreign books**—ksena vivleeah; **books in English**—vivleeah st'anglika; **second-hand books**—metaheerismena vivleeah

bookstore, a (the)—ena (toh) vivliopoleeoh

boot, a (the)—mia (ee) bohta (pl. ee bohtess); **leather boots**—dhermatiness bohtess; **rubber boots**—galohsess

border (frontier)—ta seenora

bored (I am)—Variemay (also means "tired," "lazy")

born (I was)—Yeneethika; **(in America**—steen Amerikee); **He (she) was born**—Yeneethikeh

borrow (I)—Dhahneezomay; **May I borrow this (for a moment)?**—Boroh na dhaneestoh aftoh (ya mia stigmee)?; **You may borrow it**—Borees na toh dhaneestees.

boss, the—toh ahfendikoh; **Who's the boss?**—Piohs eenay t'ahfendikoh?

both—kay ee dheeoh

bottle, a (the)—ena (toh) boukahli (pl. ta boukalia); **a bottle of water (wine)**—ena boukahli nehro (krahsee); **an empty bottle**—ena ahdhio boukahli; **a petrogas bottle**—mia fiahli; **a hot water bottle**—mia thermofora

Most bottles in Greece have a deposit (prokatavolee) on them, sometimes up to 25% of the initial price one pays. Thus, they are highly prized, and it would not be appreciated if you should walk away with one from a café or taverna without paying for the bottle as well as its contents.

bottle opener, a (the)—ena (toh) ahnikteeri *or* klee-**dhee** (lit. "key"); **bottle top, a (the)**—e**na** (toh) kah**pah**ki

bottom, the—oh **pah**tos; **rear end**—oh peesi**nos**

bowl, a (the)—e**na** bohl; **plastic**—plasti**koh**; **soup**—tees **sou**pas

box, a (the)—e**na** (toh) kou**tee**; **cardboard**—harti**noh**; **wooden**—**ksee**lino

boy, a (the)—e**na** (toh) ah**goree** (pl. ta ah**goria**)

boy friend, a (the)—e**nas** (oh) **feelos** *or* ahgahpeen**menos**; **my boy friend**—oh **feelos** (ahgah**pimenos**) mou

Inasmuch as feelos can also mean "friend," it is perhaps better, if you wish to be quite specific, to use the term ahgahpee**menos** ("loved one"), although this, to a Greek mind, is rather strong and personal. For a discussion of the confusions and fine distinctions involved, see under **friend**. See also "**gomenos**" in **Part 4** for another variation.

bra, a (the)—e**na** (toh) soutien (as in the French, "*soutien gorge*")

bracelet, a (the)—e**na** (toh) vrakhee**ohlee** (In Greek, brace**leh** means "watchband.")

brazier, a (the)—e**na** (toh) man**gah**lee.

bread—pso**mee**; **white**—**ahs**pro pso**mee**; **dark**—**mah**vro pso**mee**; **country**—horiahtiko pso**mee**; **dry, twice-baked**—paksimah-**dhee**

break (I)—**Spah**zo; **Don't break it!**—Mee toh **spah**sees!; **I broke**—**Es**pasa; **He (she) broke it**—Toh es**paseh**; **breakage**—**spahs**imo (See also BREAKING PLATES.)

breast, a (the) human and animal—e**na** (toh) **stee**thos (pl. ta **stee**thee); **slang**—ta vee**zeeah**; **breast feeding**—vee**zagma**

bride, a (the)—**mia** (ee) **neefee**; **bridegroom**—e**nas** (oh) gam**brohs**

bridge, a (the)—**mia** (ee) ye**fira**; **card game**—breetz

briefcase, a (the)—e**nas** (oh) hartofee**lakas**

bring (I)—**Fehr**no; **I will bring it**—Tha toh **feh**ro; **Will you bring it?**—Tha toh **feh**rees?; **Will you bring me...?**—Tha mou **feh**reteh...?; **Bring me**—**Feh**reh mou; **Did you (he/she) bring it?**—Toh eh-hees (eh-hee) **feh**ree?; **He (she) will bring it**—Tha toh **feh**ree.

British—Vretanos (m), Ahnglee-dha (f), Vretaniko (n); I am British—Eemay Vretanos (Ahnglee-dha)

broke, I'm (out of money)—Eemay tahpee

broken—spahsmeno

bronze—broondzohs

brooch, a (the)—mia (ee) porpee (can also mean "buckle" or "clasp")

broom, a (the)—mia (ee) skoupa

brother, a (the)—enas (oh) ah-dhelfohs (pl. ee ah-dhelfee—which can also mean "the sister"); my (your) brother—oh ah-dhelfohs mou (sou); brother-in-law, a (the)—enas (oh) kouniah-dhos

brown—kafeh (but "brown" bread is called "black"—mahvro psomee)

brothel, a (the)—ena (toh) bordello

For further information, see PROSTITUTE.

brunette (color)—kastano; a brunette—mia kastanee

brush, a (the)—mia (ee) voortsa; nail brush—mia voortsa nikhion; paint brush—ena peenello; toothbrush—mia o-dhon-dohvoortsa

buckle (belt), a (the)—enas (oh) halkas

bucket, a (the)—enas (oh) kouvas

bug, a (the)—ena (toh) zoeefio (pl. ta zoeefia); bedbugs—koriee

bulb (light), a (the)—mia (ee) lahmpa (pl. lahmpess); burnt out—kaikeh; bayonet/screw (base)—byonnet/vee-dhotoh; watts vaht

bull, a (the)—enas (oh) tahvros

bullet, a (the)—mia (ee) sfayra (pl. sfayress)

bunch of, a—ena mahtso; a bunch of flowers—ena bouketoh loulou-dhia; a bunch of grapes—ena tsambee stafeelia

bureau, a (the)—ena (toh) grafeeoh; Tourist Bureau—Grafeeoh Toorismou (written as: ΓΡΑΦΕΙΟΝ ΤΟΥΡΙΣΜΟΥ)

burn, a—ena engavma; sunburn—ena eeliakoh engavma

burn, I—Kayoh; I am burning from the sun—Kayomeh ahpo ton eelio; to burn—na kahpso; Where can I burn this?—Poo boroh na toh kahpso?; I burned myself—Kaikah; It burned—Kaikeh.

bus, a (the)—ena (toh) leh-ohforeeoh; bus statlon—stathmos leh-ohforeeon; bus stop—ee stahsee leh-ohforeeou

but—ahla *or* **mah**

butcher, a (the)—enas (oh) hasahpees; **butcher shop, a (the)**—ena (toh) kreh-opoleeoh (written as: ΚΡΕΟΠΟΛΕΙΟΝ)

butter—vooteero

button, a (the)—ena (toh) koombee (pl. koombiah)

buy (to)—na agorahso; **I want to buy**—Thelo na agorahso; **Where can I buy...?**—Poo boroh na agorahso...?; **I will buy it**—Tha toh agorahso; **Will you buy it?**—Tha toh agorahsees?; **I bought**—Ahgorasa; **I bought it**—Toh ahgorasa; **Did you buy it?**—Toh ahgorasess?; **She (he) bought it**—Toh ahgoraseh.

by (next to, near)—Kondah; **by the sea**—konda steen thalasa; **Sit by me**—Kahtseh kondah mou.

by (travel)—meh; **by foot**—meh ta po-dhia; **by train**—meh toh trayno

by (rental)—meh; **by the day**—meh teen eemehra; **by the week**—meh teen ev-dhomah-dha; **by the month**—meh ton meena

by tomorrow—ohs ahvrio; **by now**—eh-os torah

by myself—mohnos mou

Byron—Oh Veeron

Byzantine—Veezantinos (m), Veezantinee (f), Veezantino (n)

C

cabin, a (the)—mia (ee) cabeena (pl. cabeeness); **single**—mohnohklinee; **double**—dheeklinee; **1st (2nd) class**—protee (dhefteree) thessee cacao—kakao

café, a (the)—ena (toh) kafeneeoh (written as: ΚΑΦΕΝΕΙΟΝ)

caffeine—cafeh-eenee; **decaffeinated**—horees cafeh-eenee

caique, a (the)—ena (toh) kah-eeekee

cake, a (the)—ena (toh) cayk

calendar, a (the)—ena (toh) eemerolohghio (See **Part 5** for a Greek Festive Calendar.)

call, to (yell)—na fonakso; **to telephone**—na teeleh-foneeso

calm—eeremos *or* eesihos (m), eeremee *or* eesihee (f); **calm weather or sea**—bonahtsa

camera, a (the)—mia (ee) fotografikee meekhanee (See PHOTOGRAPHER.)

camping—kahmping

can (I)—Boroh; I can't—Dhen boroh; You can—Borees; He (she) can— Boree; We can—Boroomeh; You can—Boreeteh; They can—Borooneh; Can (may) I?—Epitrepeteh? I could (not)—(dhen) borousa; Could you?—Tha borousess?

can (tin), a (the)—ena (toh) teneke-dhenio koutee (pl. koutess); a large can—enas (oh) tenekess; a can of fruit—ena koutee froota; canned fruit—froota conserva; can opener, a—ena anikteeri conservas

cancel (to)—na akiroso; I want to cancel the reservation—Thelo na akiroso toh kleesimo

candle, a (the)—ena (toh) kehree (pl. ta kehriah)

candy—karamella; candies—karamelless

A generic term for all types of candy, not just caramels.

cane (walking), a (the)—ena (toh) bastoonee

canvas—moosamahs

cap, a (the)—ena (toh) kahpello

capitol, a (the)—mia (ee) protevousa

car (auto), a (the)—ena (toh) aftokeenitoh

car ferry, a (the)—ena (toh) feriboht

carafe, a (the)—mia (ee) karafa; a small carafe—ena karafaki

captain, the—oh kahpetanios

caravan (motor home), a (the)—ena (toh) trohospeetoh

carbonated—anthrakiko; non-carbonated—dheehos anthrakiko

card (business), a—ena episkepteerio

cards (playing)—trapouloharta; card game, a (the)—mia (ee) hartopekseea

carnival, a (the)—ena (toh) carnivahlee: Carnival Season—Apokriess

carpet, a (the)—ena (toh) halee

carry (to)—na sikoso; I can (not) carry it—(dhen) boroh na toh sikoso; Can you carry (transport) it?—Borees na toh metafehrees?

cashier, a (the)—enas (oh) tahmeeas (m), mia (ee) tahmeeas (f)

casino, a (the)—ena (toh) kahzeeno

casserole, a (the)—ena (toh) yoovetsi

cassette, a (the)—mia (ee) cassetta (pl. cassettess)

castle, a (the)—ena (toh) kahstro

cat, a (the)—mia (ee) **gah**tah (pl. **gah**tess)

catch (to)—na **pi**ahso *or* na pro**lah**vo; **I want to catch some fish**—**Thel**o na **pi**ahso **psar**ia; **Did you catch any fish?**—**Epi**ases **psar**ia?; **I must catch the boat**—**Prep**ee na pro**lah**vo toh ka**rah**vee.

caught (I)—**Epi**asa *or* pro**lav**a; **I've caught a cold**—Eh-ho ar**pak**see **kree**oh *or* Eh-ho **kree**ohsi.

Catholic—Katho**lik**os (m), Katho**lik**ee (f), Katho**lik**oh (n); **Is there a Catholic church?**—Eepar**hee** Katho**lik**ee eklis**ee**a?; **I'm Catholic**—**Ee**may Katho**lik**os (Katho**lik**ee).

caution—pro**soh**ee (written on signs as: ΠΡΟΣΟΧΗ)

cave, a (the)—mia (ee) spee**li**ah

CD, a (the)—ena (toh) **see**dee (pl. ta **see**dee)

cemetary, a (the)—ena (toh) nekro**taf**eeoh

center, a (the)—ena (toh) **ken**tro (written as: KENTPON)

century, a (the)—enas (oh) ay-**oh**nas; **Which century?**—**Pee**ohn ay-**oh**na?; **The Fifth Century, B.C.**—Oh **pemp**tos ay-**oh**nas, pro **Hree**stoo

ceramic (adj.)—kera**mik**oh; **ceramics**—kera**mik**a

certain (sure)—**see**goura; **certainly**—**vev**ayos

certificate, a (the)—ena (toh) pistopee-**it**ikon; **a birth/health/ marriage**

certificate—ena pistopee-**it**ikon yenee**seh**-ohs/**eeg**yeeas/**gah**moo

chain, a (the)—mia (ee) ali**see**-dha; **gold**—**hree**see; **silver**—ahsi-**men**ia

chair, a (the)—mia (ee) ka**rek**la (pl. ka**rek**less)

chamomile (tea)—hamo**meel**ee (**tsa**-ee)

change (coins)—**psee**la; **from a bill**—ta **res**ta; **change (to)**—na**ah**lahkso; **I want to change money**—**Thel**o na a**lah**kso **hree**mata; **Can you change this?**—Bo**ree**teh na a**lah**kseteh af**toh**?; **I want to change my clothes**—**Thel**o na a**lah**kso ta **rouk**ha mou; **I've changed my mind**—Ah**lah**ksa gno**mee**; **Have you any change?**—Eh-**het**eh **psee**la?; **Keep the change**—**Krat**a ta **res**ta.

charge (to)—na hreh-**ohso**; **How much do you charge for...?**—**Pos**o hreh-**ohn**eteh ya...?; **Can I charge this until tomorrow?**—**Bor**oh na toh hreh-**ohso** **mehk**ree ah**vrio**?

charm (good-luck), a—ena fee**lak**toh

charter, a—ena tsartehr *or* ena **nah**vloma

charter (to)—na navloso; **I want to charter**—**The**lo na navloso

cheap—fteeno (the "f" must be pronounced, as in "fffteeno")

check, a (the) bank—ena (toh) tehk; **restaurant**—**en**as (oh) logari-asmos

cheese—teeree; **grated**—treemeno

chemist's, a (the)—ena (toh) farma**kee**oh (See PHARMACY.)

chess—**skah**kee; **chess board, a**—ena ska**kie**ra; **chess piece, a**—ena pioh**nee** (pl. ta **pioh**nia)

chest, the (anat.)—toh **stee**thos; **box**—ki**vo**tio *or* ba**oo**lo

chestnut—**kah**stano (pl. **kah**stana)

chic—seek; **That's very chic**—Eenay polee seek

chewing gum—**tseek**less

chicken, (the)—ena (toh) koto**pou**lo (pl. koto**pou**la *or* ko**tess**) (See also MENU.)

child, a (the)—ena (toh) pay-**dhee**; **the children**—ta pay-**dhiah**; **my child**—toh pay-**dhee** mou. (Please see my remarks under BABY.)

chilled (drinks)—pago**me**no; **chilly** (adv.)—**pseek**hra

chips (potato) **American**—(patatess) tseeps; **English**—patatess tigani**tess**

chocolate—soko**lah**ta; **bar, a**—mia **plah**ka soko**lah**ta; **box of, a**—ena kou**tee** soko**lah**tess

Christ—Oh **Hree**stos; **Christian**—Hree**stia**nos (m), Hreestia**nee** (f)

Christmas—Hree**stoo**yena; **at Christmas**—ta Hree**stoo**yena

church, a (the)—mia (ee) ek**lee**seea

C.I.A.—**Seeah** *or* **See-aee-ay**

cigar, a—ena **poo**ro (pl. **poo**ra)

 Can be found at sidewalk kiosks in most cities and towns.

cigarette, a (the)—ena (toh) tsi**ga**ro (pl. tsi**ga**ra)

cinema, a (the)—ena (toh) si**ne**ma *or* enas (oh) kinemato**grah**fos

cistern, a (the)—mia (ee) **steh**rna; **is empty**—eenay ah-**dhia**

city, a (the)—mia (ee) poh**lees**

class—**thes**see; **1st (2nd/3rd) class**—pro**tee** (dhefte**ree**/tree**tee**) **thes**see; **deck/deluxe/tourist**—kata**stro**ma/**louks**/tooristi**kee** (See also TICKET.)

classical—classi**koh**; **classical music**—classi**kee** moosi**kee**; **Classical Greece**—arheh-a **Ella**-dha (lit. "ancient Greece") clean (to)—na kathareeso; **Can you clean this?**—Borees na katha-reesees aftoh?

clean (adj.)—katharos (m), katharee (f), katharoh (n)

cleaners, the—toh pleenteerio

cleaning, the—toh katharisma

cleaning woman, a (the)—mia (ee) kathareestria.

clever—ekseepnos (m), ekseepnee (f), ekseepno (n)

climate, the—toh kleema

climax, a (the) sexual—enas (oh) orgasmos; **Did you reach a climax?**—Ee-hess orgasmo?

clinic, a (the)—mia (ee) kleenikee (See HOSPITAL.)

clock, a (the)—ena (toh) roloy; **alarm clock, a (the)**—ena (toh) kseepniteeree

close (to)—na kleeso; **When do you close?**—Poteh kleeneteh?; **When does it close?**—Poteh kleenee?: **Is it closed?**—Eenay kleesto?

closed—kleesto (written on door signs as: ΚΛΕΙΣΤΟΝ)

clothes—rouha (also a euphemism for "sanitary napkin"); **my clothes**—ta rouha mou; **clothes hanger, a**—ena kremastari; **clothes line**—ena skeenee ya ahploma; **clothes pins**—man-dalahkia

cloth, a—ena pahnee; **cloth (material)**—eefasma

cloud, a (the)—ena (toh) seenefo (pl. ta seenefa)

coach (bus)—leh-oforeeo; **train**—vagonee

coast, the—ee paraleeah

coat, a (the) men's—ena (toh) sakahkee; **women's**—mia (ee) zahketta; **overcoat, a (the)**—ena (toh) paltoh

cockroaches—katsareedhess

cocoa—kahkao

coffee, a (the)—enas (oh) kafess (pl. kafeh-dhess) (See under DRINK.)

coin, a (the)—ena (toh) nomisma *or* ena (toh) kehrma (pl. nomeesmata *or* kehrmata)

cold (adj.)—kreeoohs (m), kreeah (f), kreeoh (n); **It (the weather) is cold**—Kahnee kreeoh; **It (a thing) is cold**—Eenay kreeoh; **I am cold**—Kreeohno; **Are you cold?**—Kreeohnees?; **I have a cold**—Eh-ho kreelog-yima

collect (I)—Mazevoh; **collection, a**—mia seelog-yee

color, a (the)—ena (toh) **hroma** (pl. ta **hromata**)

column, a (the)—**mia** (ee) kolona (pl. ee koloness)

comb, a (the)—**ena** (toh) ktenee

come (to)—n'artho; **I want to come**—Thelo n'artho; **Will you come?**—Th'arthees?; **Is he (she) coming?**—Th'arthee?; **Are they coming?**—Th'arthoon? **I'm coming** (arriving)—Erhomeh; **He (she) is coming**—Erhetay; **Come!**—Ella; **Come here!**—Ella dhoh!; **Come with me**—Ella mahzee mou; **Come in**—Ella messa; **I came**—Eeltha; **You came**—Eelthess; **She (he) came**—Eeltheh

Come back (to)—na yireeso or na ksanartho; **I'll be back**—Tha yireeso; **I'll come back next year**—Tha ksanartho tou **hronou**; **When will you be back?**—Poteh tha yireesees?

comfortable—ahnetohs (m), ahnetee (f), ahnetoh (n)

Common Market, the—Ee Kinee Agora or Ehohk

communism—komoonismos (See also COMMUNISM.)

company, a (the) business—**mia** (ee) etayreea; **of friends**—**mia** (ee) pareh-a; **I have company**—Eh-ho pareh-a

complaint, a—ena parapono; **I have a complaint**—Eh-ho parapono

compliment, a—**ena** komplimento; **my compliments**—ta singharitiriah mou

composer, a (the)—**ena**s (oh) seenthetees

concert, a (the)—**mia** (ee) seenavleea

condom, a—ena profilaktikoh (pl. profilaktika)
    Available both in pharmacies and sidewalk kiosks.

conductor, the (orch.)—oh mah-**estros**; **bus**—oh eespraktor leh-oforeeou

confectionary store, a (the)—ena (toh) zakharoplasteeoh

"Congratulations!"—"Sing-hariteeria!"

consul, a (the)—**ena**s (oh) proksenos; **consulate, a (the)**—**ena** (toh) prokseneeon

continual—seeneh-hees; **continually**—seenehos

contraceptive, a (the)—**ena** (toh) andisiliptikoh; **birth control pills**—andisiliptika; **male prophylactics**—profilaktika

contract, a (the)—**ena** (toh) seenvolayo

convenient—volikos (m), volikee (f), volikoh (n); **Is it convenient**

for you?—Seh volevee?; **It's not convenient for me**—Dhen meh
volevee

cook, a (the)—**en**as (oh) **mahg**-yeeras

cook (to)—na magyee**rep**so

cookies—bis**kott**a

cool—dhro**ser**os (m), dhro**ser**ee (f), dhro**ser**oh (n)

copper—**hal**kos

copy, a (the)—**en**a (toh) antee**graf**o (pl. ta antee**graf**a)

cork, a (the) bottle—**en**a (toh) **poma**; **corkscrew, a (the)**—**en**a (toh)
teer**boo**son

corner, a (the)—**mia** (ee) go**nee**a; **on (in) the corner**—stee go**nee**a;
around the corner—**meta** tee go**nee**a

correct (adj.)—**sos**toh or ah**kri**vees; **the correct time**—ee ah**kri**vees
ora

cosmetics—ka**leen**dika

cost (to)—na cos**tee**si; **How much does it cost? Poso** cos**tee**si?; **It
costs too much**—Cos**tee**si **pohla**

cot, a (the)—**en**a (toh) koo**kett**a

cotton—vam**bah**kee

cough, a—**en**as **veekh**as; **I have a cough**—Eh-ho **veekh**a; **She (he)
has a cough**—Eh-hee **veekh**a; **cough drops**—pas**teel**yes ya toh
veekha; **cough syrup**—see**rop**ee ya toh **veekh**a

country, a (the)—**mia** (ee) pa**treedh**a; **my country**—ee pa**treedh**a
mou; **state, a (the)**—**en**a (toh) **krah**tos

country(side), the—ee ek**soh**ee

couple, a (the) pair—**en**a (toh) zev**gar**ee; **a married couple**—**en**a
pan**dreh**meno zev**gar**ee; **a couple of days (hours)**—**kana**
dheeoh **meh**ress (**oress**)

course (of)—**fis**ika or veva**yos**

court, a (the) of law—**en**a (toh) dheekas**teer**io

cousin, a (the)—**en**as (oh) **ksa**-**dhel**fos (m), **mia** (ee) ksa-**dhel**fee (f)

cove, a (the)—**en**a (toh) lim**nah**kee

cover, a (the)—**en**a (toh) **ske**pasma (pl. **ske**pas**ma**ta)

cow, a (the)—**mia** (ee) agh-**yela**-dha (pl. agh-**yela**-dhess)

crack, a—**en**a rah**ghis**ma; **It is cracked**—**Een**ay ra**ghis**meno

crash, a (auto)—**mia** sin**grou**see

crash helmet, a—**en**a **krah**nos

crazy—trehlos (m), trehlee (f); He's crazy—Eenay trehlos

cream—krema; a cream pudding—mia krema; cold cream—krema neektos; face cream—krema prosopoo; salve—ahlifee

credentials—dhia-pistev-teeria; my credentials—ta dhia-pistev-teeriah mou

credit—peestosis; credit card, a—mia peestotikee karta; credit cards—peestotikess kartess

Most tourist shops, car rental agencies, and some hotels, even on the smaller islands, have arrangements with one or more of the major credit card companies and should accept yours without any problem.

crime, a—ena englima; a pity—ena kreema

crochet—kroseh; I crochet—Pleko meh kroseh; crochet needle, a—ena velonahki (pl. velonahkia)

cross, a (the) Christian—enas (oh) stavros

crossroad, a (the)—ena (toh) stavro-dhromee

cruise, a (the)—mia (ee) krou-asiera; I'm on a cruise—Kahno krou-asiera; cruise ship, a (the)—ena (toh) krou-asieropleeoh

cry (to)—na klahpso; I will cry—Tha klahpso; I cried—Eklapsa; She (he) is crying—Klay-ee

crystal—kreestalo

cuckold, a—enas keratas

cuddle together (to)—na mazevomay konda

culture—kooltoora

cunning—pohneeros (m), pohneeree (f), pohneeroh (n)

cup, a (the) coffee, tea—ena (toh) fleetzahnee (pl. fleetzahnia); a cup (amount)—mia koupa

Cupid—Oh Ehros

curiosity—peri-er-ghia

curious—peree-ergos (m), peree-erghee (f), peree-ergo (n); strange—paraksenos (m), paraksenee (f), parakseno (n)

current, a (the) air, water, elec.—ena (toh) revma

curse, a (the)—mia (ee) kahtara or mia (ee) vlahsteemia ("blasphemy")

curtain, a (the)—mia (ee) kourteena (pl. ee kourteeness)

cushion, a (for sitting)—ena maksilari (ya kathisma)

custom, a (the)—mia (ee) sineethia

customs, the (border)—toh teloneeoh

customer, a (the)—enas (oh) pelahtees (pl. ee pelahtess)

cut (to)—na kohpso; **I cut**—Ekopsa; **I cut myself**—Kohpika; **He (she) cut himself**—Kohpikeh

cute—haritomenos (m), haritomenee (f), haritameno (n)

cypress, a (the)—ena (toh) keepareesi (pl. ta keepareesia)

D

daddy—babahs (while papahs means "priest")

daily—katheh mehra

dairy store—gahlaktopoleeoh (written as: ΓΑΛΑΤΟΠΟΛΕΙΟΝ)
These usually sell eggs, yogurt, cheese, various grocery items, and bottled or fresh milk. The latter is usually available only in the early morning, and it must be boiled at least 5 minutes before drinking.

damaged (it is)—Eenay halasmeno

"Damn!"—"Sto dheeahvalo!"

dance, a (the)—enas (oh) horos; **I don't know how to dance**—Dhen ksero na horevo; **I want to learn to dance**—Thelo na mahtho na horevo; **Will you teach me?**—Tha meh mahthees?;**I want to see folk dances**—Thelo na dhoh la-ikoos horoos.

danger—keen-dhinos (written on signs as: ΚΥΝΔΙΝΟΣ)

dangerous—epikeen-dhino

Danish (adj.)—Dhahnikoh; **Danish man**—Dhahnezos; **Danish woman**—Dhahneza; **language**—Dhahnika

dark (color)—skooro; **without light**—skotino

darling, my—ahgahpee mou; mahtia mou (lit. "my eyes"); poulahkee mou (lit. "my little bird" but beware that this is also a euphemism for "penis".)

date, the—ee eemeromineea; **What's the date?**—Tee eemeromineea eenay?; **appointment**—rahndehvoo; **Shall we make a date?**—Tha dhosoumeh rahndehvoo?
Calendar dates are always spoken of with the day first and the month second, as in: **July 20th, 1999**—eekosee Yuleeo heelia enayakosia eneneenda enaya

daughter, a (the)—mia (ee) koree (pl. koress); **My daughter**—ee koree mou; **daughter-in-law**—mia (ee) neefee

dawn, the—ee avghee; **at dawn**—teen avghee *or* ta haramata

day, a (the)—mia (ee) mehra (pl. mehress); **today**—seemera; **yesterday**—ekthess; **tomorrow**—ahvrio; **the day before yesterday**—prokthess; **the day after tomorrow**—methahvrio; **What day is it?**—Tee mehra eenay?; **every day**—katheh mehra; **today's (bread, eggs, etc.)**—seemerino; **daytime, the**—ee eemehra; **in the daytime**—teen eemehra

Days of the Week:

Monday—Dheftera; **Tuesday**—Treetee; **Wednesday**—Tetartee; **Thursday**—Pemptee; **Friday**—Paraskevee; **Saturday**—Sahvatoh; **Sunday**—Kiriakee

The following patterns are followed for every day of the week except Saturday:

On Tuesday—teen Treetee; **this Tuesday**—aftee teen Treetee; **next Tuesday**—teen ahlee Treetee; **last Tuesday**—teen perasmeni Treetee

On Saturday—toh Sahvatoh; **this Saturday**—aftoh toh Sahvatoh; **next Saturday**—toh ahlo Sahvatoh; **last Saturday**—toh perasmeno Sahvatoh

dead (adj.)—nekros (m), nekree (f), nekro (n)

dead end, a—mia ah-dhiekso-dhoh

dear (beloved)—ahgahpitos (m), ahgahpitee (f); **Dear John**—AhgahpitehYanee

dear (expensive)—ahkrivos (m), ahkrivee (f), ahkrivoh (n)

death—thanatos

decide (to)—na apofaseeso; **I can't decide**—Dhen boroh na apofaseeso; **You decide**—Esee apfahseeseh; **I've decided**—Eh-ho apofaseesee

deed, a (the) house, land, etc.—ena (toh) engrafon

deep (for the sea)—'vathiah; **Is it very deep?**—Eenay polee vathiah?; **How deep?**—Poso vathiah?; **How many meters?**—Posa mehtra?

delay, a (the)—mia (ee) kathisterisee; **Why the delay?**—Yahtee ee kathisterisee?

delicious—nostimo

deliver (to)—na fehro; **Will you deliver this?**—Tha toh fehreteh?

deluxe—louks

democracy, a—mia dheemokrateea

For a brief history of the vicissitudes of democracy in modern Greece, see MONARCHY.

dent, a—ena vathooloma

dentist, a (the)—enas (oh) o-dhondee-atros

deodorant, an (under-arm)—**ena** aposmitiko; **room**—aposmitiko dhomateeoo **department store, a (the)—ena** megahlo katasteema

dependable—aksiohpistos (m), aksiohpistee (f), aksiohpisto (n); **Is he dependable?—Eenay** aksiohpistos?; **I'm depending on you**—Eksartohmay ahpo sena

dessert, a (the)—ena epi-dhorpio (pl. epi-**dhorpia**)

devil, the—oh dhiahvolos; **Go to the devil!**—Sto dhiahvolo!

A strong curse. See **moondza**.

diamond, a (the)—ena (toh) dhia**mahnd**ee (pl. dhiamahndia)

diapers—pahness

diarrhea—dheeahria

dice (playing)—zaria

dictionary, a (the)—ena (toh) leksikoh; **English-Greek**—Ahnglo-Eleenikoh

die (to)—na pethahno; **I'm dying of hunger (the heat)**—Pethayno apo teen peena (zestee); **Is he (she) dying?**—Pethaynee? **He (she, it) died**—Pethaneh

diet, a—mia dhee-ayta; **I'm on a diet**—Kahno dhee-ayta

difference, a (the)—mia (ee) dheeafora; **It doesn't make any difference**—Dhen peerahzee

different—dheeaforetikoh

difficult—dheeskolos (m), dheeskolee (f), dheeskolo (n)

digestion, the—ee honepsi

dinner, a (the)—ena (toh) yevma (also means "lunch")

direct (adv.)—Kaht'eftheeahn; **Does this (bus, ship, etc.) go direct to...?**—Paee kaht'eftheeahn stee...?

director, a (the)—enas (oh) dhee-eftheentees

directory, a (the) telephone, etc.—**enas** (oh) kahtahlogos

dirt (earth)—homa; **grime**—vromiah; **dirty**—vromikos (m), vromikee (f),vromiko (n)

disappointed—ahpogo-eetevmenos (m), ahpogo-eetevmenee (f)

dish, a (the) plate—**ena** (toh peeahtoh (pl. peeahta); **a dish of (macaroni)**— **mia** mereedha (makaronia)

dishonest—ahnen**dimos** (m), ahnen**dimee** (f), ahnen**dimo** (n)

disenfectant, a (the)—**ena** (toh) apolimandikoh

disk, a (the) of any sort—**enas** (oh) **dhees**kos (pl.**dhees**kee)

dive (I)—Voo**toh** (See SCUBA DIVING.)

divorce, a—**ena** dhiazeeg-yio; **divorced (I am)**—Eemay horismenos (m), horis**menee** (f)

dizzy—zalis**menos** (m), zalis**menee** (f), zalis**menoh** (n)

do (I)—**Kah**no; **I am doing**—**Kah**no; **I want to do**—Thelo na kahno; **I will do it**—Tha toh **kah**no; **I must do it**—Prepee na toh kahno; **Can he (she) do it?**—Boree na toh **kah**nee?; **Will you do it?**—Tha toh **kah**nees?; **Don't!**—Mee!; **Don't do it!**—Mee toh kahnees!; **I did it**—Toh ekana; **She (he) did it**—Toh ekaneh; **Did you do it?**—Toh ekaness?; **What can we do?**—Tee na **kah**noomeh?

doctor, a (the)—**enas** (oh) yiahtros

dog, a (the)—**enas** (oh) **skee**los

doll, a (the)—**mia** (ee) **kou**kla (pl. **kou**kless)
Also used, as in English, to describe little children and females. The diminuative is kou**klakee**, i.e. "little doll": Kou**klakee** mou— **My little doll.**

dollar, a—**ena** dhohlario (pl. dhohlaria). (See also MONEY.)

donkey, a (the)—**enas** (oh) **gaee**-dharos *or* **ena** (toh) **gaee**-**dhooree**
Don't!—Mee!

door, a (the)—**mia** (ee) **porta** (pl. ee **portess**)

double—**dheeplo**; **a double bed**—**ena** dheeplo krevahtee (but: **a double room**—**ena** **dheeklino**); **a double ouzo**—**ena** dheeplo oozo

dowry, a (the)—**mia** (ee) **preeka**

drain a (the)—**enas** (oh) okhe**tos**; **stopped up**—kleesmenos

draw (I)—Ske-dhiahzo; **Will you draw it (a map)?**—Tha toh skesiahseteh (**ena hartee**)?

dream, a (the)—**ena** (toh) **ohneero** (pl. ta ohneera); **Sweet dreams!**—Ohneera gleeka!

dream (I)—Oneerevomay; **I dreamed**—Oneereftika; **Last night I dreamed (about you)**—Ekthess vrah-dhee (seh) oneereftika

dress, a (the)—ena (toh) forema (pl. foremata); **a beautiful dress**—ena orayo forema

dressmaker, a—mia moh-dheestra

dress (I)—Deenomay; **I must dress**—Prepee na deethoh

dried (vegs., fruits, etc.)—kseroh; **no water**—stegnoh

drink (I)—Peeno; **I don't drink**—Dhen peeno; **drink (to)**—na pioh; **I want something to drink**—Thelo kahtee na pioh; **Can I drink this?**—Boroh na toh pioh?; **Drink up!**—Ahspro pahtoh!; **Is the water drinkable?**—Toh nehro eenay posimo?

drive (I)—Odheego; **I will drive**—Tha odheeg-yeeso

driver, a (the)—enas (oh) odheegos; **driver's license**—ena (toh) dheeploma

drugstore, a (the)—ena (toh) pharmakeeoh

drunk (adj.)—metheesmenos (m), metheesmenee (f)

drunk, a (the)—enas (oh) bekrees

dry (vegs. & fruit)—ksero; **no water**—stegno; **wine**—broosko

dummy (pacifier), **a (the)**—mia (ee) peepeela

duty (tax), **a (the)**—enas (oh) foros or dhasmos

dye—vafee or boh-ya (the latter meaning "paint")

E

each—kahtheh; **each one**—kahtheh ena (*or* mia *or* enas)

early—enorees; **early in the morning**—proee-proee

earring, a (the)—ena (toh) skoolareekee (pl. ta skoolareekia)

earthquake, an (the)—enas (oh) seesmos

earthenware—peeleena

east—anatolee

Easter—Paskha *or* Lambree; **at Easter**—toh Paskha; **Happy Easter**—Kalo Paskha; **Easter Sunday**—Keeriakee tou Ah-you Paskha; **Easter Monday**—Dheftera tou Paskha; **Easter bread**—tsoorekee; **Easter egg**—Paskalino avgo

The most important religious event of the year, outranking even Christmas.

easy—efkolos (m), efkolee (f), efkolo (n)

eat (I)—Trogo; **to eat**—na fao; **I want something to eat**—Thelo kahtee na fao; **When (Where) shall we eat?**—Poteh (Poo) tha fahmeh?; **What shall we eat?**—Tee tha fahmeh?; **What is he**

eating?—Tee troee?; **I ate**—Efagah; **Did you eat?**—Efaghess?;
Did she (he) eat?—Efageh?

egg, an (the)—**en**a (toh) av**go** (pl. av**ga**)

electric (adj.)—eelek**troh**; **electric current, the**—toh **rev**ma; **electrician, an (the)**—**en**as (oh) eelek**trologos.**

The electric current in Greece is almost entirely 220 volts A.C.,
although on a few remote islands you might find 110 volts D.C.
The plugs are of the European, round-prong type, and the bulb
sockets almost always bayonet. To unscrew, push them in and
turn them counterclockwise a quarter-inch. Then lift out.

elevator, a (the)—**en**a (toh) ahsan**sehr** (as in the French "ascenseur")
In Greece, the first floor is the floor above street level; in elevators,
the ground floor is indicated by this sign: I.Σ. and the basement
by this sign: Υ.Π.

embarassed (I am)—Vreeskomay seh ahmikha**nee**a

embroidery—**ken**dima

emergency, an—**mi**a ah**nang**hee

emery board, an—**en**a yalo**hartoh** (lit. "sandpaper')

empty—ah-**dhee**oh

end, the—toh **tehr**ma or toh **tell**os; **the end of the summer**—toh
tellos tou kalokay**ri**oo; **the end of the affair**—toh **tell**os tees
skehsees; **end of April**—**tell**os Ahpree**lee**oo

engaged (to marry)—aravonias**men**os (m), aravonias**men**ee (f); **I'm
engaged**—Eemay aravonias**men**os (aravonias**men**ee)

engine, an (the)—**mi**a (ee) mee**khan**ee

English (lang.)—Ahng**lika**; **Do you speak English?**—Meelahteh
Ahng**lika**?

English (adj.)—Ahng**likoh**; **Englishman, an (the)**—**en**as (oh) **Ahn**glos; **Englishwoman, an (the)**—**mi**a (ee) Ahng**lee-dha**

engraving, an (the)—**mi**a (ee) harak**tikee**

enough—ar**ketoh**; **Do you have enough money?**—Eh-hees ar**keta**
hreemata?; **That is enough**—Fthah**nee**; **Enough!**—Ar**keta**!

entrance, an (the)—**mi**a (ee) **ee**sodhos (written on signs as:
ΕΙΣΟΔΟΣ; **No Entrance**—ΑΠΑΓΟΡΕΥΕΤΑΙ ΕΙΣΟΔΟΣ)

envelope, an (the)—**en**as (oh) **fah**kelos (pl. **fah**kelee); **air mail**—
ah-ehropo**rikoh** **fah**kelo; **large**—me**gahl**o **fah**kelo

envy (I)—Zilevo; **I envy you**—Seh zilevo; **I envy him (her)**—Ton (teen) zilevo

espadrilles—skenenia papootsia

etcetera—kay leepa

etching, an (the)—mia (ee) gravoora (pl. gravooress)

Euripides—Oh Evripee-dhees

evening—vrah-dhee; **this evening**—toh vrah-dhee; **yesterday evening**—ekthess vrah-dhee; **tomorrow evening**—ahvrio vrah-dhee

In Greece, evening begins when the sun sets; in other words, in the summertime, seven o'clock in the evening is still afternoon to a Greek. Therefore, when making a rendezvous, specify the hour, not the time of day.

every—kahtheh; **everybody**—ohlee; **every day**—kahtheh mehra; **every other day**—mehra parah mehra; **everything**—ohla; **everywhere**—pandoo

evil—kako (which also means, simply, "bad"); **evil eye, the**—toh kako mahtee (See **Part 4**.)

exactly—ahkrivos or sosta; **It's exactly six o'clock**—Eenay ahkrivos eksee ee ora; **Exactly!**—Sosta! (or Ahkrivos!)

excavation, an (the)—mia (ee) anaskafee

exchange (to)—na alahkso; **Can I exchange this?**—Boroh na toh alahkso?; **foreign exchange**—seenahlagma; **the exchange rate**—ee teemee seenalagmatos

exciting—sinarpastikoh

excursion, an (the)—mia (ee) ek-dhromee

excuse, an (the)—mia (ee) profasee; **Excuse me**—Seegnomee or Meh singhoreeteh

exhibition, an (the)—mia (ee) ekthesi
(written on signs as: ΕΚΘΕΣΕΙΣ)

exit, an (the)—mia (ee) eksodhos (written on signs as: ΕΞΟΔΟΣ)

expecting (I am)—Perimeno; **I am expecting a baby**—Perimeno paydhee

expensive—ahkreevoh; **It's very expensive**—Eenay pohlee ahkreevoh

expenses, the—ta ekso-dha; **my expenses**—ta ekso-dha mou extension (of a visa, holiday, etc.)—**mia** paratasee

extra—e**k**stra

eye, an (the)—e**na** (toh) **mah**tee (pl. ta **mah**tia); **my (your) eyes**—ta **mah**tia mou (sou). "**Mah**tia mou" being also a way of saying "My darling."

eyebrow pencil, an—e**na** molee**vee** ya ta **mah**tia; **eyeglasses**—yah**liah**; **eyelash, an**—**mia** vlefa**ree**dha (pl. vlefa**ree**dhess); **eyelid, the**—toh vle**fa**ro; **eye liner**—eye liner; **eye shadow**—skiah mah**tee**on; **eyesight**—ee o**ra**see; **eyestrain**—ee koo**ra**ssee ton mah**tee**on; **eyewash**—kolee**rio**; **evil eye, the**—toh ka**ko mah**tee

F

fabric—ee**fas**ma

face, a (the)—e**na** (toh) **pro**sopo; **my (your) face**—toh **pro**sopo mou (sou)

fact, a (the)—e**na** (toh) ye**go**nos

faint (dizzy)—zahlis**me**nos (m), zahlis**me**nee (f)

faithful—**pee**stos (m), **pee**stee (f); **unfaithful**—ah**pi**stos (m), ah**pi**stee (f)

fake, a—**mia** apomee**mi**see

fall (to)—na **pe**so; **I fell**—E**hpe**sa; **Did you fall?**—E**hpess**s?; **He (she) fell**—E**hpe**seh

fall (autumn)—fthee**no**poro; **in the fall**—toh fthee**no**poro; **this fall**—toh fthee**no**poro

false (untrue)—la**the**meno; **not real**—**psef**tiko

family, a (the)—**mia** (ee) eeko-**ye**nia; **my family**—ee eeko-**ye**niah mou

famous—feemis**me**nos (m), feemis**me**nee (f), feemis**me**no (n)

fan, a (tte) electric—e**nas** (oh) ahnemis**tee**ras; **hand**—**mia** (ee) ven**dah**lia

fantasy, a—**mia** fanta**see**a

far—mah**kriah**; **Is it far?**—Ee**nay** mah**kriah**?; **How far?**—**Po**so mah**kriah**?; **on foot**—meh ta **po**dhia; **by car**—meh toh aftokee**nitoh**; **by bus**—meh toh leh-ohfo**ree**oh; **by boat** (ship)—meh tee **var**ka (toh ka**rah**vee); **by train**—meh toh **tray**no; **How many minutes?**—**Po**sa **lef**tah?; **How many hours?**—**Po**sess o**ress**?

When asking any of the above questions, a good rule of thumb is to add to the answer received about 20% in time or distance. For the reasons why, see FACT.

fare, the (ticket price)—ta **nah**vla; **What is the fare?**—Poso eenay ta **nah**vla?

farm, a (the)—mia (ee) **far**ma

farmer, a (the)—**en**as (oh) yeh-or**gos**

farther—mahkreetera; **How much farther?**—Poso mahkreetera?

fashion, the—ee moh-dha; **fashionable**—tees moh-dhahs

fast (speedy)—**gree**gora; **Not so fast**—**Oh-**hee **toh**so **gree**gora; **faster**—pee-**oh gree**gora

fat (adj.)—pa**hees** (m), pa**hiah** (f), pa**hee** (n); **I'm too fat**—**Ee**may poh**lee** pa**hees** (pa**hiah**); **animal fat**—**lee**pos

fate—**meera**; **It is (was) fate**—**Ee**nay (**Ee**tahn) mee**rayo**

father, a (the)—**en**as (oh) pah**teh**ras *or* **en**as (oh) bah**bahs**; **father-in-law**—**en**as (oh) pe**theros**

faucet, a (the)—mia (ee) **vree**see; **The faucet is broken**—Ee **vree**see **ee**nay spahs**menee**

fault, a (the)—**en**a (toh) **sfal**ma; **It's my fault**—**Ee**nay **sfal**ma mou; **It's not your fault**—Dhen **ee**nay **sfal**ma sou; **It's his (her/their) fault**—**Ee**nay **sfal**ma tou (tees/tous); **faulty**—Dhen **pa**ee **kala** (lit. "It doesn't go well.")

favor, a (the)—mia (ee) **hah**ree; **Will you do me a favor?**—Tha mou **kah**nees mia **hah**ree?

favorite (It's my)—**Ee**nay toh kah**lee**tero mou; **What's your favorite?**—Pee**oh ee**nay toh kah**lee**tero sou?

feast, a—**en**a tra**peh**zee (lit. "a table"): **feast day, a**—mia **yor**tee *or* **en**a panig-**yeer**ee

feel (to) touch—na ang**hee**so; **Feel this**—Ahn**ghik**seh toh; **feel (to)** emotional, physical—na estha**hno**may; **I feel terrible**—Estha**hno**may ahs**kheema** (also means "ashamed"); **How do you feel?**—Pohs estha**hnese**?; **I felt**—Estha**hn**thika

feeling, a (emotion)—**en**a seenes**thima**; **my feelings**—ta seenes**thima** mou; **I don't want to hurt his (her) feelings**—Dhen **the**lo na ton (teen) plee**goso**

feet, the—ta **po**-dhia; **a foot**—**en**a **po**-dhee; **on foot**—meh ta **po**-dhia

female, a (the)—mia (ee) yee**nay**ka

feminist, a—**mia** femineestria

ferry, a (the)—**ena** (toh) fehree boht; **Is there a ferry to...?**—Eh-hee fehree boht ya tee...?

fever—peeretoh; **I have a fever**—Eh-ho peeretoh; **She (he) has a fever**—Eh-hee peeretoh

fiancé, a (the)—**en**as (oh) aravoniasti**kos** (m), **mia** (ee) aravoniastikiah (f)

fight, a (quarrel)—**en**as kavgahs; **We had a fight**—Eehamay **ena** kav**gah.**

figure (body), **a**—**mia** silouetta; **a beautiful figure**—**mia** oraya silouetta

file, a—**mia** leema; **nail file, a**—**mia** leema ton nikheeon

fill (to)—na yemeeso; **I will fill it**—Tha toh yemeeso; **Fill it up**—Yemiseh toh.

filling station, a (the)—**en**a (toh) venzina-dhiko

film (for a camera)—feelm.

filter (cigarettes, lens, etc.)—feeltro; **filter cigarettes**—tsigara meh feeltro

finally (at last)—epiteloos or teli**ka**; **eventually**—teli**ka**

find (to)—na vro; **I want to find**—Thelo na vro; **Where can I find...?**—Poo boroh na vro...?; **Did you find it?**—Toh vreekess?; **I found**—Vreeka; **He (she) found**—Vreekeh.

fine (thin, delicate)—leptoh or pseeloh; **pure**—katharoh; **fine art**—kahlee teknee

fine (I'm)—Eemay kala; **That's fine**—Kala eenay.

finish (to)—na teliohso; **I want to finish**—Thelo na teliohso; **I finished**—Teleeosa; **Are you finished** (Did you finish)?—Teleeosess?; **Is she (he) finished?**—Teleeoseh?; **It's finished**—Teleeoseh; **We're finished**—Teliohsameh.

fire—fotiah; **It's on fire**—Peereh fotiah; **to make a fire**—n'anahpso fotiah

fireworks—peerotekneemata

A favorite toy of the Greeks and a prominent feature of their Easter festivities, particularly on Easter Sunday morning when, following the priests' midnight announcement that Christ has risen, the entire country explodes in pyrotechnic displays. (See EASTER.)

first—**pro**tos (m), **pro**tee (f), pro**toh** (n); **at first**—steen arkhee; **first of all**—prot' ap' ohla; **first aid**—protee voeethia; **first class**—

protee thessee; **first name**—meekro ohnoma

fish, a (the)—ena (toh) psaree; **the fishes**—ta psaria

fish (to)—na psarevo

fish market, a (the)—mia (ee) psaragora

fit (It doesn't)—Dhen teriahzee; **fitting, a** (clothes)—mia **prova**

fix (to)—na episkevahso; **I can't fix this**—Dhen boroh na toh episkevahso; **Can you fix it?**—Boreeteh na toh episkevahseteh?; **fixed (It is)**—Eenay ehteemo (lit. "It is ready.")

flag, a (the)—mia (ee) seemaya

flash—flahs; **flashbulb**—lampa flahs; **flash cube**—keevo flahs; **flashlight, a**—(the)—enas (oh) fahkos

flavor, a (the)—ena (toh) ahroma

fleas—pseelee; **flea market, the**—ta paliazee-dhika (But, in Monastiraki in Athens, it is called "toh yousooroom.)

flight, a (the) airplane—mia (ee) pteesee

flint, a (the) lighter—mia (ee) petra (pl. petress); **Do you have flints (for a lighter)?**—Eh-hees petress (ya ahnapteera)?
Available at all sidewalk kiosks, either loose or in Ronson-type packets.

flippers—vatrak-ho-**peh**-dhila

flirt (I)—Flehrtaro; **I wasn't flirting**—Dhen **flehr**tara

flirt, a—enas flehrtakhias (m), mia koketta (f)

floor, the (of a room, etc.)—toh **pah**toma; **of a building**—oh orofos; **2nd floor**—**dhef**teros orofos; **3rd floor**—**tree**tos orofos
As in Europe, the first floor is the one above street level.

florist's shop, a (the)—ena (toh) anthopoleeoh

flower, a (the)—ena (toh) louloo-dhee (pl. ta louloo-dhia)

flu, the—ee greepee; **I have the flu**—Eh-ho greepee; **He (she) has the flu**—Eh-hee greepee

flush (to) (the toilet)—trahvaee; **The toilet doesn't flush**—Dhen trahvaee toh kazanahkee

flute, a (the)—ena (toh) flaooto

fly, a (the)—mia meega (pl. ee meeghess); **flypaper**—meegopaghee-dha; **fly spray**—ah-ehrosol; **fly swatter**—meegoo-dhee-ohktees

fly (to)—na taksi-**dhep**so ah-ehroporikos; **I want to fly to...**—Thelo na taksi-**dhep**so ah-ehroporikos stee...

folk dance—la-eekos horos; **folk song**—dheemotiko trahgoo-dhee food—fahghitoh; **food poisoning**—trofikee dheelitireeasi

foot, a (the)—**en**a (toh) po-dhee (pl. podhia); **on foot**—meh ta po-dhia; **football** (soccer)—po-**dhos**fero

for—ya; **for me**—ya **men**a; **for you**—ya **sen**a; **for all of you**—ya sahs; **for her**—ya af**teen**; **for him**—ya af**ton**; **for us**—ya mahs; **for them**—ya af**tous**; **for this**—ya af**toh**; **for that**—ya e**kee**no; **What for?**—Ya tee?; **What is this for?**—Ya tee **ee**nay af**toh**?

forbidden—ahpago**rev**eteh (written on signs as: ΑΠΑΓΟΡΕΥΕΤΑΙ)

forecast, the—ee prov**lep**sees

foreign—**ksen**o; **foreigner, a (the)**—**en**as (oh) **ksen**os (m), **mi**a (ee) **ksen**ee (f). (See FOREIGNER.)

forever—ya **pahn**da

forget (I)—**Ksek**no; **Don't forget!**—Mee ksek**has**ees; **forgot (I)**—Ksek**has**a˙; **You forgot**—Ksek**has**ees; **He (she) forgot**—Ksek**has**eh; **We forgot**—Ksek**has**ameh

forgive (I)—Sing**hor**o; **I forgive you**—Seh sing**hor**o; **Please forgive me**—Parakalo, meh singho**ree**teh

fork (eating), a (the)—**en**a (toh) pee**roo**nee (pl. pee**roo**nia)

fountain, a (the)—**en**a (toh) sindri**vah**nee

fox, a—**mi**a ah**lep**oo; **fox fur**—**goo**na ahle**poos**

fragile—ef**thraf**-stoh (written as: ΕΥΘΡΑΣΤΟ)

frame (picture), a (the)—**mi**a (ee) kor**nee**za

free—ellef**ther**o; **for free** (gratis)—**tzam**ba; **unoccupied**—ellef**ther**o; **free love**—ellef**ther**os eh**rot**as: **freedom**—elefther**ee**a

freighter (ship), a (the)—**en**a (toh) for**tee**go **plee**on

French (lang.)—Gali**kah**; **French** (adj.)—Gali**koh**; **Frenchman, a**—**en**as **Gah**los; **Frenchwoman, a**—**mi**a Gahlee-dha; **French-fries**—patah**tess** tigani**tess**

fresh (not stale)—**fres**ko; **fresh today**—seeme**rin**o; **Is it fresh today?**—**Ee**nay seeme**rin**o?; **fresh water** (not salty)—**glee**ko **neh**ro

Friday—Parask**ev**ee

fried—tigani**toh**; **fried eggs**—**av**ga **mah**tia

friend, a (the)—**en**as (oh) **feel**os (m), **mi**a (ee) **feel**ee (f). **friend-ship**—feel**ee**a

from—**ah**po; **Where are you from?**—**Ah**po poo **ees**teh?; **From whom?**—**Ah**po **pee**on?; **from now on**—**ah**po **tor**ah frozen—kahtep-sigmeno

fruit—froota; **fruit juice**—heemos frooton

full (bottle, box, etc.)—yemahtoh; **hotel, stomach**—fool; **complete**—ohloklero; **full-length**—mahkree; **full moon**—pahselinos

funeral, a (the)—mia kee-dheea

funnel, a—ena honee

funny—komikos (m), komikee (f), komikoh (n); **strange**—paraksenos (m), paraksenee (f), parakseno (n)

fur—goona; **fur coat, a**—ena goonino paltoh

furnished—epeeplomeno; **Is it furnished?**—Eenay epeeplomeno?

furniture—ehpeela

fuse, a (the)—mia (ee) ahsfahlia (pl. ahsfahliess); **The fuse is blown**—Kah-eekeh ee asfahlia.

future, the—toh mellon; **in the future**—stoh mellon

G

gale, a (the)—mia (ee) thee-ela; **gale warning**—anangheleea thee-elees

gallery, a (the) art—mia (ee) peenakotheekee

gamble (to)—na **payzoh** or na **pekso** (both literally meaning "to play"); **gambling**—tzohgohs

game, a (the)—ena (toh) payknee-dhee (pl. paykneedhia)

garage, a (ahe)—ena (toh) garahz

garbage, the—ta skoupee-dhia; **Where can I put the garbage?**—Poo boroh na **vahlo** ta skoupeedhia?

garden, a (the)—enas (oh) **keepos**

garlic—skor-dhoh

gas (cooking)—gahzee; **gas cooker, a (the)**—mia (ee) koozeena (also the word for "kitchen"); **a bottle of gas**—mia feeahlee gahzee

gasoline—venzeenee; **diesel**—petrelayo meekhanees; **regular**—kanonikee; **super**—soopehr

gas station, a (the)—ena (toh) venzeenah-dhiko

gay (happy)—haroomenos (m), haroomenee (f); **homosexual**—teeootos

general (adj.)—yenikah; **generally**—yenikah

general store, a (the)—ena (toh) yeni**koh** embor**io** or pahn-dopolee**oh**

These stores are life-savers and contain a mindboggling assortment of goods from animal foods to groceries, hardware items and barreled ouzo and paraffin. But never meats or cigarettes.

generous—yenna**yos** (m) yenna**ya** (f), yenna**yo** (n)

gentle—ev-yeni**kos** (m), ev-yeni**kee** (f), ev-yeni**koh** (n); **gently**—eerema

German (lang.)—Yeh**rmani**ka; **a German man (woman)**—enas Yehr**manos** (mia Yehrman**ee-**dha); **German** (adj.)—Yehr**mani**koh

gesso—yeepso ya kalite**knee**

get (to) bring—na fehro; **I'll get it**—Tha toh fehro; **Will you get it?**—Tha toh fehrees?; **Did you get it?**—Toh effehress?; **Do you get (understand) it?**—Kah**tahla**vess?;—**I get up**—See**koh**nomay; **I get sick**—Yeenomay ahrostos; **Get well!**—Perastikah!; **Let's get together**—Na kah**noo**meh pahreh-a; **I got it**—Toh eh-ho pahree (**I understood**—Kah**tahla**va); **Have you got it?**—Toh-hees?; **Has she (he) got it?**—Toh-hee?

gift, a (the)—ena (toh) dhoro (pl. dhora)

gilded—hreeso**meno**

gipsy, a (the)—enas (oh) tsingah**nos** (m), mia (ee) tsing**ah**na; **gipsies**—tsing**ah**nee

girl, a (the) little—ena (toh) koree**tsee** or koreet**sakee**; **young lady**—mia (ee) ko**pella**; **girl friend, a**—mia feelee or feelenah-dha; **my girl friend**—ee feelee (feelenah-dha) mou

give (to)—na dhoso; **I want to give this to you (him/her)**—Thelo na sou (tou/tees) toh dhoso aftoh; **Did you give it to her (him)?**—Tees (tou) toh eh-dhosess?; **Will you give me (a cigarette)?**—Tha mou dhosees (ena tsigahro)?; **Give me**—Dhohs mou; **Give me that**—Dhohs mou aftoh; **I give up** Para-dhee-dhohmay; **I gave**—Eh-dhohsa; **I gave it to her (him)**—Tees (tou) toh ehdhohsa

glass, a (the)—ena (toh) pohtee**eere** (pl. pohtee**eeria**); **a glass of water (wine)**—ena pohtee**eere** nehro (krah**see**); **glass (the substance)**—yah**lee** or kree**stalo**; **eyeglasses**—yah**liah**; **sunglasses**—yah**liah** tou eeli**oo**

glaze, a (the) pottery—ena (toh) glasarisma; **glazed**—glasarismeno

glue—kohla: **all-purpose**—Oohoo (UHU—a brand name become generic)

gnats—skneepess

go (to)—na pao; **I am going (to/for)**—Pao or Peeg-yeno (sto/ya); **I am going** (leaving)—Fevgo; **I want to go**—Thelo na pao; **I will go**—Tha pao; **I have gone to** (visited)—Eh-ho paee. **Are you going?**—Pahs? or Peeg-yenees?; **Are you going** (leaving)?—Fevghees?; **Do you want to go?**—Thelees na pahs?; **Will you go?**—Tha pahs?; **When will you go?**—Poteh tha pahs?; **Where will you go?**—Poo tha pahs?; **Did you go?**—Peeg-yess?; **Have you gone** (visited)?—Eh-hees paee? **He (she/it) is going (to/for)**—Paee or Peeg-yenee (sto/ya); **He is going** (leaving)—Fevghee; **He wants to go**—Thelee na paee; **He will go**—Tha paee; **When will he go?**—Poteh tha paee?; **Where will he go?**—Poo tha paee?; **Has he gone** (visited)? Eh-hee paee?; **He went**—Peegyeh; **He has gone** (left)—Leepee or Efeegeh; **It (prices, the sun, etc.) is going up (down)**—Ahnevehnee (Kahtevenee).

Note: Since all three third persons (he, she, it) take the same verb form and since the pronoun is rarely used, you must, if you want to be specific, preface the verb with its proper pronoun: **He**—Aftohs; **She**—Aftee; **It**—Aftoh.

We are going (to/for)—Pahmeh or Peeg-yenomeh (sto/ya); **We are going** (leaving)—Fevgomeh; **Let's go**—Pahmeh; **We want to go**—Thelomeh na pahmeh; **We will go**—Tha pahmeh; **When will we go?**—Poteh na pahmeh? **Where are we going?** Poo tha pahmeh?; **We have gone** (visited)—Eh-homeh paee; **We went**—Peegameh

They are going (to/for)—Peeg-yenoon (sto/ya); **They are going** (leaving)—Fevgoon; **They want to go**—Theloon na pahneh; **They will go**—Tha pahneh; **When will they go?**—Poteh tha pahneh?; **Where are they going?**—Poo tha pahneh?; **They have gone** (visited)—Eh-hoon paee; **They've gone** (left)—Leepoon or Efeegahn; **They went**—Peeganeh.

Here we go!—Pahmeh!; **What's going on?**—Tee seemvaynee?; **Go on** (go ahead)—Prokhora; **It's (a fire, etc.) gone out**—Esviseh; **It's gone** (disappeared)—Eksa-fahneesthikeh goat, a (the)—ena (toh) kaht-seekee (pl. kaht-seekess)

God—Oh Theh-ohs; My God!—Theh mou!; God willing—Prota Oh Theh-ohs; God only knows—Oh Theh-ohs ksehree; Thanks (glory) be to God—Dohksa toh Theh-oh

goddaughter, a (the)—mia (ee) vaptisteera; godfather, a (the)—enas (oh) nonohs; godmother, a (the) mia (ee) nonah; godson, a (the)—enas (oh) vap-tisimiohs

gold—hreesohs; golden—hreesoh; gold leaf—feelo hreesou; gold-plated—epihreesomeno

golf—golf; golf ball—golf bahla; golf club—golf club; golf club (organization)—leskhee tou golf; golf course—yeepe-dhoh tou golf

There are four golf courses in Greece: one in the Athens suburb of Glyfada, two on the island of Rhodes, and one in Chalkidiki in Northern Greece. Please see the local Greek National Tourist Organization (E.O.T.—pronounced eh-oht) for further details.

good (adj.)—kahlos (m), kahlee (f), kahlo (n); very good—polee kahlo; Good!—Kala! (used in the sense of "okay" as well as in the adverbial form of "good," i.e. "well")

Goodbye—Ahndeeo or Yasoo or Sto kahlo or, in the sense of "Nice meeting you"—Harika polee

good looking—ohmorfos (m), ohmorfee (f); Good morning—Kahlee mehra; Good afternoon—Hayreteh; Good evening—Kahlee spehra

gouache—nehro boh-yahs (lit. "water paint")

gourd, a—ena nehro-kolokeethee or ena flahskee

government, a (the)—mia (ee) keevehrnisee

grafitti—grafeetee

gram, a—ena gramario (pl. gramaria)

In Greece, everything from grocery items to screws, nails and ropes are sold by the gram and kilo.

granddaughter, a (the)—mia (ee) engonee; grandfather, a (the)—enas (oh) papoos; grandmother—mia (ee) ya-ya; grandson—enas (oh) engonos

grated (cheese, etc.)—treemeno; grater, a—enas treeftes

grave, a (the)—enas (oh) tahfos; the grave of...—oh tahfos tou (tees)...

grease (fat)—**lee**pos; **greasy** (food)—lee**par**o; grease (lubricant)—**grah**so; **greasy** (oily)—lah-**dhoh**meno

Greece—E**lla**dha; **of Greece**—tees E**lla**dhas; **in Greece**—steen E**lla**dha; **from Greece**—ahpo teen E**lla**dha. **Greek** (lang.)—E**leeni**ka; **I don't speak (understand) Greek**—Dhen mee**lao** (kata**lavay**no) E**leeni**ka; **Greek man, a (the)**—**en**as (oh) E**lleen**as; **Greek woman**—**mi**a (ee) E**leenee-**dha

green—**prah**sino; **greens** (veg.)—**hor**ta

grill, a—**mi**a s**ka**ra; **grilled**—tees s**ka**ras or psee**toh**

grocer, a (the)—**en**as (oh) bah**kah**lees; **groceries**—ee-dhee bah**kali**kees; **grocery store, a (the)**—**en**a (toh) bah**kah**liko

ground, the (earth)—toh **ho**ma or eeg-**yee**; **ground, the** (electrical)—ee **yee**ose; **ground** (spices, etc.) adj.—**tree**meno

group, a (the) tourist, etc.—**en**a (toh) group; **of friends**—**mi**a (ee) pa**reh**-a

guarantee, a (the)—**mi**a (ee) eng-**yee**-eesee (although the word "gahrahn**dee**" is increasingly coming into use); **I guarantee it**—Toh eng-**yee**oomay

guess, to—na man**dep**so; **Guess!**—**Mahn**depseh!; **I guess** believe)—No**mee**zo

guest, a (the)—**en**as (oh) ksenos (m); **mi**a (ee) ksenee

guide, a (the)—**en**as (oh) o-**dhi**gos; **a tourist guide**—**en**as (oh) ksenagos; **a guide book**—**en**as o-**dhi**gos (vee**vlee**o)
To add to the confusion, the driver of any vehicle, including your tourist bus, is also called **en**as o-**dhi**gos.

guitar, a (the)—**mi**a (ee) kee**tha**ra; **guitarist, a (the)**—**en**as (oh) kitha**ree**stas

gynecologist, a (the)—**en**as (oh) yeenay-ko**loh**gos

H

hair, a—**mi**a **tree**kha; **hair** (on the head)—mah**li**ah; **the hair**—ta mah**li**ah; **my hair**—ta mah**li**ah mou; **hairy**—mali**ar**os; **hairbush, a**—**mi**a **voort**sa mah**li**on; **haircut, a**—**en**a koo**re**ma; **hair dresser**—ko**mo**tria; **hair drier, a**—**en**a se**swar** or peesto**la**kee; **hairnet, a**—**en**a **fe**leh; **hairpins**—foor**ket**tess

half—meeso; **the half**—toh meeso; **half a kilo**—meeso kilo; **half a bottle**—ena meeso boukahlee; **half the bottle**—toh meeso boukahlee; **half-and-half**—meeso-meeso

ham—zambon

hamburger patty, a—**en**a beef**tek**ee; **hamburger, a** (with bread)—ena beef**tek**ee sandoo-**eet**s; **hamburger meat** (raw)—**keem**a

hammer, a (the)—**en**a (toh) s**feer**ee

hand, a (the)—**en**a (toh) **heh**ree (pl. ta **heh**ria); **a handful**—**mi**a **fouk**ta; **handmade**—**heer**opee-eetoh; **second-hand**—metahehrismeno

handbag, a (the)—**mi**a (ee) t**sahn**da (also means plastic *or* paper bag)

handicrafts—heerotek**nee**a

handkerchief, a (the)—**en**a (toh) mahn**deel**ee (pl. mahn**deel**ia)

handsome—o**ray**os *or* oh**mor**fos

hangover, a—**en**as ponokefalos ahpo me**thee**si

harbor, the—toh lee**mah**nee; **harbor master, the**—oh lime**nark**hees

hard—s**kleer**oh; **difficult**—**dhees**kolo

hardware—see-dheri**ka**; **hardware store**—maga**zee** poo po**lae**e seedheri**ka**

harpoon, a—**en**a kamah**kee**

harvest, the—oh theris**mos**

hashish—hah**see**see

hat, a (the)—**en**a (toh) kah**pel**lo

hate (I)—**Mee**so; **I hate it**—Toh **mee**so; **I hate you**—Seh **mee**so; **I hate him (her)**—Ton (teen) **mee**so; **Do you hate me?**—Meh mee**see**s?

have (to)—na eh-ho; **I want to have**—**Thel**o na eh-ho

Present:	Past	Infinitive
I have—**Eh**-ho	I had—**Ee**-ha	na eh-o
You have—**Eh**-hees	You had—**Ee**-hess	na eh-ees
He has—**Eh**-hee	He had—**Ee**-heh	na eh-ee
We have—**Eh**-homeh	We had—**Ee**-hameh	na eh-omeh
You have—**Eh**-heteh	You had—**Ee**-hateh	na eh-eteh
They have—**Eh**-hoon	They had—**Ee**khahn	na eh-oon

Future—put "tha" before the present: **I will have**—Tha **eh**-ho.

Negative—put "dhen" before the verb: **I don't have**—dhen **eh**-ho; **I won't have**—Dhen tha **eh**-ho.

have to (I) must—Prepee; **I have to go**—Prepee na **pao**. See also **must**.

he—aftohs *or* when "he" is over there somewhere: ekeenos

head, a (the)—ena (toh) kefahlee; **my head**—toh kefahlee mou; **headache**—ponokefalos; **head, the** (boss)—toh ahfendikoh

hear (I)—Ahkoo-oh; **Do you hear?**—Ahkoo-ees?; **I heard**—Ahkoosa; **Did you hear?**—Ahkoosess?; **He (she) heard**—Ahkooseh

hearing—ahkoee; **hearing aid**—ahkoostika varikoee-as; **hard of hearing**—vareeko-ohs

heart, the—ee kardhiah; **my heart**—ee kardhiah mou (but, in the more passionate sense: **My heart!**—Kar-dhoola mou!—literally "My soul!")

heat, the—ee zestee; **heater, a (the)**—mia (ee) thehrmahstra

heaven—ooranos; **I'm in heaven**—Eemay sta oorahnia; **heavenly**—oorahnio

heavy—vahree; **very heavy**—polee vahree

heel, the (foot)—ee ftehrna; **shoe**—toh takoonee

heir, a (the)—enas (oh) kleeronomos (m), mia (ee) kleeronomos (f)

heirloom, a—ena keemeelio

helicopter, a (the)—ena (toh) elikoptero

hell—kolasees; **Go to hell!**—Sto dheeahvolo!

Hello!—Yasoo *or* Yasahs

helmet, a (the)—ena (toh) krahnos

help—voeethia—**to help**—na voeetheeso; **I want to help**—Thelo na voeetheeso; **I want help**—Thelo voeethia; **Can you help me?**—Boreeteh na meh voeetheeseteh?; **helper, a**—enas voeethos

hem, the (dress)—toh streefoma

her—ahftee; **for her**—ya ahftee; **hers**—dheekoh tees; **her** (possessive)—tees; **object of verb**—teen (di rect), tees (indirect); **her sweater**—toh pulohver tees; **It's hers**—Eenay dheekoh tees; **I saw her** Teen ee-dha; **I gave it to her**—Tees toh eh-dhosa; **Give it to her**—dhohs tees toh

herb, a (the)—**en**a (toh) vo**ta**no (pl. ta vo**ta**na)

Hercules—Oh Eerak**lees**

here—eh-**dhoh**; **Come here**—Ella dhoh; **Here it is**—Nah toh

Hi!—Ya**soo**!

high—**psee**la

highway, a (the)—**mi**a (ee) ethni**kee** o-**dhohs**

hill, a (the)—**en**as (oh) **lo**fohs

him—ah**fton**; **for him**—ya ah**fton**; **object of verb**—ton (direct), tou (indirect); **It's for him**—**Ee**nay ya ah**fton**; **I saw him**—Ton ee**dha**; **I gave it to him**—Tou toh eh-**dho**sa; **Give it to him**—**dhohs** tou toh

his—**dhee**koh tou; **possessive pronoun**—tou; **It's his**—**Ee**nay **dhee**koh tou; **his sweater**—toh pul**loh**ver tou

history, the—ee eesto**ree**a; **historical**—eesto**ri**koh

hitch-hike (to)—na **kah**no au**to**stop

hold (to)—na kra**tee**so; **I'll hold (or keep) it**—Tha toh kra**tee**so; **Will you hold (or keep) it for me?**—Tha toh kra**tee**sees ya **me**na?

hole, a (the)—**mi**a (ee) **tree**pa (pl. ee tree**pess**); **It has a hole**—Eh-hee **tree**pa

holidays—dhee-ako**pess**

holy—ee-**eroh** (n) *or* a**hyos** (m), a**hgyee**a (f), and a**hyo** (n)—all of which also means "saint"

home—**spee**tee; **my home**—toh **spee**tee mou

homeland—ee pah**tree**dha; **homemade**—spee**tee**sio; **homesick**—nostal**gos** (m), nostal**ghee** (f); **I'm homesick**—Nostal**go** teen pah**tree**dha

Homer—Oh Oh**mee**ros

homosexual, a (the)—**en**as (oh) omofilo**fi**los (m), **mi**a (ee) omofilo**fi**lee (f); **homosexuality**—omofilofi**lee**a

honest—**en**dimos (m), **en**dimee (f), **en**dimo (n); **honesty**—**en**dimo-tees

honey—**mel**lee; **honeymoon**—**mee**nahs tou **mel**itohs

hood, a (hat)—**mi**a koo**koo**la; **with a hood**—meh koo**koo**la

hook, a (the) all types—**en**a (toh) ahn**ghee**stree (pl. ahn**ghee**stria)

hookah (water pipe), a (the)—**en**as (oh) nargi**less**

hope (noun)—elpee-**dha**; **I hope**—el**pee**zo; **I hope so**—Toh elpeezo; **I hoped**—Eelpeeza; **Is there any hope?**—Eepar-hee elpee-dha?

horn (animal), **a (the)**—**en**a (toh) ker**a**toh; (pl. ta ker**a**ta); a cuckold—**en**as kera**tahs**

horny (sexually)—eretheesmenos (m), eretheesmenee (f)

hornet, a (the)—**mi**a (ee) s**fee**nga (pl. ee sfeenghess); **hornet's nest, a (the)**—**mi**a (ee) sfeengofoli**ah**

horoscope, a (the)—**en**a (toh) oraskopio

horrible—freektoh (n)

hors d'oeuvres—mezeh *or* meze-dhahkia

horse, a (the)—**en**a (toh) ahlogo (pl. ta ahloga)

horsepower—eepo-**dhee**namee; **How many horsepower?**—Posee eepodheenamee?

hospital, a (the)—**en**a (toh) nosokom**ee**o

hospitality—filok-seneea

hostel (youth)—kseno-nahs neh-ohtitos

hot—zestos (m), zestee (f), zestoh (n); **hot weather, the**—oh zestos kayros; **hot water**—zestoh nehro; **It (food, water, etc.) isn't hot enough**—Dhen eenay arketa zestoh; **hot water bottle**—thermo-fora

hotel, a (the)—**en**a (toh) kseno-dhok**hee**o
(written as: ΞΕΝΟΔΟΧΕΙΟΝ)

hour, the—ee ora; **one o'clock**—mia ee ora; **in an hour**—seh mia ora; **hours**—oress; **in five hours**—seh (*or* meta ahpo) pendeh oress; **hourly**—katheh ora

house, a (the)—**en**a (toh) sp**ee**tee (pl. sp**ee**tia); **a 2- or 3-story house**—**en**as peergos (lit. "tower"); **an apartment house**—**mi**a pohlikahtik**ee**a

how—pohs; **How many?**—Posa?; **How mucb (is it)?**—Poso eenay)?; **How far?**—Poso mahkiah?; **How long (time)?**—Poso kayro?; **How are you? Pohs pahs?; How are you doing?**—Tee kahnees?; **How do you do?**—Hayro polee?

humid—eegroh; **humidity**—eegraseea

humor—humor; **a sense of humor**—**mi**a aysthisee humor

hunger—peena; **I'm hungry**—Peeno; **I'm not hungry**—Dhen peano; **Are you hungry?**—Peenahs?; **Is she (he) hungry?**—Peenaee?; **We're hungry**—Peenoomeh hunting—keeneeghee; **I want to go hunting**—Thelo na pao kee-neeghee

hurry (I'm in a)—Veeahsomay; **Hurry!**—Veeahsou!

hurt, a—mia pleeghee; **It hurts**—Ponaee; **Does it hurt?**—Ponaee?

husband, a (the)—enas (oh) ahn-dhras; **my husband**—oh ahn-dhras mou; **your husband**—oh **ahn**-dhras sou; **her husband**—oh **ahn**-dhras tees

I

I—Ehgo; **I am**—Eemay; **I have**—Eh-ho; **I want**—Thelo; **Not I**—Oh-hee ehgo

Icarus—Oh Eekaros

ice—pahgos; **ice cold**—pahgameno; **ice cubes**—pahgahkia

ice cream—pahgotoh; **chocolate**—sokolata; **vanilla**—vaneelia; **cone, a**—ena honahkee; **cup, a**—ena keepelahkee; **stick**—ksee-lahkee

icon, a (the)—mia (ee) eekona (pl. eekoness)

idea, a (the)—mia (ee) ee-dheh-a; **I have an idea**—Eh-ho mia ee-dheh-a

identity card, a (the)—ena dhelteeo tahftohtitos

if—ahn (used exactly as in English); **If you want**—Ahn thelees

Iliad, the—Ee Eeleeahs

ill—ahrostos (m), ahrostee (f); **illness, an (the)**—mia (ee) ahrosteea

illegal—paranomo; **illegally**—paranoma

imagine (I)—Fantahzomay; **I don't imagine so**—Dhen fantah-zomay; **Imagine!**—Fantahsou!

imitation, an—mia ahpomeemisee; **imitation leather**—dhehrma eemitasiohn

immediately—ahmehsos

important – spou-**dhay**os (m), spou-**dhaya** (f), spou-**dhay**o (n)

impossible—ah-dheenatoh; **It's impossible**—Eenay ah-dheenatoh; **It was impossible**—Eetahn ah-**dhee**natoh

in (In the sense of "at")—sto (n), stee (f), etc.

in (in the sense of "inside")—mehsa sto (stee, etc.); **He is in the hotel**—Eenay mehsa sto ksenodhokheeo; **What's in the bottle?**—Tee eenay mehsa sto boukahlee?; **He (she) is inside**—Eenay mehsa

incense—leevahnee (available at kiosks and grocery stores)

independent—ahneksartitos (m), ahneksartitee (f), ahneksartito (n)

inflate (to)—na fooskono; **Can you inflate this?**—Boreeteh na toh fooskoseteh aftoh?

information—pleeroforeea (written as: ΠΛΗΡΟΦΟΡΕΙΑΙ); **I would like some information**—Tha eethela mia pleeroforeea

ingredients, the—ta seestatika

ink—melahnee; **black**—mahvro; **blue**—bleh; **red**—kokino; **India ink**—seenikee melahnee

inner tube, an—mia sambrella

innocence—ahtho-ohtita; **innocent**—ahtho-os (m), ahtho-a (f)

insect, an—ena endomo; **the insects**—ta endoma; **insecticide**—endomoktohno

inside—mehsa; **the inside**—toh esoteriko; **inside out**—ahnahpo-dha

instant, an—mia steegmee; **instant** (adj.)—steegmee-ayo; **instant coffee**—steegmee-ayos kafess *or* Nescafeh

insult, an—mia prosvolee; **insulting**—prosvlitikoh

insurance, the—ee ahsfahlia; **life insurance**—ahsfahlia zoees

intelligent—meeahlomenos (m), meeahlomenee (f)

intercourse (sexual)—seenouseea

interested (I am)—Endheeaferomay; **It interests me**—M'endheeaferee; **Are you interested?**—Endheeaferesay?; **Is he (she) interested?**—Endheeaferetay?; **interesting**—endheeaferon; **very interesting**—polee endheeaferon

international—dhee-ethnees

interpreter, an (the)—enas (oh) dhee-ermineh-ahs

into—mehsa

introduce (I)—Seesteeno; **I want to introduce you**—Thelo na seh seesteeso; **Do you want me to introduce you?**—Thelees na seh seesteeso?; **Will you introduce me?**—Tha meh seesteesees?

introduction, an—mia seestasees

invite (to)—na kahleso; **I would like to invite them (him/her)**—Tha eethela na tous (ton/teen) kahleso

Irish (adj.)—Eerlan-dhikoh; **an Irishman**—enas Eerlan-dhohs; **an Irish woman**—mia Eerlan-dhee; **the Irish**—ee Eerlan-dhee

iron (the metal)—see-dhero; a flat iron—ena see-dhero; iron (to)—
    na see-dheroso; Can you iron this?—Borees na toh see-
    dherosees?

I.O.U., an—ena grahmahtio

irritating—erethistikos (m), erethistikee (f), erethistikoh (n)

island, a (the)—ena (toh) neesee; the island of Patmos—toh
    neesee Pahtmos

isolated—ahpomero; an isolated spot—ena ahpomero mehros; an
    isolated beach—mia ahpomeree phahz

Israeli, an—enas Eesra-eelinos (m), mia Eesra-eelinee (f)

it—aftoh (n), aftee (f), aftohs (m), aftess (f pl.), aftee (m pl.), aftah
    (n pl.); object of verb (direct)—toh (n), teen (f), ton (m); pos-
    sessive pronoun—tou (n), tees (f), tou (m); Its batteries—Ee
    bathareeess tou; I have it—Toh eh-ho; I gave it to him—Tou toh
    eh-dhosa

Italian (adj.)—Eetalikoh; an Italian man—enas Eetalos; an Italian
    woman—mia Eetalee-dha; the Italian language—Eetalika

itch, an—mia fagoora

itemize (to)—na analeeso; Can you itemize the bill, please?—
    Boreeteh na analeeseteh toh lohgariasmo, parakalo?

itinerary, an (the)—ena (toh) dhromologhio; What is the itin-
    erary?—Tee eenay toh dhromologhio?

ivory—elefantostoon

J

jacket, a (the)—mia (ee) zahketta or ena (toh) sah-kahkee

jade—nefreetees

jammed (blocked)—blok-harismeno

January—Yenaris

Japanese (adj.)—Yahponikoh; a Japanese man enas Yahponehsos; a
    Japanese woman—mia Yahponehsa; the Japanese language—
    Yahponika

jar, a (the) glass—ena (toh) vahso

jelly—zelleh; jelly fish—tsouktra (large—meh-dhousa

Jesus—Oh Yeesoos

jewelry—kosmeemata; jeweler's—kosmeematapoleeo

jetty, a (the)—mia (ee) prokimeh-a or enas (oh) molos

job, a—mia dhooliah; **I'm looking for a job**—Psahkno ya dhooliah

joke, a.—ena ahsteeo; **I'm joking** – Ahstee-ehvomay; **It was only a joke**— Eetahn mohno ahsteeo

journey, a (the)—ena taksee-dhee; **I'm journeying**—Taksi-**dhevo**

joy, a—mia hara; **It's a joy**—Eenay mia hara

juice—heemos

juke box, a (the)—**ena** (toh) juke box

July—Yoolios

June—Yoonios

junta, a (the)—**mia** (ee) hoonda

just (correct, fair)—sostoh; **exact**—ahkrivess; **just** (barely, recently)—mohlees; **just now**—mohless torah; **He just left**— Mohlees efeegeh; **I just arrived**—Mohlees eeltha; **just a little**— tohso dhah; **just you and me**—emees mohnon

K

kaftan, a (the)—**mia** (ee) kaftahnee; **with a hood**—meh kookoola

keep (to)—na krahteeso; **Can I keep it?**—Boroh na toh krahteeso? **You can keep it**—Borees na toh krahteesees; **Keep it**—**Krah**tiseh toh; **to keep (take care of)**—na feelahkso; **Will you keep it for me?**—Tha toh feelahksees ya mena?; **for keeps**—ya pahnda

keepsake, a—ena entheemio

kennel a (the)—**ena** (toh) speet**ah**kee skee**e**lou (lit. "a little dog house")

kerosene—kahtharo petrelayo; **a kerosene lamp**—mia lampa petrelayoo

Kerosene can almost always be bought loose in grocery stores; you should your own can or bottle.

key, a (the)—**ena** (toh) klee-**dhee**; **key ring, a**—**ena** breh-**lohk**

kiln, a (the)—**ena** (toh) kameenee

kilo, a (the)—**ena** (toh) kilo

kilometer, a—**ena** heeliohmetro (pl. heeliahmetra)

kind (good-hearted)—kahlos (m), kahlee (f); **kindness**—ee kahloseenee; **You're very kind to me**—Eesay polee kahlos (kahlee) mazee mou

king, a (the)—**enas** (oh) vasilayefs; **kingdom, a (the)**—**ena** (toh) vaseelio; **King Constantine**—Oh vasilayefs Constanteenos

There is no longer a king or a kingdom of Greece, the people having voted by referendum in 1974 to abolish the monarchy.

kiosk, a (the)—**ena** (toh) pere**ep**tero; **Where is the nearest kiosk?**—Poo eenay toh pleesee-**es**tero pere**ep**tero?; **Is there a kiosk open?**—Eeeparkhee ahneektoh pere**ep**tero?

kiss, a—**ena** feelee (pl. feeleeah); **many kisses**—pola feeleeah; **to kiss**—na feel**ee**so; **I want to kiss you**—**Thelo** na seh feel**ee**so; **Kiss me**—Feel**ee**seh meh!

kitchen, a (the)—**mia** (ee) koozeena; **in the kitchen**—steen koozeena

kite, a (the)—**enas** (oh) **harta**-etohs (pl. ee **harta**—etee)

A very popular sport for kids of all ages in Greece, particularly during Lent and particularly on the first day of Lent, **Clean Monday**.

knife, a (the)—**ena** (toh) mah**kheh**ree (pl. mah**kheh**ria); **penknife, a**—**enas** soog**hiahs**

knit (I)—Pl**ekoh**; **I Like to knit**—M'ah**resee** na pl**ekoh**; **Did you knit that?** Toh ehpl**ek**sess?; **How did you knit that?**—Pohs toh ehpl**ek**sess?; **I want to learn**—**Thelo** na **matho**; **Can you knit me one?**—Borees na mou pl**ek**sees ena?

knitting needles—veloness ya pl**ek**simo; **size number**—noomero; **knitware**—pl**ek**toh *or* treekoh

knot, a (the) of a rope, etc.—**enas** (oh) **kom**bohs

know (I)—Ks**ehro**; **I don't know**—Dhen ks**ehro**; **I will know**—Tha ks**ehro**; **I want to know**—**Thelo** na **mathoh**; **Do you know?**—Ks**eh**rees?; **Do you want to know?**—**Thel**ees na ks**eh**rees?; **He (she) knows**—Ks**eh**ree; **I knew it**—Toh **eek**sera; **Did you know?**—**Eek**seress? **I know (am familiar with)**—gnor**eezo**; **I know her (him)**—Teen (toh) gnor**eezo**; **Do you know him (her)?**—Ton (teen) gnor**ee**zees?; **He (she) knows me**—Meh gnor**ee**zee

L

labyrinth, a (the)—**enas** (oh) lave**erin**thos; **The Labyrinth of Minos**—Oh Lave**erin**thos tou **Mee**noa

lace—dahn**del**la

lacquer (hair)—lahk

ladder, a (the)—mia (ee) **skah**la (also means "stair"and "stairway")

lady, a (the)—mia (ee) keereea; **the ladies**—ee keeree-ess; **Ladies' Room, the**—toh yeenaykon (written as: IYNAIKON)

lake, a (the)—mia (ee) leemnee

lamb, a (the)—ena (toh) arnee; **baby lamb**—ena (toh) arnahkee

lamp, a (the)—mia (ee) lahmpa (also means "lightbulb")

land (ground) the—ee gyee; **property**—kteema; **my land**—toh kteema mou

landlord, the—oh speeto-neeko-keerees; **landlady, the**—ee speeto neeko-keera; **landowner, the**—oh kteemateeas

language, a (the)—mia (ee) glosa (pl. glosess); **the Greek language**—ee Eleenikee glosa; **the English language**—ee Ahnglikee glosa

lantern, a (the)—ena (toh) fahnaree (pl. fahnaria)

large—megahlos (m), megahlee (f), megahlo (n)

last, the—toh teleftayo; **at last**—epiteloos; **last night**—ekthess toh vrah-dhee; **last week**—teen perasmenee ev-dhohmah-dha; **last month (year)**—ton perasmeno meena (hrono); **last name, your (her/his/my)**—toh epeethetoh sou (tou/tees/mou)

late—argah; **I'm late**—Arghisa; **It's late**—Eenay argah; **It's never too late**—Poteh dhen een'argah; **We'll be late**—Tha argheesoumeh; **later**—eestera or argoteera; **See you later**—Tha seh dhoh argoteera

laugh, a—ena yellio

laundromat, a (the)—ena (toh aftohmatoh pleenteerio

laundry, a (te)—ena (toh) pleenteerio

laundry, the (dirty clothes)—ta rou-ha ya pleesimo; **Where can I clean my laundry?**—Poo boroh na pleeno ta rou-ha mou?; **Is there a laundress?**—Eeparhee mia pleestra?

law, a (the)—enas (oh) nomos (pl. ee nomee); **lawyer, a (the)**—enas (oh) dheekigoros

lazy—tembellees (m), tembella (f)

leak, a (the)—mia (ee) dheeafighee; **It's leaking**—Trekhee

learn (to)—na matho; **I want to learn Greek (to dance)**—Thelo na matho Eleenika (na horevo); **I learned**—Emmatha

lease, a (the)—mia (ee) meesthosee; **to lease**—na ekmisthoso

leather—dhehrma; **leather** (adj.)—dhehrmahtinos (m), dhehrmahtinee (f), dhehrmahtino (n)

leave (to)—na feego; **I have to leave**—Prepee na feego; **I want to leave**—Thelo na feego; **I don't want to leave**—Dhen thelo na feego; **I'm leaving**—Fevgo; **I will be leaving**—Tha feego; **When are you leaving?**—Poteh tha feeghees?; **When is he (she/it) leaving?**—Poteh tha feeghee?; **Are you leaving?**—Fevghees? **We're leaving**—Fevgomeh; **We will be leaving**—Tha feegomeh. **I left**—Efeegah; **You left**—Efeeghess; **He (she/it) left**—Efeegheh *or* Leepee; **We left**—Feegameh; **They left**—Efeeghan; **Leave me alone!**—Ahseh meh!; **on leave**—meh ahdheea

left (direction)—ahreestera; **Turn left**—Streepseh ahreestera.

leg, a (the)—ena (toh) poh-dhee (pl. ta poh-dhia) which also mean "foot" and "feet"; **leg** (of lamb, etc.)—toh bootee

legal—nomimo; **It is legal?**—Eenay nomimo?

legend, a (the)—enas (oh) meethos; **legendary**—meethikoh

lemon, a (the)—ena (toh) lemohnee; **lemons**—lemohnia; **lemonade**—lemohna-dha; **lemon juice** (fresh)—freskos heemos lemon-yoo

lend (to)—na dhah-neeso; **I'll lend it to you**—Tha sou toh dhah-neeso; **Can you lend me...?**—Borees na mou dhahneesees...? **I lent**—Eh-dhahneesa; **She (he) lent it to me**—Mou toh Eh-dhahneeseh

length, the—toh mahkros

Lent—Sarakostee; **Lenten**—Sarakostiano

lesbian, a—mia lesveea

less—leegotero; **a litttle less**—leego leegotero

lesson, a (the)—ena (toh) matheema (pl. ta matheemata)

Let's go—Pahmeh; **Let me do it**—Ahseh meh na toh kahno; **Let me be!**—Ahfiseh meh! *or* Ahseh meh!

letter, a (the)—ena grahma (pl. grahmata) also refers to the letters of the alphabet; **Do I have any letters?**—Eh-ho grahmata? Passports are required when picking up mail.

lettuce—maroolee

liar, a (the)—enas (oh) pseftees (m), mia (ee) pseftra (f); **He (she) is a liar**—Eenay pseftees (pseftra)

library, a (the)—mia (ee) vivliotheeke

license, a (the) permit—mia ah-dheea; **driver's license**—dheeploma

lie, a (the)—ena (toh) psema; **Lies!**—Psemata!; **It's a lie**—Eenay psema; **a white lie**—ena ahtho-oh psema

lie down (to)—na ksaploso; **I want to lie down for a while**—Thelo na ksaploso ya leego; **She (he) is lying down**—Eenay ksaplomenee (ksaplomenos); **Lie down**—Ksahploseh

life—ee zoee; **life insurance**—ahsfahlia zoees; **a lifetime**—mia zoee

lift (I)—Seekono; **I can't lift it**—Dhen boroh na toh seekoso; **Can you lift it?**—Borees na toh seekosees?

lift a (the) elevator—ena (toh) ahsansehr (as in the French "ascenseur")

light, a (the)—ena (toh) fohs; **Do you have a light? Eh-hees fotiah?** (lit. "fire"); **to light**—na ahnahpso; **light** (not heavy)—elafro

lighter, a (the) cigarette—enas (oh) ahnapteeras; **lighter fluid**—venzeenee ya ton ahnapteera; **gas**—ah-ehrio ya ton ahnapteera

lightning—ee astrahpee

like (I)—M'ahrehsee (a reflexive verb literally meaning "It likes me."); **I like you (but I don't love you)**—M'ahrehsees (ala dhen seh ahgapo); **I don't like**—Dhen m'ahrehsee; **I like to dance**—M'ahrehsee na horevo; **Do you like the wine?**—S'ahrehsee toh krahsee?; **Do you like me?**—S'ahrehso?; **Don't you like it?**—Dhen s'ahrehsee?; **He (she) likes**—Tou (tee) ahrehsee; **I liked it**—Mou ahreseh; **Did you like it?**—Sou ahreseh?: **Did he (she) like it?**—Tou (tees) ahreseh?; **We liked it**—Mahs ahreseh; **like** (preposition)—sahn; **like that**—sahn aftoh.

linen (the fabric)—leeno; **the bed linen**—ta sendohnia

lip, the—toh heelos; **your (my) lips**—ta heelee sou (mou); **lipstick**—krahg-yon

liquid (n. & adj.)—eegro

list, a (the)—enas (oh) kahtahlogos (also means "catalogue" and "directory," so nowadays one often hears "mia (ee) leesta" instead).

listening (I am)—Ahkoo-oh; **I was listening**—Ah-koo-a; **Listen!**—Ahkooseh!

little (adj.)—meekros (m), meekree (f), meekro (n); **a little**—leego; **a little wine**—leego krahsee; **just a little**—mohno leego; **a little**

piece—ena koma**tah**kee; **in a little while**—seh lee**gah**kee

As in some of the above examples, there are various diminutives which can be added—often indiscriminately to almost all nouns, including names. The most common of these are: -**ah**kee, -**oo**la, -**oo**lahkee, and -**eet**sa. Thus, a baby lamb (ar**nee**) is called ar**nah**kee, while I myself (on fortunately few occasions) have been called "Toh**mah**kee" and my daughter Samantha, variously, Saman**thah**kee, Saman**thou**la, and Saman**teet**sa. The variations are endless.

live (to)—na zoh; **He (she) lives**—Zee; **to live (dwell, stay)**—na **mee**no; **I want to live (stay) in Greece**—**The**lo na **mee**no steen Ellah-dha; **I am living at (in)**—**Me**no sto, stee, etc.; **Where do you live?**—Poo me**nees**?; **Where does he (she) live?**—Poo me**nee**?

live (adj)—zon**da**nos (m), zonda**nee** (f), zon**da**no (n)

lizard, a (the)—**mia** (ee) **sah**vra (pl. ee **sah**vress)

loan, a (the)—**ena** (toh) **dhah**nio; **It's a loan**—Eenay **dhah**nio

lobby, the (hotel)—oh pro**thal**amos; **in the lobby**—ston pro**thal**amo

local—to**pi**koh

lock, a (the)—**mia** (ee) kleed**hari**ah; **to lock**—na klee-**dhoh**so

locket, a (the)—**ena** (toh) men**dagh**ion

lonely (I am)—Es**thah**nomay mo**nak**siah

long (length)—mah**krees**; **How long?**—**Po**so **mah**kros?; **How long (time)?**—**Po**see **o**ra?

look (to)—na kee**tahk**so; **I am looking**—Kee**tah**zo; **Look!**—**Kee**ta! **I am looking for**—**Psah**kno; **I'm looking forward to**—Pros-**dho**koh

loose (not packaged or bottled)—**hee**ma; **loose wine**—**hee**ma **krah**see; **loose (not tight)**—ha**la**ro; **loose (clothing)**—**far**dhee; **loose-leaf notebook, a**—**ena** doh**sieh**

lose (to)—na **hah**so; **I don't want to lose it**—Dhen **the**lo na toh **hah**so; **Don't lose it**—Mee toh **hah**sees!; **I lost**—Eh-**ha**sa; **I lost my wallet (passport)** Eh-**ha**sa toh porto**lee** (dheeahvatee**rioh**) mou; **lost (adj.)**—**hah**meno; **The Bureau of Lost Property**—Toh Gra**fee**on Apolesthen**don** Ahndiki**me**non

lot, a (very much)—po**lee** or ena so**ro**; **I want lots**—**The**lo po**lee**; **a lot of money**—po**la** hree**ma**ta; **a parking lot**—**mia mahn**dra ya parkarisma; **a lot (land)**—ena komahtee gyee

lotion—losion; **suntan lotion**—losion eeleeoo

lottery, a (the)—ena (toh) lakheeoh

loud—dheenatoh; **The music is too loud**—Ee moosikee eenay
polee dheenata

loudspeaker, a (the)—ena (toh) megahfono

lounge, the—toh sahlonee

love (n)—ahgahpee; **My love**—Ahgahpee mou; **I love**—Ahgapoh; **I
love you**—S'ahgapoh; **Do you love me?**—M' ahgapahs?

lover, a (the)—enas (oh) ehrastees (m), **mia** (ee) ehromenee (f)

low—hahmiloh; **lower**—peeoo hahmiloh

lozenges (throat)—pahsteel-yes

lubricant, a—ena leepahndiko or **grah**so (the latter meaning "grease")

luck—teekhee; **Good luck!**—Kahlee teekhee!; **lucky**—teekhehros
(m), teekhehree (f), teekhehro (n)

luggage, the—ee ahposkevess; **my luggage**—ee ahposkevess mou;
the left-luggage department—ee apotheekee ahposkevon

lunch, a (the)—ena (toh) yevma (Also means "dinner" and "meal";
therefore a more exact phrase would be "mesimeria**no** fagheetoh,"
but hardly anyone uses it)

Lunch is eaten by Greeks anywhere between 10 A.M. and 3 P.M.,
depending on the kind of job they have. It is traditionally the
biggest meal of the day, intended to store up energy for the work
ahead. Consequently, most Greeks also take a 2-hour nap after
eating.

M

machine, a (the)—mia (ee) meekhanee

Madame—Keereea; **of a brothel**—ee tzatzah

Madonna, the—Ee Pahnag-yeea

magazine, a (the)—ena (toh) periodhikoh (pl. penodhika); **English
(American) magazines**—Ahnglika (Amerikanika) perio-dhika

maid, a (the)—mia (ee) eepeeretria

mail, the—toh taki-dhromeeo; **mailbox, a**—ena gramatokivotio;
mailman, the—oh takhee-**dhroh**mos

make (to)—na kahno; **I want to make**—Thelo na kahno; **Will you
make it?**—Tha toh kahnees?; **Can he (she) make it?**—Boree na
toh kahnee?; **I made it**—Toh ehkana; **You made**—Ehkaness; **She**

(he) made—Ehkaneh; **to make love**—na kahnoumeh ehrota; **make up (cosmetics)**—mahkeeyahz; **to make up** (after a quarrel)—na ksana-ftiahkno; **Let's make up, shall we?**—Ahs tha ftiahksoomeh?; **To make up my mind**—na ahpofaseeso; **I can't make up my mind**—Dhen boroh na ahpofaseeso

make, the (brand)—ee **mar**ka

male, a—**en**as ahn-dhrahs

man, a (the)—**en**as (oh) ahn-dhrahs (pl.ee **ahn-**dhress)

manager, a (the)—**en**as (oh) dhee-eftheen**dees**; **I want to see the manager, please**—**The**lo toh dheeeftheen**dee**, parakalo; **management, the**—ee dhee-eftheensees

manners, good—**kah**lee tropee; **bad manners**—**kak**ee tropee

map, a (the)—**en**as (oh) har**tees**; **Do you have a map of Greece (of Athens)?**—Eh-heteh **en**a har**tee** tees Ellah**dhas** (tees Ah**thee**nas)?

marble—**mar**maro

March—**Mar**tios

margarine—margah**ree**nee

marionette, a (the)—**mia** (ee) mario**net**ta (pl, mario**net**tess)

market, a (the)—**mia** (ee) ah**gor**a

marmalade—marme**lah-**dha

marriage, a (the)—**en**as (oh) **gah**mo

Mary (Mother of Jesus)—Ee Mah**ree**a *or* Ee Panag-**yee**a

mascara—**mas**kara

masturbation—mala**kee**a; **masturbator, a (the)**—**en**as (oh) mal**ah**kas
These are very loaded words in Greek and you will hear them being constantly used, pejoratively or not, by Greek men.

mat, a—**mia**—**psa**tha; **mat** (non-glossy)—**maht**

match, a—**en**a **speer**toh (pl. **speer**ta)
Can only be bought at sidewalk kiosks or the occasional cigarette store; kitchen matches are non-existent

maternity clinic, a (the)—**en**a (toh) may-ef**tee**rio

matter (What's the...?)—Tee seem**vay**nee?

mattress, a (the)—**en**a (toh) **stro**ma (pl. **stro**mata)

May—Ma**hees**

May I?—Bo**roh**?; You may—Bo**rees**

maybe—**ee**sohs

mayonnaise—ma-yoneza

mayor, a (the)—enas (oh) dheemarkhos; **mayory, the (City Hall)**—
Toh dheemar-**heeo**

me—mou, mena, *or* meh; **for me**—ya mena; **with me**—mazee mou;
give me—dhohs mou; **Help me**—Voeethiseh meh; **Tell me**—
Pehz mou; **Me, too**—Kay ehgo (lit. "And I")

meal, a (the)—ena (toh) yevma

mean (I)—Eno-oh; **What do you mean?**—Tee theleees na pees?;
What does she (he/it) mean? Tee eno-ee?; **I meant**—Eethela na
poh *or* Eno-oosa; **meaning, the**—toh noeema

meat—kreh-ahs; **meatballs**—kefteh-dhess

mechanic, a (the)—enas (oh) meekhani**kos**

Medea—Ee Mee-**dheea**

medicine—farmaka

medieval—mesayonikoh

medium (sweet or dry)—**meh**trio; **medium rare**—**meh**trio pseemeno

Medusa—Ee Meh-dhoosa

meet (to)—na seenanteeso; **I want to meet him (her)**—Thelo na
ton (teen) seenanteeso; **I will meet you at...**—Tha seh seenanteeso stees...; **I met**—Seenahnteesa; **I've met him (her)**—Ton
(teen) eh-ho seenanteesee; **Have you met Dolly (Dick)?**—Eh-
hees seenanteesee teen Dolly (ton Dick)?

memento, a—ena entheemio

men—ahn-dhress; **MEN'S ROOM, the**—tohn Ahn-**dhrohn** (written
as: ANΔPON)

mentholated—meentholee

menu, a (the)—ena (toh) menoo *or* enas (oh) kahtahlogo

message, a (the)—ena (toh) meenima; **Is there a message for
me?**—Eh-ho kanena meenima?; **I'll leave you a message**—Tha
sou ahfeeso ena meenima; **Leave me a message at...**—Ahfeeseh
mou ena meenima sto (stee, etc.)...

metal—**meh**talo

meter, a (the) gas, elec.—enas (oh) metri**tees**; **taxi meter, the**—toh
roloy

middle, the—toh mehso; **in the middle**—sto mehso

midwife, a (the)—mia (ee) mahmee

might (I)—Eesohs; I might not—Eesohs oh-hee

milk—gahla; evaporated milk—gahla evaporeh; skimmed milk—gahla apovootiromeno; chocolate milk—gahla sokolata

Any fresh milk bought in dairy stores (galaktopoleeoh) or from farmers must be boiled for at least 5 minutes to kill various microbes and viruses, particularly the ones which could give you tuberculosis.

minaret, a (the)—enas (oh) meenaress

mind, the—to meealo *or* oh nous; I've something on my mind—Eh-ho kahtee sto meealo mou; I've changed my mind—Ahlaksa gnomee; Never mind—Dhen peerahsee

mine (possessive)—dheeko mou; It's mine—Eenay dheeko mou; It's not mine—Dhen eenay dheeko mou

miniature—meeniatoura *or* meekrografeea

Minos—Oh Meenoahs; Minoan—Meenoeekoh

Minotaur, the—Oh Meenotavros

mint—dheeohsmohs; peppermint—menta

minus—pleen

minute, a—ena leptoh (pl. lepta); in a minute—seh ena leptoh; just a minute—mia steegmee ("steegmee" meaning "moment")

miracle, a—ena thavma; miraculous—thavmastoh

mirror, a (the)—enas (oh) kathreptees; hand mirror, a—enas kathreptees hehrioo; pocket mirror, a—enas kathreptees tees tsepees

miscarriage, a—mia ahpovlee; I'm afraid of having a miscarriage—Fovoomay ohtee tha ahpovalo

Miss—Dhespeenees *or* dhespeenee-dha (written as: Δις)

Missus (Mrs.)—Keereea (written as: Κα).

miss (to) long for—mou leepee; I'm going to miss you (Greece) very much—Tha mou leepsees ehsee (leepsee ee Ellah-dha) polee; Will you miss me?—Tha sou leepso?; I missed you—Mooleepsess; Have you missed me?—Meh petheemisess?

miss (to) not catch—na hahso; I don't want to miss the boat—Dhen thelo na hahso toh karahvee; I missed the bus—Eh-hasa toh leh-oforeeo

mistake, a (the)—ena (toh) lathos; I made a mistake—Ekana lathos; It's a mistake—Lathos eenay

Mister—Keerios (written as: **Κος**)

mixed—ahnahmikta; **mixture, a (the)**—ena (toh) meegma

modern—mohdehrno

moment, a—mia steegmee; **just a moment**—mia steegmee

monarchy, the—ee mohnarkheea

monastery, a (the)—ena (toh) mohnasteeree

Monday—Deftehra

money—hreemata *or* hreema *or* lefta; **I want to change money**—Thelo na ahlahkso hreemata

money order, a (the)—mia (ee) takhidhromikee epitagyee

monk, a (the)—enas (oh) kalohg-yeros (pl. ee kalohg-yeree)

month, a (the)—enas (oh) meenas (pl. meeness); **In a month**—meta ahpo ena meena; **a month ago**—preen ena meena; **last (next) month**—ton perasmeno (ton **ahlo**) meena

Months have both formal and colloquial names. In the listing below, the formal is in parenthesis: **January**—Yenarees (Yanooarios); **February**—Flevarees (Fevooarios); **March**—Martees (Martios); **April**—Ahpreelees (Ahpreelios); **May**—Maees (Ma-yos); **June**—Yoonio (Yoonios); **July**—Yoolio (Yoolios); **August**—Ahvgoosto (Ahvgoostos); **September**—Setemvrees (Septemvrios); **October**—Oktohvrees (Oktohvrios); **November**—Noemvrees (Noemvrios); **December**—Dhekemvrees (Dhekemvrios). **In May**—ton Maee (**Mah**-yo); **beginning of May**—arkhess tou Maee (Mah-eeyoo); **end of May**—telee tou Maee (Mah-eeyoo); **May 5th**—pendeh Mahyoo; **the 23rd of October**—stees eekosee-treess Oktovreeoo; **last (next) May**—ton parasmeno (ton ahlo) Maee

moon, the—toh fengahree; **the full moon**—ee pahnselinos; **moonlight, the**—toh selinofohs *or* ee fengara-dha

more—kay ahlo, perisotero, *or* ahkoma: **I want more wine**—Thelo kay ahlo krahsee; **another beer**—ahkoma mia beera; **I want more (additional)**—Thelo perisotero; **more than that**—perisotero ahpo aftoh; **The more the better**—Ohso perisotero tohso kahleetero

"Peeoh" is used to make adjectives comparative: **That is good**—Aftoh eenay kahlo; **That is better**—Aftoh eenay peeoh kahlo (although one may also say, "Aftoh eenay kahleetero")

morning, the—toh proee; **in the morning**—toh proee; **this morning**—toh proee; **yesterday morning**—ekthess proee; **tomorrow morning**—ahvrio toh proee; **"Good morning"**—Kahlee mehra

"Kahlo proee" is a term used when parting at night and wishing someone a good morning for the following day.

mortar and pestle—goo-dhee kay goo-dho-**hehree**

mosque, a (the)—ena (toh) tzamee

mosquito, a (the)—**ena** (toh) koonoope (pl. ta koonoopia) **mosquito net, a**—mia koonoopiehra; **mosquito repellent**—prostaseea ya ta koonoopia; **mosquito spray**—ah-erosol

mother, a (the)—mia (ee) meetehra *or* mia mana; **my mother**—ee meetehra (mana) mou; **your mother**—ee meetehra (mana) sou

mother-in-law, a (the)—mia (ee) pethera

motor, a (the)—mia (ee) meekhanee; **motorbike**—ena (toh) moto-po-**dheelatoh**; **motorboat**—mia venzeenakatos; **motorcycle**—mia (ee) motoseekletta; **motor oil**—lah-dhee keeneeteeros; **motor scooter**—ena (toh) scootehr *or* vespa

mountain, a (the)—ena (toh) voono; **the mountains**—ta voona; **to go mountain climbing**—na kahno orivaseeah; **I want to go mountain climbing**—Thelo na kahno orivaseeah

mourning—penthos

mouse, a (the)—ena (toh) pondeekee; **the mice**—ta pondeekia; **mousetrap, a (the)**—mia (ee) fahka

moustache, a (the)—ena (toh) moostahkee

mouth, the—toh stohma; **mouthwash, a**—mia gargahra

movie, a (the)—ena (toh) feelm

much—polee; **I don't want much**—Dhen thelo polee; **very much**—para polee; **too much**—para polee; **How much?**—Poso?; **How much is it?**—Poso kahnee?

mule, a (the)—ena (toh) moolahree; **the mules**—ta moolahria

muse, a (the)—mia (ee) moosa; **The Nine Muses**—EeEneh-a Moosess

museum, a (the)—ena (toh) mooseeo; **Where is the museum?**—Poo eenay toh moseeo?

mushrooms—mahnitaria

music, the—ee moosikee; **I like the music**—M'ahrehsee ee moosikee; **What music is it?**—Tee moosikee eenay?; **Greek** music—Eleenikee moosikee; **classical music**—classikee moosikee; **pop music**—moosikee pohp; **musician, a (the)**—enas (oh) moosikos; **the musicians**—ee moosikee

must—prepee; **I must go**—Prepee na feego; **I must not**—Dhen prepee na

mustache, a (the)—ena (toh) moostahkee

mustard—moostar-dha

my—mou *or* dheekoh mou

"Mou" follows the noun possessed; "dheekoh mou" precedes it:

My sweater—toh pullohver mou *or* toh dheekoh mou pullohvehr

myself (by)—mohnos mou (m), mohnee mou (f)

myth, a (the)—enas (oh) meethos; **mythical**—meethikoh; **mythology**—meethologheea; **mythological**—meethologhikoh

N

nail, a—mia proka (pl. prokess)

nail, a (the) finger—ena (toh) neekhee (pl. ta neekhia); **nailbrush**—voortsa neekheeon; **nail scissors**—psali-dhahkee ya neekhia

naked—yeemnos (m), yeemnee (f), yeemno (n)

name, a (the)—ena (toh) ohnoma (pl. ta ohnomata); **first name, the**—toh meekro ohnoma; **last name, the**—toh ehponimo; **full name, the**—toh ohnoma kay ehponimo; **maiden name, the**—toh eekooyeniakoh ohnoma; **my name**—toh ohnoma mou; **your name**—toh ohnoma sou; **her (his) name**—toh ohnoma tees (tou)

Although it is perfectly correct to say "My name is..." (Toh ohnoma mou eenay...), Greeks usually say, "I am called..." (Meh leneh...):

My name is Tom—Meh leneh Tom; **What is your name?**—Pohs seh leneh?; **What is his (her) name?**—Pohs ton (teen) leneh?; **What is it called?**—Pohs toh leneh ("It" being any neuter object, including a child.)

In addition, when referring to someone by hame, one prefaces it with either the feminine or masculine article: "ee" Samantha, "oh" Oliver or in their objective forms: **I saw Samantha and Oliver**—Ee-dha teen Samantha kay ton Oliver.

But when speaking directly to a person, the article is not used nor, in names ending in "s", is the final "s": **Where is Zorba?**—Poo eenay oh Zorbas?; **Hello, Zorba!**—Yasoo Zorba!

name day, a (the)—mia (ee) yortee

namesake—seenonomatos (m), seenonomatee (f), seenonomato (n). The passing down of names is an important and cherished tradition in Greece.

nap, a—enas eèpnakos; **I want to take a nap**—Thelo na pahro ena eepnako

napkin, a (the)—mia (ee) petseta (pl. petsetess); **paper napkins**—hartohpetsetess

Narcissus—Oh Narkisos

natural (not artificial)—feesikoh; **naturally**—vevaya

navy, the—toh naftikoh

near—konda; **near to**—konda sto; **nearby**—polee konda

necessary—ahparaytitoh; **It's necessary**—Eenay ahparaytitoh

necklace, a (the)—ena (toh) kolieh; **necktie, a (the)**—mia (ee) grahvahta

needle, a (the)—mia (ee) velona (pl. veloness); **knitting needles**—veloness plekseematos; **sewing needle, a**—mia velona ya rahpsimo; **needlework**—ehrgoheero

neighbor, a (the)—enas (oh) yeetonahs (pl. ee yeetoness)

neither—ooteh; **neither one nor the other**—ooteh toh ena, ooteh toh ahlo

nervous—nevrikos (m), nevrikee (f), nevriko (n); **I'm nervous**—Eemay nevrikos (nevrikee)

net, a (the)—ena (toh) dheektee

never—poteh; **never mind**—dhen peerahzee

new—neh-os (m), neh-a (f), neh-o (n) *or* kenoorios (m), kenooria (f), kenoorio (n)

news, the—ta neh-a; **What news?**—Tee neh-a?; **good (bad) news**—kala (ahskheema) neh-a

newspaper, a (the)—mia (ee) efimeree-dha

next, the—toh epomeno; **When is the next boat?** Poteh eenay toh epomeno karavee?; **next day (week)**—teen ahlee mehra (evdhomah-dha); **next month**—ton ahlo meena; **next year**—tou hronoo; **next to**—dheepla nickname, a (the)—ena (toh) paratsooklee

night, the—ee neekta; tonight—ahpohpseh (lit. "this evening");
last night—ekthess vrah-dhee or (after about 11 P.M.) ekthess
neekta; tomorrow night—ahvrio toh vrah-dhee; at night—toh
vrah-dhee or tee neekta

nightmare, a—enas efialtees; I had a nightmare—Ee-ha efialtee

nipple, a (the) breast—mia (ee) theelee (pl. ee theeless); for a baby
bottle—theelee toh beeberon

no—oh-hee or oy-hee

nobody—kahnees or kahnenahs; Nobody was there—Kahnees
dhen eetan ekee

noise—thoreevos; noisy—thorivo-dhees

none—katholoo; There's none—Dhen eh-hee katholoo

nonsense—ahnoeesee-ess

non-stop—ahnev stathmoo; direct—kat-eftheea

noon—messimehree

"Noon" in Greek does not mean "exactly 12 o'clock." Its literal
meaning is "middle of the day," which to a Greek means anytime
from about 12:00 to about 2:00. So, when making an appointment for noon, it is best to specify the exact time—but even then,
you shall probably end up waiting.

normal—kanonikoh; normally—kanonika

north—oh voriahs

nose, the—ee meetee

nostalgia—nostalgyeea; nostalgic—nostalg-yikos (m), nostalg-
yikee (f), nostalg-yikoh (n)

not—dhen or mee or oh-hee; I am not—dhen eemay; I will not
be—dhen tha eemay; Don't do that!—Mee kahnees aftoh!;
Don't—Mee! Not that—Oh-hee ekeenoh; Not that book—Oh-
hee ekeenoh toh vivleeo

notary public, a (the)—enas (oh) seemvolayografos

note, a—mia nota; a banknote—ena hartonomisma; a notebook—
ena tetra-dhio; a notepad—ena blohk

nothing—teepota; It's nothing—Dhen eenay teepota

"Teepota" also means "something" or "anything," as in: Do you
want something?—Theleteh teepota?; Nothing, thank you—
Teepota, efhareestoh

novel, a (the)—**en**a (toh) meethi**stor**eema (lit. "myth-history")

November—Noemvrees

now—**tor**ah; **right now**—ah**meh**sos; **now and then**—kahpoo-**kahpoo**

nowhere—**poo**thena

nude (adj.)—**yeem**nos (m), yeem**nee** (f), yeem**no** (n); **nudity**—yeem**nia**; **a nudist**—**en**as yeem**nee**stees, **mia** yeemnee**stria**; **nudist beach, a (the)**—**mia** (ee) para**lee**a yeem**nee**ston

nuisance, a—**mia** enok**lee**see; **an annoying person**—**en**as enokli-**tik**os (m), **mia** enokli**tee**kee (f); **It's a nuisance**—**Ee**nay enok**lee**see; **What a nuisance!**—**Tee** enok**lee**see!

number, a (the)—**en**as (oh) ah**rith**mos or **en**a (toh) **noo**mero

"Ah**rith**mos" is used for street and telephone numbers, while "**noo**mero" is used for all other numbers, including clothing and needle sizes: **What's his (her/your) telephone number?**—**Pi**ohs **ee**nay oh ah**rith**mos tou (tees/sou)?; **What number?**—**Tee noo**mero?; **Number six**—**Noo**mero ek**see**

nurse, a (the)—**en**as (oh) no**sok**omos (m), **mia** (ee) no**sok**oma (f)

nurse (to) breast-feed—na thee**lah**so; **I'm nursing the baby**—thee**lah**zo toh mo**roh**

nuts (food)—kah**ree**-dhia; **peanuts or pistachios**—fees**teek**ia; **nut, a (the) bolt**—**en**a (toh) pahk**sim**a-dhee (pl. pahk**sim**a-dhia)

nylon—na**ee**lon

O

oar, an (the)—**en**a (toh) koo**pee** (pl. ta koo**pi**ah)

occupied (taken)—peeahs**men**ee

ocean, the—oh oke**ah**nos

o'clock—ee **or**a; **one o'clock**—**mia** ee **or**a

October—Oktovrees

octopus, an (the)—**en**a (toh) htapo-**dhee**

Odysseus—Oh Ohdhee**seh**-efs; **The Odyssey**—Ee Oh-**dhee**sia

Oedipus—Oh Ee-**dhee**poos

of—tou, tees, or ton

Almost never used as it is in English: **a glass of water**—**en**a po**tee**ree **neh**ro; **a bottle of wine**—**en**a boo**kah**lee **krah**see; **a**

friend of mine—**en**as feelos mou. But it is used in the possessive and genitive cases: **Florence's house**—toh **spee**tee tees Florence; **The light of the house**—Toh fohs tou speetioo

off (turned)—kleestoh; **cancelled**—ahkirothikeh

offer (to)—na kerahso; **What can I offer you?**—Tee seh kerahso?

office,a (the)—**en**a (toh) grah-**fee**o

officer, a (the) of the law—**en**as (oh) astinomos; **of a ship**—**en**as (oh) ahksiomati**kos**

official, a (the) goverment, bank, etc.—**en**as (oh) eepah**lee**los

oil—lah-dhee; **olive oil**—elayoh-lah-dhoh; **seed oil**—sporelayo; **machine oil**—lah-dhee tees meekha**nees**; **suntan oil**—lah-dhee eeleeoo; **oil paint**—lah-dhoh-boh-**yah**; **oil painting, an (the)**—mia (ee) elayografeea; **oily**—lah-dhehro

ointment—ahli**fee**

okay—end**ah**ksee *or* kahlah

old (not new)—pahliohs (m), pahliah (f), pahlioh (n); **old friends**—pahliee feelee; **old man, an (the)**—enas (oh) yehros; **old woman**—mia (ee) greeah; **old-fashioned**—dehmodeh; **old (spoiled)**—halasmeno; **How old are you (is he/she/it)?**—Posohn hronohn eesay (eenay)?; **I'm 20 years old**—Eemay eekosee hronohn

olive, an (the)—mia (ee) eliah (pl. eliess); **olive oil**—elayoh-lah-dhoh; **olive tree, a (the)**—elayoh-dhentro (pl. elayoh-dhentra)

Olympic Games, the—Ee Oleempiakee Ahgoness

on (top of)—pahno sto; **It's on the table**—Eenay pahno sto trah-pehzee; **lying on**—sto; **It's on the floor (beach)**—Eenay sto **pah**toma (stee plahz); **switched on**—ahneektoh; **The radio is on**—Toh rah-dheeohfono eenay ahneektoh; **on Friday (etc.)**—teen Paraskevee; **on time**—steen ora tou; **on the right (left)**—sta dheksiah (ahreestera); **on the house**—kehrasma

once (one time)—mia fora; **once more**—ahlee mia fora; **once a week**—mia fora teen ev-dhohmah-dha; **once (before)**—kah-poteh; **at once**—ahmehsos

one (the number)—enas (m), mia (f), ena (n); **that one**—ekeenos (m), ekeenee (f), ekeeno (n); **this one**—aftohs (m), aftee (f), aftoh (n); **That man (girl) over there**—Ekeenos (ekeenee)

only—mohno; only this—mohno aftoh; only you (sub.)—mohno esee, (obj.) mohno esena; only for me—mohno ya mena; only for you—mohno ya sena

open—ahneektoh (written in shop windows as: ANOIKTON); When is it open?—Poteh eenay ahneektoh?; Is it open?—Eenay ahneektoh?

open (to)—na ahneekso; When will you open?—Poteh tha ahneeksees?

opener, an (the) can, bottle—ena (toh) ahneekteeree *or*klee-dhee ("key")

operator, the (telephope)—ee teelehfoneetria

opposite, the—toh ahnteethetoh; opposite (across from)—ahpenandee ahpo

optician, an (the)—enas (oh) optikos

or—ee (used exacrly as in Englishj: Yes or no?—Nay ee oh-hee?

oracle, an (the)—ena (toh) manteeon; the Oracle of Delphi—toh manteeon ton Dhelfohn

orange, a—ena portokahlee (pl. portokahlia); orange juice—portokala-dha heemos; orangeade—portokala-dha (pl. portokala-dhess)

order, an (the)—mia (ee) parangheleea; order (to)—na parangheelo; I want to order—Thelo na parangheelo; I've ordered—Eh-ho parangheelee; Have you ordered?—Eh-hees parangheelee?

oregano—reeganee

orgasm, an—enas orgasmos

oriental rug, an (the)—ena (toh) anatoleetiko halee

original, an (the)—enas (oh) protohteepos; originally—arkheeka

Orpheus—Oh Orfeh-efs *or* Orfeh-ahs

Orthodox Church, the—Ee Ortho-dhoksos Ekleeseea

other, the—toh ahlo

our—mahs; ours—dheekoh mahs; It's our house—Eenay toh speetee mahs; It's ours—Eenay dheekoh mahs

out—ekso; outside—ekso; Out!—Ekso!; Let's go out—Pahmeh ekso

over (above)—ahpo pahno; finished—teliomeno; over there—ehkee pehra

overcharged (I was)—Meh hrehosahn parapahno

overcoat, a (the)—ena (toh) paltoh

owersleep (to)—na parakimitho; **I don't want to oversleep**—Dhen thelo na parakimitho; **I overslept**—Parakimeethika; **Don't oversleep!**—Mee parakimithees!

owe (I)—Hrostoh; **How much do I owe you?**—Poso sou hrosto?; **You owe me**—Mou hrostahs

owl, a (the)—mia (ee) kookoovah-ya

The symbol of Athena, the Goddess of Wisdom, who is also the goddess of Athens, which is why one sees so many reproductions of owls lurking in tourist shops.

own (I)—katekho; **I own it**—Eenay dheekoh mou; **my own**—dheekoh mou; **your own**—dheekoh sou; **her (his) own**—dheekoh tees (tou); **our own**—dheekoh mahs; **owner, the**—oh edhiokteetees

P

pack, a (the) back—ena (toh) sahkee-dhio; **of cards**—mia (ee) trahpoola

pack (to) luggage—na pahketahro; **I must pack**—Prepee na pahketahro; **to pack a package**—na kahno **dhema**

package, a (the)—ena (toh) **dhema** (pl. ta **dhemata**); **small package, a (the)**—ena (toh) dhema**tahkee** or pahketoh

padlock, a (the)—ena (toh) louketoh; **combination**—seen-dheeasmoo

pain, a (the)—enas (oh) pohnos (pl. ee pohnee); **It's painful**—Ponaee; **I have a pain here**—Eh-ho pohno eh-dhoh

paint—bohya; **oil paint**—lah-dhoh-bohya; **plastic paint**—plastikee bohya; **waterpaint**—nehrobohya or acquarella; **glossy**—yaleestero; **mat**—maht; **paint brush, a (the)**—ena (toh) peenello (pl. peenella)

paint (I) paintings—Zografeezo; **walls, doors, etc.**—Boh-yateezo

painting, a (the)—enas (oh) peenakahs (pl. ee peenakess)

painter, a (the)—enas (oh) zograhfos; **female**—mia zograhfos; **I'm a painter**—Eemay zograhfos

pair, a (the)—ena (toh) zevgahree (not used for pants or scissors)

palace, a (the)—ena (toh) pahlahtee

palette, a (the)—mia (ee) pahletta; **palette knife**—mia (ee) spah-toola zograhfoo

pan, a (the) frying—ena (toh) teegahnee

pants (trousers)—pantalonee; **underpants** (men's)—sovrako; **woman's**—keelota

panty hose—kalsohn

Papa—Bahbahs (while Pahpahs is Greek for a priest, as in our use of the word Father")

paper, a (the)—ena (toh) hartee; **a sheet of paper**—mia kola hartee; **air mail paper**—hartee ahlilo-grafeeas ah-ehroporikoh; **paperback book, a**—ena hartoh-dhetoh veevleeo; **paper bag, a**—mia hartosakoola; **paperclips**—seendheteeress; **onion-skin paper**—leptess koless or tsigarokoless; **typewriter paper**—koless grafomeekhanees; **identity papers**—pistopee-eetika

paradise—pahrah-dheesos

paraffin (kerosene)—katharo petrelayo

Pardon me—Singnomee or Meh singhoreeteh; **Pardon me?**—Parakaloh?

"Singnomee" is the most commonly used expression, "Meh singhoreeteh" being extremely polite.

parent, a (the)—enas (oh) gonefs (pl. ee gonees)

park, a (the)—ena (toh) parko

park (to)—na parkaro; **Where can I park?**—Poo boroh na parkaro?; **Am I allowed to park here?**—Epitrepeteh na parkaro eh-dhoh?: **parking lot, a (the)**—mia mahndra ya parkarisma

But PARKING, both the sign and the word, has now been adopted by virtually everyone in Greece.

part, a (the)—ena (toh) komahtee

partner, a (the)—enas (oh) seeneteros; **partnership**—etayreea

party, a (the)—ena (toh) partee or ena (toh) glendee; **a birthday party**—ena partee (glendee) yenethleeon; **a name day party**—mia yortee; **a religious festival**—ena panig-yeeree; **political party, a (the)**—ena (toh) kohma

passenger, a (the)—enas (oh) epivahtees (pl. ee epivahtess)

Passover—Evraeekoh Pahska

passport, a (the)—ena (toh) dheeavateerio

past (beyond)—alpo pehra; **in the past**—sto pahrelthon

pastels—pahstel

pastilles—pahsteelyes

patch, a (the)—**en**a (toh) **bah**loma

patience—eepomo**nee**

partiarch, the—oh pahtri**ar**khees

pay (to)—na plee**ro**so; **I want to pay**—**The**lo na plee**ro**so; **I paid**—
  Plee**ro**sa; **He (she) paid**—Plee**ro**seh; **Did you pay?**—
  Plee**ro**sess?; **Who paid?**—Pee**ohs** plee**ro**seh? **It's paid for
  (by)**—Eenay plee**ro**meno (**ah**po)

peace (not war)—ee**ree**nee; **quiet**—eesee**khee**a; **peaceful**—**ee**see-ho

peanuts—fees**tee**kia (also the name for pistachio nuts)

pearl, a (the)—**en**a (toh) margari**tah**ree (pl. margari**tah**ria); **pearl
  necklace, a (the)**—**en**a (toh) koli**eh** **ah**po margari**tah**ria

pedal, a (the)—**en**a (toh) pe**tah**lee

pediatrician, a (the)—**en**as (oh) pay-dhee-**ah**tros (written as:
  ΠΑΙΔΙΑΤΡΟΣ)

pee (urine)—**oo**ra or **pee**pee; **It (the child) wants to make peepee**—
  Thelee na **kah**nee **pee**pee.
  As in English, this is a harmless euphemism that is not considered
  at all vulgar except in terribly polite company.

peeler, a—**en**a kathari**stee**ree

pen, a (the)—**en**a (toh) stee**loh**; **black/blue/red**—**mah**vro/bleh/**ko**kino

pencil, a (the)—**en**a (toh) mo**lee**vee; **pencil sharpener, a**—**mia
  ksee**stra

penis, the—toh peh-**ohs**; **slang**—ee pso**lee**, ee **poo**tsa, toh poo**lee**,
  toh poo**lah**kee (the latter two mean "bird" and "little bird" and are
  usually used with children; the first two are quite vulgar)

penknife, a (the)—**en**a (toh) soog-ya-**dhah**kee

pension, a (the) **rooming house**—**en**a (toh) **pah**nsion (written as:
  ΠΑΝΣΙΟΝ)

pension (retirement)—**seen**taksee

people—ee **ahn**thropee or oh **kos**mos; **lots of people**—poh**lee**
  kosmos

pepper (spice)—pee**peh**ree

percent—tees eka**toh**; **ten percent**—**dhek**a tees eka**toh**

performance, a (the) **theatre**—**mia** (ee) pa**ras**tasee; **When does it
  begin?**—**Po**teh ar**khee**see?; **How many times a day?**—**Po**sess
  fo**ress** teen ee**meh**ra?

perfume, a (the)—**en**a (toh) **ah**roma; **of a flower**—ee meerod**hee**ah

perhaps—eesohs

period (full-stop)—teleea; **a period of time**—mia epokhee *or* pehree-odhohs; **menstrual period, the**—ee pehree-odhohs; **I'm having my period**—Eh-ho teen pehreeo-dhoh mou; **I missed my period**—Dhen eeh-ha pehree-odhoh; **periodically**—pehreeo-dhikos

permanent—mohnimos; **permanently**—mohnimos

permit, a (the)—mia (ee) ahdheea; **work permit**—ahdheea ergaseeahs

personal—prosopikoh; **personal effects, the**—ta prosopika pragmata

perspiration—ee-dhrotahs; **I'm perspiring**—Ee-dhrono. **pesticide**—ah-ehrosol

pestle, a (the)—ena (toh) goodhohehree

pet, a (the)—ena (toh) kahtikeedhio zo-oh

petrol—venzeenee; **petrol station**—venzinah-dhiko

pharmacy, a (the)—ena (toh) farmakeeo
(written as: ΦΑΡΜΑΚΕΙΟΝ)

philosopher, a (the)—enas (oh) feelosofos; **philosophy**—feelosofeea

phone (to)—See telephone.

phonograph, a (the)—enas (oh) fonograhfos *or* ena (toh) peekahp; **record, a (the)**—enas (oh) dheeskos

photocopy, a (the)—mia (ee) fototipeea (pl. fototipee-ess); **I want a photocopy (of this)**—Thelo mia fototipeea (ahpo aftoh)
Photocopying machines are becoming ubiquitous in Greece and can often be found at stationary and book stores.

photograph, a (the)—mia (ee) fotografeea (pl. fotografee-ess)

photographer, a (the)—enas (oh) fotograhfos; **photography shop, a (the)**—ena (toh) fotografeeoh

phrase, a (the)—mia (ee) frahsee; **phrase book, a**—ena vivleeo meh ekfrasees; **English-Greek phrasebook**—ena vivleeo meh Ahnglo-Eleenikess ekfra-sees

pick up (to) someone—na kahno kamahkee

picnic, a (the)—ena (toh) peekneek; **Let's have a picnic**—Ahs pahmeh ya ena peekneek

picture, a (the)—mia eekona (pl. eekoness); **painting, a (the)**—enas (oh) peenakas; **a photograph**—mia fotografeea

pie, a (the)—mia (ee) peeta (pl. peetess); apple pie—melopita; cheese pie—teeropita; meat pie—kreh-ahtohpita; spinach pie—spanakopita

piece, a (the)—ena (toh) kamahtee

pier, the—oh mohlos

pig, a (the)—ena (toh) gooroonee (pl. ta gooroonia)

pill, a (the)—ena (toh) hahpee (pl. ta hahpia)

pillow, a (the)—ena (toh) mahksilahree (pl. ta mahksilahria); pillow case, a (the)—mia (ee) maksilaro-theekee

pin, a (the)—mia (ee) karfeetsa (pl. karfeetsess)

pinch, a (a little)—mia prehza; a finger pinch—mia tseebeeah; He pinched me—Meh tseembiseh; The shoes (boots, etc.) pinch— Meh peeahnoon. pipe, a (the) metal—enas (oh) soleenahs; pipe, a (the) smoking—ena (toh) tseemboukee; pipe tobacco—kahpnohs peepahs; pipe cleaners—katharisteeria ya tseemboukee Pipe tobacco and cleaners, etc. are rarely available except in the larger cities, so if you are traveling around, take a supply with you.

pitcher, a (the)—mia (ee) karafa; a pitcher of water—mia karafa nehro

pity—kreema; What a pity!—Tee kreema! I pity you (him/her)— Seh (ton/teen) leepahmeh

place, a (the)—ena (toh) mehros (pl. ta mehree) "Toh mehros" also being an euphemism for "the toilet."

plan, a (the)—ena (toh) skeh-dhio (pl. skeh-dhia); My plans are...—Ta skeh-dhiah mou eenay...; What are your plans?— Piah eenay ta skeh-dhiah sou?; I plan to...—Skedhiahzo na...

plane (airplane)—ah-ehroplahno; plane tree, a (the)—enas (oh) plahtanos

plaster (n)—yeepso; bandaid—lefkoplahst or hansa-plast

plastic (adj.)—plastikos (m), plastikee (f), plastikoh (n)

plate, a (the)—ena (toh) peeahtoh (pl. ta peeahta); a plate of potatoes—mia meree-dha patatess

Platò—Oh Plahton

play, a (the) theatre, film—ena (toh) ehrgo (pl. ta ehrga)

play (to)—na paykso; I want to play—Thelo na paykso; I don't know how to play—Dhen ksehro na paykso; Let's play—Ahs payksoomeh

playground, a (the)—mia (ee) paydhikee hara

please—parakalo (also means "You're welcome")

pliers—pensa

plug, a (the) electric—mia (ee) **preeza; for a hole** (basin, barrel etc.)—mia (ee) **tah**pa

plumber, a (the)—**en**as (oh) ee-dhravli**kos; plumbing, the**—ta eedhravli**ka; The plumbing doesn't work**—Ta eedhravli**ka** dhen dhoolevoon

plus—seen; **two plus two**—dheeo seen dheeo; **plus that**—mahzee meh af**toh**

pocket, a (the)—mia (ee) tsepee (pl. ee tsepess)

pocketbook (purse)—ena (toh) portofolee

poem, a (the)—**en**a (toh) **pee**ma (pl. ta pee-**ee**mata)

poet, a (the)—**en**as (oh) pee-ee**tees** (m & f)

poison—dheeliteerio; **poisonous**—dheeliteerioh-dhees

police, the—ee ahstinomeea; **policeman, a (the)**—**en**as (oh) ahstinomos **or en**as (oh) horofeelakas; **police station, the**—toh ahstinomi**koh** t**mee**ma; **Tourist Police, the**—ee Tooristikee Ahstinomeea

polio—poliomee-e**lee**tees; **polio vaccine**—emvolio poliomee-**elee**tee

Oral polio vaccines are available virtually everywhere in Greece where there is a doctor, so if you have a child who needs a booster, don't hesitate to ask.

polish—loostro; **nailpolish**—vehr**nee**kee neekhee**on; shoe polish**—vehr**nee**kee ya ta papootsia

pollution—mohleensees

polytechnic, the—toh pohleetek**nee**on

pool, a (the) swimming—mia (ee) pee**see**na; **pool (the game)**—beeliar-dhoh; **football pool**—ProPo

poor (adj.)—fftok**hos** (m), fftok**hee** (f) fftok**ho** (n); **the poor**—ee fftok**hee**

pop (popular)—pohp; **popcorn**—pohp-korn

pope, the—oh **Pah**pahs

popular—dheemofi**lees**

pork—heerino

pornography—pornografeea; **pornographic**—pornografi**koh**

The laws regarding pornographic films and magazines are very liberal in Greece.

port, a (the)—ena (toh) leemahnee; **port police, the**—toh leemenarkheeo

portable—foreetoh

porter, a (the)—enas (oh) ahk-thoforos

portion, a (of food)—mia meree-dha (pl. meree-dhess)

portrait, a (the)—ena (toh) portraytoh

postman, a (the)—enas (oh) takhee-dhromos

post office, a (the)—ena (toh) takheedhrameeo (written on yellow signs with black letters as: ΤΑΧΥΔΡΟΜΕΙΟΝ or ΕΛΤΑ)

pot, a (the) cooking—mia (ee) heetra; **flower pot, a (the)**—mia (ee) glahstra

potter, a (the)—enas (oh) kerameestas; **pottery**—keramikee; **pottery shop, a (the)**—ena (toh) keramopee-eeo

powder—skonee; **cosmetic or baby**—poo-dhra

prefer (I)—Proteemoh; **What do you prefer?**—Tee proteemahs?

pregnant—enghios

prescription, a (the)—mia (ee) seentagyee

preserves—marmela-dha or gleeka kootal-you

president, the—oh proeh-dhrohs; **of the United States**—tees Amerikees

pressure—pee-esees

price, the—ee teemee; **price list, the**—toh teemolo-ghio

pride (self-respect)—feelotimo; **conceit**—eeperoseea

priest, a (the)—enas (oh) papahs (pl. ee papa-dhess)

prison—feelakee

problem, a (the)—ena (toh) provleema (pl. provleemata)

program, the—toh programma

Prometheus—Oh Promeethefs

promise, a—mia eeposkhesees; **I promise**—Eeposkhomay; **I promise you**—Sou eeposkhomay; **Promise?**—Eeposkheseh?

prompt (popctual)—steen ora (lit. "on the hour"); **promptly**—takheh-os

Inasmuch as nothing is ever punctual or immediate in Greece, these words should be taken as euphemisms for "as soon as possible."

propeller, the—ee propella

property—periooseea; **land**—kteema; **It's my property**—Eenay dheekee mou periooseea; **I want to buy some property**—Thelo na agoraso ena kteema; **It is your property?**—Eenay toh dheekoh sou kteema?; **property owner, the**—oh eedheeookteetees

prophylactic, a (the) contraceptive—**ena** (toh) profilactikoh (pl. profilactika)

These can be purchased both in pharmacies and at sidewalk kiosks.

proposal, a (the)—**mia** (ee) seeghisee; **marriage proposal**—mia protasee gahmoo

prostitute, a (the)—**mia** (ee) pootahna

prostration (heat)—eeleeasee

Can be life-threatening. For emergency first aid, please see under **sunstroke**.

Protestant—Prohtestahntees

proud—pereefanos (m), pereefanee (f), pereefano (n)

pullover, a (the)—**ena** (toh) poolohvehr

pump, a (the)—**mia** (ee) ahndleea

pumpkin, a—**ena** kokino kolakeethee

puncture, a—mia treepa

pupil, a (the) school—**enas** (oh) mathitees (m), **mia** matheetria (f) (pl. ee mathitess, ee matheetriess)

puppet, a (the)—**mia** (ee) marionetta (pl. marionettess)

pure (clean)—katharo; **unmixed**—ahnotheftoh

purse, a (the)—**ena** (toh) portofolee (also the word for "wallet"); **I've lost my purse**—Eh-ho hahsee toh portofolee mou; **My purse has been stolen**—Mou klepsaneh toh portofolee

purser, the—oh loghistees

put (to)—na valo; **to put back**—na valo peeso; **Where can I put this?**—Poo boroh na toh valo aftoh?; **Can I put it here?**—Boroh na toh valo eh-dhoh?; **Put it there**—Valeh toh ekee; **I'll put it back**—Tha toh valo peeso; **I put it back**—Toh ehvala peeso; **Where did you (he/she) put it?**—Poo toh ehvaless (ehvaleh)?

putty—stokos

puzzle, a—**ena** aynigma; **game**—**enas** greefos

Pygmalion—Oh Peegmaleeon

pyjamas—peezahmess
Pythagoras—Oh Peethagoras

Q

quality—peeohtees; good quality—kalee peeohtita

quarrel, a—enas kavgahs; I don't want to quarrel—Dhen thelo na kahno kavgah; We had a quarrel—Eekhameh ena kavgah

quarter, a (the)—ena (toh) tetartoh; a quarter-kilo—ena tetartoh; in a quarter of an hour—seh ena tetartoh; a quarter to three—treess para tetartoh; a quarter past three—treess kay tetartoh

queen, a (the)—mia (ee) vahseelisa; Queen Elizabeth—Ee Vahseelisa Eleesavet

queer (strange)—parakseno; homosexual, a—enas beeness

question, a (the)—ena (toh) ehrotima (pl. ehroteemata); I have a question—Eh-ho mia ehrotisee

queue, a (the)—mia (ee) oorah

quick—greegoro; quickly—greegora

quiet, the—ee eeseekheea or ee eeremeea; quiet (still)—eeseek-ho; peaceful—eeremo; Quiet!—Eeseekha!

quit (I)—Engataleepo; He (she) has quit—Eh-hee engataleepsee.

R

rabbi, a (the)—enas (oh) rahveenos

rabbit, a (the)i ena (toh) koonelee (pl. koonelia)

rabies—leesa

racket, a (the) tennis, etc.—mia (ee) raketta (pl. rakettess)

radiator, a (the)—ena (toh) kalorifehr; of a car—toh pseegheeo

radio, a (the)—ena (toh) rahdhiohfono

railroad, the—oh seedheero-dhromos; railroad station, a (the)—enas (oh) stathmos traynou

rain, the—ee vrokhee; It's raining—Vreh-hee; Will it rain?—Tha vreksee? It rained—Ehvrekseh; rainbow, a (the)—ena (toh) oorahnio tokso; raincoat, a (the)—ena (toh) ah-dhiahvrokho

rape—veeasmos

rare (special, not often found)—spahnio; rarely—spahnia

rat, a (the)—enas ahroorayos (pl. ahrooray-ee); rat poison—pondikofarmako; rat trap, a—mia fahka

rate of exchange, the—ee teemee seenalagmatos

ravine, a (the)—**en**a (toh) fa**rahng**hee

raw—**ahp**seetoh *or* omo (the latter for fruits, etc.)

razor, a (the)—**en**a (toh) ksee**rah**fee; **razor blades**—kseeristi**kess** lepee-**dhess**

read (to)—na **dhee**avaso; **I want to read**—**Thel**o na **dhee**avaso

ready—**eh**timo; **It is ready?**—**Ee**nay **eh**timo?; **When will it be ready?**—**Pot**eh tha **ee**nay **eh**timo?

real—ahlee**thee**no; **Really?**—Ahlee**thi**a?

real estate—eekope-**dha**

reason, the—oh **loh**gos; **reasonable**—loh**ghi**koh

receipt, a (the)—**mi**a (ee) ahpo-**dhik**see; **May I have a receipt?**—Boroh na **eh**-ho **mi**a ahpo-**dhik**see?

receive (to)—na **lah**vo; **I received**—**Ell**ava

reception desk, the—ee resep**siohn**

recipe, a (the)—**mi**a (ee) seen**tag**yee; **Can I have the recipe?**—Boroh na **eh**-ho teen seen**tag**yee?

recognize (I)—Ahnagno**ree**zo; **I didn't recognize you (her/him)**—Dhen seh (teen/ton) ahnag**nor**isa; **Don't you recognize...?**—Dhen ahnag**nor**isees...?

recommend (I)—Seen**stoh**hi; **What do you recommend?**—Tee seen**istahs**?

record, a (the) music—**en**as (oh) **dhees**kos (**dhees**kee); **record player, a (the)**—**en**a (toh) pee**kahp**; **record (to)**—na kata**grap**so; **I want to record**—**Thel**o na kata**grap**so

reef, a (the)—**mi**a (ee) **kseh**ra

reel, a (the) fishing—**mi**a(ee) ah**nem**ee; **tape, film,etc.**—**en**a (toh) ka**roo**lee

refill, a (pen, etc.)—**en**a ahndalak**ti**koh

refrigerator, a (the)—**en**a (toh) psee**ghee**o

regards—hayre**tees**mata

registered (at a hotel, etc.)—grah**men**os (m), grah**men**ee (f); **Is Mr. Smith registered here?**—**Ee**nay oh **keer**ios Smith grah**men**os eh-**dhoh**?; **a registered letter**—**en**a see**stim**eno **grah**ma

regular—tak**ti**koh *or* kano**ni**koh; **regularly**—tak**ti**ka *or* kano**ni**ka

relative, a (the)—**en**as (oh) sing**yen**ees (m), **mi**a (ee) sing**yen**ees; (pl. ee sing**yen**ees)

relationship, a (the)—**mi**a (ee) **skheh**see; **our relationship**—ee **skheh**see mahs

relax (to)—na ksekoora**s**toh; **I need to relax**—Prepee na ksekoora**s**toh; **Relax!**—Ksekoora**h**sou!; **Calm down!**—Eeremi**s**eh!; **relaxed**—ksekoorastos (m), ksekoorastee (f)

reliable—ahksiohpistos (m) ahksiohpistee (f), ahksiohpistoh (n)

religion—three**s**kevma; **religious**—threeskeftikos (m), threeskeftikee (f), threeskeftikoh (n)

rely (to...on)—na vahsee**s**toh; **I'm relying on you**—Vasee**z**omay seh **s**ena

remember (I)—Theema**h**may; **I don't remember**—Dhen theema**h**may; **I will remember**—Tha theemee**t**ho; **Do you remember?**—Theema**h**say?; **Will you remember?**—Tha theemee**t**hees?; **I remembered**—Theemee**t**hika; **Did you remember?**—Theemee**t**hikess?

remind me—Thee**m**eeseh mou; **It reminds me of...**—Mou theeme**e**zee...

remover, a (for paint, etc.)—eksalipti**k**oh meh**s**o; for fingernail polish—ahse**t**ohn

rendezvous, a (the)—**ena** (toh) rahnde**h**voo; **Shall we make a rendezvous?**—Tha dhoh**s**oomeh rahnde**h**voo?

rent, the—toh eneekio or toh neekee

repair (to)—na episkeva**h**so; **Can you repair this?**—Boreeteh na toh episkeva**h**seteh aftoh?

repairman, a—enas episkeva**s**tees; **repair shop, a**—ena seen-ergh**ee**o

repay (to)—na ahndapo-**dhoh**so; **to repay money**—na kseplee**r**oso; **How can I repay you?**—Pohs boroh na sou ahndapo-**dhoh**so? Repaying Greeks for anything (except money) is almost impossible.

repellent, a (insect)—**ena** apothiti**k**oh endohmon

replica, a (the)—**ena** (toh) panomio**h**tipo

reply, a—mia ahpahn**d**isee; **It (the telephone) doesn't reply**—Dhen ahpahn**d**aee

reproduction, a (the)—**ena** (toh) ande**e**grafo

resemble (I)—Meea**h**zo; **You resemble**—Meea**h**zees; **Sbe (he/it) resembles you**—Sou. meea**h**zee

reservation, a (the)—**ena** (toh) klee**s**imo; **I have a reservation**—Eh-ho klee**s**imo; **reserve (to)**—na klee**s**o; **I want to reserve (make a reservation)**—Thelo na klee**s**o (**a room/table**—ena dhohmahtio/trahpehzee); in reserve—rehzerva; reserved (taken)—kleesmeno

responsibility, the—ee eftheenee; responsible (accountable)—eepefthinos (m) eepefthinee (f); I am responsible—Eemay eepefthinos; Who is responsible?—Piohs eenay eepefthinos? responsible (reliable)—ahksiohpistos (m) ahksiohpistee (f)

rest, a—mia ksekoorasee; I want to—Thelo na ksekoorastho; I am resting— Ksekoorahzomay

rest, the (of something)—toh eepolipo

restaurant, a (the)—ena (toh) estiatorio; Where is a good (cheap) restaurant?—Poo eenay ena kalo (fftheeno) estiatorio?
Good, cheap restaurants are fortunately not yet a thing of the past in Greece, nor are they terribly difficult to find: they are usually located in or near the market place, and the best are the ones that have the most Greeks in them.

result, the—toh ahpotelesma

Resurrection, the (of Christ)—Ee Ahnahstasis

retainer, a (fee)—mia prokatavolee

retired—seendaksiookhos (m & f)

return (to) come back—na yeereeso or na ksanartho; I want to return—Thelo na ksanartho; I will return—Tha yeereeso; When will you (she/he/it) return?—Poteh tha yeereesees (yeereesee)?;

return (to) give back—na epistrepso; I'll return it—Tha toh epistrepso; return ticket, a (the)—ena (toh) eesiteerio met'epistrofeess

reward, a (the)—mia (ee) ahmivee; I'll give a reward—Tha dhohso mia ahmivee

rhythm, a (the)—enas (oh) reethmos

ribbon, a (the)—mia (ee) cor-dhella

rich (wealthy)—ploosios (m), ploosia (f)

right (correct)—sostoh or dheekayo; It's right (correct)—Eenay sostoh; I'm right—Eh-ho dheekayo; You're right—Eh-hees dheekayo; He (she) is right—Eh-hee dheekayo; right (opp. of left)—dheksiah—the political Right—Ee dheksiah; all right—endahksee; right away—ahmehsos

ring, a (the) finger—ena (toh) dhaktilee-dhee; a diamond ring—ena dheeamandenio dhaktilee-dhee; engagement and wedding

ring, a (the)—mia (ee) **veh**ra

The engagement ring is also the wedding ring, worn on the left hand before the wedding and on the right hand afterwards.

river, a (the)—**ena** (toh) po**tah**mee or **enas** (oh) pota**mos**

roach, a (the)—mia (ee) katsaree-dha (pl. katsaree-dhess)

road, a (the)—**enas** (oh) **dhromos**; **main road, the**—oh keerios dhromos; **road map, a**—enas odhikos hartees

robbed (I was)—Meh **lee**stepsahn; **robbery, a (the)**—mia (ee) leesteea

robe, a (the)—mia (ee) rohba

rollers (hair)—**rolla**

Roman (adj.)—roma-ikos (m), roma-ikee (f), romaikoh (n)

romance, a (the)—**ena** (toh) ro**mahn**dzo; **romantic**—romandikos (m), romandikee (f), romandikoh (n)

roof, a (the)—mia (ee) skepee

room, a (the)—**ena** (toh) dho**hmah**tio (pl. dho**hmah**tia)

rooster, a (the)—**enas** (oh) peti**nos**

rope, a (the)—**ena** (to) skeenee (pl. ta skeeniah)

rosary, a (the)—**ena** (toh) kombolo-ee katholikon

Not to be confused with kombolo-ee, the Greek worry beads

rose, a (the)—**ena** (toh) tree-anda**fi**lo (pl. tree-anda**fi**la)

rouge—kokina-dhee

rough (uneven)—trak**hee**; **not gentle**—trak**hees**; **a rough sea**—mia **ahg**ria tha**la**sa

round (adj.)—strong**hi**loh; **a round of drinks**—mia volta; **roundabout, a (the)**—mia (ee) kiklikee dheea-**stav**rosee; **roundtrip, a**—**ena** taksee-dhee met'epistro**feess**; **a roundtrip ticket**—**ena** eesiteerio met' epistro**feess**

route, a (the)—**ena** (toh) dhromolohghio; **What's the best route?**—Pioh eenay toh kaleetero dhromolohghio?

rowboat, a (the)—mia (ee) **var**ka meh koupiah

rubber (the substance)—ka-oot-**souk**; **rubber** (adj.) ehlastikoh; **rubberband, a**—**ena** lastikho (pl. **las**tikha); **rubbers** (overshoes)—gahlohtsess; **prophylactics**—profilaktika

rubbish, the—ta skoopee-dhia; **Rubbish!**—Ah-ee-**dhee**-ess!

rucksack, a (the)—**ena** (toh) sahkee-dhio

rude (impolite)—ahghenees

rug, a (the)—**en**a (toh) hal**ak**ee

rule, a (the)—**en**as (oh) kan**o**nahs (pl. ee kan**o**ness)

ruler, a (the) straight-edge—**en**as (oh) har**ak**ahs

rumor, a (the)—**mi**a (ee) **fee**mee (pl. ee **fee**mess)

run (to)—na trek-ho; I like to run—M'ah**reh**see na trek-ho; I ran—
Eh**trek**sa; He (she/it) ran—Eh**trek**seh; We ran—**Trek**sameh; I
have to run (go)—**Pre**pee na **fee**go; Is it (the bus, train, etc.)
running?—Keeklo**fore**e?

rusk (dried, baked bread)—paksi**mah**-dhee

rust—sk**oo**riah; rusty—sk**oo**nas**men**o

S

saccharine—sakhar**ee**nee (while **zak**haree is "sugar")

sad—leepi**men**os (m), leepi**men**ee (f), leepi**men**o (n)

saddle, a (the)—**mi**a (ee) **sel**la

safe (adj) not dangerous—ah**keen**-dhino; secure, out of danger—
ahsf**al**ees; for safe-keeping—ya ahs**fal**ia; safety pin, a—**mi**a
para**man**a (pl. para**man**ess)

sail, a (the)—**en**a (toh) **pah**nee (pl. ta pah**ni**ah) or **en**a (toh) ee**ste**eo
(pl. ee**ste**ea); sailboat, a (the)—**mi**a (ee) **var**ka meh **pah**nee;
sailor, a (the)—**en**as (oh) **naf**tees; sailing—eestiopl**oe**ea; I want
to go sailing—**The**lo na **kah**no eestiopl**oe**ea

saint, a (the)—**en**as (oh) **ah**-yos (m), **mi**a (ee) **ahg**-yia (f)

salad, a (the)—**mi**a (ee) sal**at**a

salary, a (the)—**en**as (oh) **mees**thos

sale, a (the)—**mi**a (ee) **ekp**tohsee (written as: ΕΚΠΤΩΣΕΙΣ)
Traditionally take place in August and February, although, as elsewhere, there may be spot sales throughout the year.

same, the—toh ee-**dhee**o

sand—**ah**mos; sandy—**ah**mo-dhess; fine sand—ps**ee**lee **ah**mos;
sandpaper—yalo**har**toh

sandal, a (the)—**en**a (toh) san-**dah**lee (pl. san-**dah**lia) sandwich,
a (the)—**en**a (toh) **sah**ndwits (pl. **sah**ndwits); a toasted sandwich—**en**a tohst (pl. tohst); cheese—**te**eree; ham—**zam**bon

sanitary—eeg-yee-**een**oh; sanitary napkins—sehr-vi**et**ess

Santa Claus—**Ah**-yos Vas**ee**lees

sardines—sar-**dhel**less

sauce, the—ee **sahl**tsa

saucer, a (the)—**ena** (toh) peeah**tah**kee

sausage—loukah**ni**ko (pl. loukah**ni**ka)

saw, a (the)—**ena** (toh) pree**oh**nee

say (to)—na poh; How do you say...?—Pohs leneh...?; What did you (he/she) say?—Tee eepess (eepeh)?; I said—Eepah; I said to you—Sou eepah; You said—Eepess; She (he) said—Eepeh; Who said?—Peeohs eepeh?

scale, a (the) weighing—**mia** (ee) zeegariah

scarf, a (the)—**mia** (ee) **sar**pa or **ena** (toh) kas**kohl**

The latter being for warmth, the former for style.

scenery, the—toh toh**pee**o

schedule, a (the)—**ena** (toh) **pro**grama; The bus (train/boat) schedule—toh dhromoloh**ghi**o

school, a (the)—**ena** (toh) sko**lee**o

scissors—psa**lee**-dhee

scorpion, a (the)—**enas** (oh) skor**pi**ohs (pl. skorpee-**ee**)

Scotsman—Skot**se**zohs; Scotswoman—Skot**se**za; Scottish—Skot**se**zikoh

Scotch tape—**sel**lotayp

screw, a (the)—**mia** (ee) **vee**-dha (pl. **vee**-dhess); screwdriver, a (the)—**ena** (toh) katsa**vee**-dhee

scuba diving—boh**tee**lyes kata-**dhee**sios

sculptor, a (the)—**enas** (oh) **glee**ptees; sculpture—gleep**ti**kee

sea, the—ee **tha**lasa; in the sea—stee **tha**lasa; calm sea—bo**nah**tza; rough sea—treeki**mee**a or ah**gri**a **tha**lasa; seafood—thala**see**na; sea nettle—**tsook**tra; seashell, a (the)—**ena** (toh) oh**stra**ko (pl. oh**stra**ka); seashore, the—ee para**lee**a

sea urchin, a (the) enas foh) a**khi**nohs (pl. ee a**khi**nee)

seasickness—naf**tee**a; I am seasick—Meh pee**ah**nee ee **tha**lasa; He (she) is seasick—Ton (teen) pee**ah**nee ee **tha**lassa

seamstress, a (the)—**mia** (ee) **rap**tria

season, the—ee epo**khee**

seat, a (the)—**ena** (toh) ka**thees**ma; Are there any seats?—Eepark**hoon** ka**thees**mata

second, a (the) time—ena (toh) dheftero-leptoh (pl. dheftero-lepta);
second (2nd)—dheftero; **second class**—dhefteree thesee;
second-hand—metaherismeno

secret, a (the)—ena (toh) meestikoh (pl. meestika); It's a secret—
Eenay meestikoh

see (I)—Vlepo; You see—Vlepees; She (he) sees—Vlepee; I saw—
Ee-dha; You saw—Ee-dhess; He (she) saw—Ee-dheh
Can also, as in English, be used to mean "understand."

seed, a (the)—enas (oh) sporohs (pl. ee sporee)

seem (I)—Faynomay; You seem—Faynesay; He (she/it) seems—
Faynetay

sell (to)—na poleeso; I want to sell—Thelo na poleeso; Do you
want to sell this?—Theleteh na toh poleeseteh?; He (she)
sells—Polaee; I sold—Pooleesa; You sold—Pooleesess; She
(he) sold—Pooleeseh; It's sold—Eenay pooleemeno; Sold
Out—Pooleethikeh.

seminary, a (the)—mia (ee) theh-ologhikee skolee

send (to)—na steelo; I want to send this—Thelo na toh steelo;
Can you send it to me?—Boreeteh na mou toh steeleteh?; I
sent—Esteela; You sent—Esteeless; She (he) sent—Esteeleh

sensual—feelee-dhonos (m), feelee-dhonee (f), feelee-dhono (n)

sentimental—seenaysthimatikos (m), seenaysthimatikee (f),
seenaysthimatikoh (n)

separate—horistee (m & f), horista (n); **separately**—ksek-horista;
separate beds (rooms)—horista kravahtia (dhohmahtia); **separate checks**—horistee logariasmee; **separated** (not divorced)—
en dhee-astasee

September—Septemvrees

serious—sovaros (m), sovaree (f), sovaro (n); **seriously**—sovarah

service, the (restaurant, etc.)—ee peripee-esi; **auto service**—seen-
teerisees; **service station, a (the)**—ena (toh) garahz

several—merikee (m), merikess (f), merika (n); **several times**—
merikess foress

sew (to)—na rahpso; Can you sew this for me?—Borees na mou
to rahpsees aftoh ya mena? **sewing**—rahpsimo; **sewing
machine**—rahptoh-meekhanee; **sewing needle, a**—mia velona
ya rahpsimo; **thread**—klostee

sex—sehx; sex appeal—sehx ahpeel; sexy—seksee

shade, the—ee skiah; in the shade—stee skiah; shady—skee-eroh; lampshade, a (the)—ena (toh) ahmbazoor

shake hands (to)—na kahno heerapseea; Let's shake on it—Na dhohsomeh ta hehria

shaker, a (the) cocktail, coffee, etc.—ena (toh) say-eekehr; salt— ahlatiehra; pepper—peeperiehra

shallow—reekho; Is it (the sea) shallow?—Eenay reekha?

shampoo—sahmpooahn

share (to)—na meerasto; We'll share it—Tha toh meerastoomeh

shark, a (the)—enas (oh) karkhareeas or ena (toh) skeelopsaro

sharp (as in "knife")—koftero; to sharpen (metal)—na akoneeso; I want to sharpen this—Thelo na toh akoneeso aftoh

sharpener, a (knife)—ena ahkonisteeri; (pencil)—mia kseestra

shave, a—ena kseerisma; shaving brush, a—ena peenelo ksireesmatos; shaving cream—krema ksireesmatos; shaving lotioh—losion ksireesmatos

shawl, a (the)—ena (toh) sahlee

she—aftee—or, when indicated from a distance—ehkeenee

sheep, a (the)—ena (toh) provatoh (pl. provata); sbeepskin— proviah

sheet, a (the) bed—ena (toh) sendohnee (pl. ta sendohnia); clean sheets—kathara sendohnia

shell, a (the) sea—ena (toh) ohstrako (pl. ta ohstraka); shellfish— thalaseena

ship, a (the)—ena (toh) pleeoh or ena (toh) kahrahvee

shirt, a (the)—ena (toh) pookahmiso (pl. pookahmisa)

shish-kebab, a—ena souvlakee

shock, a—ena sohk

shoe, a (the)—ena (toh) papootsee (pl. ta papootsia); shoe laces— kor-dhonia

shop, a (the)—ena (toh) magazee

shore, the—ee paraleea

short (not tall or long)—kondos (m), kondee (f), kondoh (n); shortly—seh leego; short circuit, a—ena vrak-hee-keekloma

shorten (to)—na kondeeno; I want to shorten this—Thelo na kondeeno aftoh should—prepee

shoulder, a (the)—enas (oh) ohmos (pl. ee ohmee); shoulder bag, a (the)—mia (ee) tsahnda kremastee; shoulder strap—ena (toh) looree

shovel, a—ena fftiahree

show (to)—na dheekso; I'll show you—Tha sou dheekso; Will you show me?—Tha mou dheeksees?

shower, a (the)—ena (toh) doos; Is there a shower?—Eh-hee doos?; With hot water?—Meh zestoh nehro?; I want to take a shower—Thelo na kahno doos

shrink (to)—na bee; Will it shrink?—Tha bee? It shrank—Meekrinee

shut (closed)—kleestoh (written as: ΚΛΕΙΣΤΟΝ); to shut—na kleeso; Shut the door—Kleeseh tee porta; Shut up!—Skaseh!

shutters, the—ta pahndzooria

shy (adj.)—drohpalos (m), drohpalee (f), drohpalo (n); He (she) is being shy—Drepetay

sick (ill)—ahrostos (m), ahrostee (f), ahrostoh (n); I feel sick—Dhen aysthahnomay kala; I think I'm sick—Nomeezo eemay ahrostos (ahrostee)

side, a (the)—mia (ee) plevra

siesta, a (the)—enas (oh) mesimvreenos eepnos or ena (toh) rehpoh

sights, the—ta ahksio-theh-ata; I want to see the sights—Thelo na dhoh ta ahksiotheh-ata

sign, a (the)—ena (toh) seema (pl. ta seemata)

sign (to)—na eepograhpso; Do I have to sign something?—Prepee na eepograhpso kahtee?; Where do I sign?—Poo eepografo?; I have signed—Eh-ho eepograhpsee; Will you sign this?—Tha toh eepograhpsees aftoh?

signature, a (the)—mia (ee) eepografee

silence, the—ee seeopee; silent—seeopiloh (n)

silk—metahksee; adj.—metaksotoh

silly—ahnoeetos (m), ahnoeetee (f), ahnoeeto (n)

silver (noun)—ahseemee; adj.—ahsimenio (n); silver-plated—ehparghiroh

sin, a (the)—mia (ee) ahmarteea (pl. ahmartee-ess)

since—**ek**toteh; **Since then**—ahpo toteh

sing (to)—na tragoo-**dhee**so; **I can't sing**—Dhen boroh na tragoo-**dhee**so; **You (he/she) sing beautifully**—Tragoo-**dhahs** (tragoo-dha-ee) thavmahsia; **singer, a (the)**—**en**as (oh) tragoo-dhees**tees** (m), **mia** (ee) tragoo-**dhees**tria (f)

single—**moh**nos (m), **moh**nee (f), **moh**no (n); **unmarried**—**ahg**amos (m), **ahg**amee (f)

sink (to)—na vooli**ahk**so; **Won't it sink?**—Dhen tha vooli**ahk**see?; **It sank**—Vooli**ahk**seh

sip, a—**mia** gooliah; **just a sip**—**moh**no mia gooliah

Sirens, the—Ee Seer**ee**ness

sister, a (the)—**mia** (ee) ah-**dhel**fee (pl. ah-**dhel**fess)

Sisyphus—Oh See**sis**fohs

sit (to)—na **kaht**so; **Where can I sit?**—Poo boroh na **kaht**so?; **Sit down** (sing. familiar)—**Kaht**seh or **Kaht**iseh; (plural or formal)—**Kaht**eesteh; (to a hyperactive child or dog)—**Kaht**seh kah**toh**!

size, the—toh **meg**-ethos; **the size number**—toh noo**me**ro

sketch, a (the)—**mia** (ee) skiagra**fee**a; **sketch book, a**—**mia** seel**og**hee **skeet**son or carneh ya **skeet**sa ("sketch pad"); **to sketch**—na **skeet**sahro; **I want to sketch you**—Thelo na seh skee**tah**ro

skewer, a (the) metal—**mia** (ee) **soov**la (pl. **soov**less); **small, wooden**—kalamah**kee** (also means "drinking straw")

ski, a (the)—**en**a (toh) skee (pl. ta skee); **I want to ski**—Thelo na **kah**no skee

Water skiing facilities are available at most major tourist spots. Mountain skiing centers exist in several parts of Greece, the newest and largest being at Mt. Parnassus. For complete information, see the local tourist bureau and ask for its excellent publication, General Information About Greece.

skin, the (human)—ee epi-dherh-**mee**-dha; **animal skin**—**dhehr**ma.

skin diving—eepovreek**hio** kol**eem**bee

skirt, a (the)—**mia** (ee) **foos**ta (pl. **foos**tess)

sky, the—oh oo**ra**nos

slacks—panta**lo**nia

sleep (noun)—**eep**nos; **to sleep**—na keemi**thoh**; **I want to sleep**—Thelo na keemi**thoh**; **Do you want to sleep?**—Thel**ees** na keemi**thees**?; **He (she) is sleeping**—Keema**tay**; **Where (when)** are you going to sleep?—Poo (poteh) tha keemithees?; **I was sleeping**—Keemomoona; **Were you sleeping?**—Keemosoona?; **I want to sleep late**—Thelo na kseepneeso argah (lit. "wake late"); **I am sleepy**—Neestahzo; **Are you sleepy?**—Neestahzees?; **He (she) is sleepy**—Neestahzee

sleeping bag, a (the)—ena (toh) sleeping bag; **sleeping car, a (the)**—ena (toh) vagon-lee *or* kleenamaksa: **sleeping pills** eepnotika hahpia

sleeve, a (the)—ena (toh) mahneekee (pl. ta mahneekia)

slice, a—mia fehta (pl. fehtess); **a slice of bread**—mia fehta psomee; **a slice of feta cheese**—mia fehta fehta

slippers—pandoofless

slow—argah; **slowly, slowly**—seegah-seegah; **Please slow down**—Parakalo, mee trekhetay; **My watch is slow**—Toh rolloy mou paee peeso

small—meekros (m), meekree (f), meekro (n)

smart (clever)—ekseepnos (m), ekseepnee (f), ekseepno (n)

smell, a (the)—mia (ee) meeroodhiah; **I smell some thing**—Meereezo kahtee; **You smell good**—Meereezees oreh-a: **It smells good**—Meereezee oreh-a

smile, a (the)—ena (toh) hahmo-yelo

smoke, the—oh kapnos; **tobacco smoke**—toh kahpnisma; **smoked (meat)**—kahpnistoh; **I smoke**—Kahpneezo; **I don't smoke**—Dhen kahpneezo; **Do you smoke?**—Kahpneezees?; **two packs a day**—dheeoh pahketta teen eemehra; **I'm trying to give up smoking**—Prospatho na kohpso toh tseegahro; **I've given up smoking**—Eh-ho kohpsee toh tseegahro

snack, a (the)—ena (toh) elafro fagheetoh; **a snack bar**—ena snahk-bahr

snail, a (the)—ena (toh) salingahree (pl. ta salingahria)

snake, a (the)—ena (toh) fee-dhee (pl. fee-dhia); **viper, a (the)**—mia (ee) okheeah; **snake bite, a (the)**—ena (toh) dhahgoma fee-dheeoo

snap, a (the) clothing—mia (ee) kohpeetsa (pl. kohpeetsess)

snob, a (the)—enas (oh) snohb (m), mia (ee) snohb (f)

snore (I)—Rokhaleezo; **You snore**—Rokhaleezees

snow—heeohnee; **It is snowing**—Heeoneezee

so (therefore)—etsee; **just so**—etsee; **so-so**—etsee k'etsee: **so big** (small)—tohso megahlo (meekro); **so much**—tohso polee; **so (this) much**—tohsos; **so (this) many**—tohsee; **so long** (goodbye)—ahndeeo

soap—sahpoonee; **a bar of soap**—mia plaka sahpoonee; **flakes**—"Tide" *or* "Rol"; **detergent**—"Ava" *or* "Trill"

sober (not drunk)—ksemetheestos (m), ksemetheestee (f)

soccer—poh-**dhos**-fero

sock, a (the) foot—mia (ee) kaltsa (pl. kaltsess)

socket, a (the)—mie (ee) breeza

Socrates—Oh Sohkrahtees

soda (bicarbonate)—so-dha; **soda water**—so-dha

soft—malakos (m), malakee (f), malakoh (n)

solder—polisee

soldier, a (the)—enas (oh) stratiohtess (pl. ee stratiohtees)

sole, a (the) shoe—mia (ee) solla (pl. ee solless); **new soles**—kenooriess solless

solvent, a (the)—ena (toh) dheealitikoh

some—merikee (m) merikess (f), merika (n); **someone**—kahpios (m), kahpia (f); **someday**—mia kahpia mehra; **somehow**—kahpos; **someplace**—kahpoo; **something**—kahtee; **sometime**—kahpoteh; **sometimes**—kahpoo-kahpoo *or* poteh-poteh; **somewhere**—kahpoo

son, a (the)—enas (oh) yohs (pl. ee yee)

song, a (the)—ena (toh) trahgoo-dhee (pl. ta trahgoo-dhia)

soon—takheh-os; **as soon as possible**—ohso toh dheenatoh greegorotera; **the sooner the better**—ohso greegorotera tohso kahleetera; **sooner or later**—argah ee greegora

sore, a (the)—mia (ee) pleeghee *or* ena (toh) travma; **sore** (adj.)—ponemeno; **a sore throat**—enas ponoh-laymos

sorry (adj.)—leepeemenos (m), leepeemenee (f); **I'm sorry**—Leep-ahmay; **I'm sorry (Excuse me)**—Singnomee

soul, a (the)—ee pseekhee

soup—soupa

sour—skeeno; **bitter**—peekros (m), peekree (f), peekro (n)

south, the—oh nohtos

spaghetti—mahkaronia

Spanish (adj.)—Eespahnikoh; **language**—Eespahnika; **Spaniard, a**—enas Eespanos; **Spanish woman**—mia Eespahnee-dha

spanner, a—ena klee-dhee

speak (to) na meeleeso; **to say or tell**—na poh; **I can't speak Greek**—Dhen boroh na meeleeso Eleenika; **Will you speak to him (her) for me?**—Tha tou (tees) meeleesees ya mena?; **I speak**—Meeloh

spear, a (the) fishing—**ena** (toh) kamahkee

special—spehsiahl or eedhikoh; **speciality, the**—ee spesialiteh

speed limit, the—toh orioh takheetitos

spend (to) money—na kso-**dhepso**; **I can't spend very much**—Dhen boroh na kso-**dhepso** pola; **I spent a lot (too much)**—Kso-dhepsa pola (pl. **parapola**); **to spend time**—na pehrahso; **I want to spend the night**—Thelo na pehraso tee **neek**ta

spice, a (the)—ena (toh) bahk-harikoh (pl. ta bahk-harika); **What spice is it?**—Tee bahkharikoh eenay?; **allspice**—bahk-**hah**ree

spider, a (the)—mia (ee) ahrahknee

spoiled (food, etc.)—halasmeno; **over-indulged**—kako-mathimeno

sponge, a (the)—**en**a (toh) sfoongahree (pl. ta sfoon**gah**ria); **sponge diver, a (the)**—**en**as (oh) sfoong**arahs**

The price of sponges may seem expensive, but one only has to visit a sponge-fishing community like Kalymnos and see the number of twisted and limping former divers to realise how much the trade can cost them.

spoon, a (the)—**en**a (toh) koo**ta**hlee; **soup spoon**—koo**ta**hlee tees **sou**pahs

sport—spor

spot, a (the) stain—**en**as (oh) lekess (pl. ee leke-**dhess**)

spring (season)—ahneeksee; **in the spring**—teen ahneeksee; **next (last) spring**—teen ahlee (teen perasmenee) ahneeksee; **spring** (coil)—elateerio

squall, a—mia borah (pl. bo**ress**)

square, a (the) city—mia (ee) plahteea; **in (on) the square**—stee plahteea

stadium, a (the)—**en**a (toh) stah-**dhee**o

stage, the (theatre)—ee skeenee

stain, a (the)—**en**as (oh) lek**ess**; **stain remover**—katharisti**koh** lekeh-dhon

stairs, the—ee sk**ala**

stamp, a (the) postage—**en**a (toh) gramatoh**simo**; **a tax stamp**—**en**a hartoh**simo**

staples (for paper)—seen-dheteer**ess**; **a stapler**—**mi**a seerapti**kee** meekha**nee**

star, a (the) planet etc.—**en**a (toh) ahsteh**ree** (pl. ta ahsteh**ria**); **the-atre, films, etc.**—**en**as (oh) st**ahr** (m), **mia** (ee) st**ahr** (f); **starfish, a (the)**—**en**as (oh) ahstere**eas**

start, the—ee ar**khee**; **at the start**—steen ar**khee**; **to start**—na ar**khee**so

starving (I'm)—Pet**hay**no ah**po** teen **pee**na (lit. "I'm dying of hunger.")

state, a (the) country—**en**a (toh) **krah**tos

station, a (the)—**en**as (oh) st**ath**mos; **bus station**—st**ath**mos leo-for**ee**ou; **subway station**—eelektri**kos** st**ath**mos; **train station**—st**ath**mos tray**nou**

statue, a (the)—**en**a (toh) ah**gal**ma (pl. ta ah**gal**mata)

stay (to)—na me**eno**; **I want to stay**—Th**elo** na me**eno**; **I will stay**—Tha me**eno**; **I'm staying at...**—Men**oh** sto...; **Where are you staying?**—Poo men**ees**?; **Stay!**—Mee**neh**!

steal (I)—Kl**evo**; **My wallet has been stolen**—Mou klep**saneh** toh portofo**lee**

steps, the (dance)—Ta ve**emata**; **Will you teach me the steps?**—Tha mou ma**thees** ta ve**emata**?

steward, the—oh kamar**otos**

stocks (investments)—ahk**see**-ess

stomach, the—toh stom**ah**kee

stone, a (theS—**mia** (ee) p**ehtra** (pl. ee p**ehtress**)

stool, a (the) sitting—**en**a (toh) sk**am**nee; **stools** (feces)—ee ken**osees**

stop, a (the)—**mia** (ee) st**asee**; **to stop**—na stamat**eeso**; **I want to stop**—Th**elo** na stamat**eeso**; **I stopped**—Stamat**eesa**; **Stop (here)!**—Stam**ata** (eh-**dhoh**)!; **stopper, a** (bottle, sink, etc.)—**en**a vool**oma**

store, a (the)—**ena** (toh) maga**zee**

storehouse, storeroom, a (the)—**mia** (ee) apo**theekee**

storm, a (the)—**mia** (ee) **thee**-ela *or* **mia** (ee) foor**toona**

story, a (the)—**mia** (ee) ee**storeea**

stove, a (the) cooking—**mia** (ee) koo**zeena** *or* **ena** (toh) petro**gahzee**;
  a heating stove—**mia somba**

straight (direct)—ef**theea**; **without anything added**—**sket**oh

strange (unusual)—pa**rakseno**

stranger, a (the)—**en**as (oh) **ksenos** (m), **mia** (ee) **ksenee** (f); **the**
  strangers—ee **ksenee**

strap, a (the)—**ena** (toh) **looree** (pl. ta loo**riah**)

straw, a (drinking)—**ena** kala**makee** (pl. kala**makia**)

street, a (the)—**mia** (ee) oh-**dhohs** (written as: ΟΔΟΣ) *or* **en**as (oh)
  dhromos; **in (on) the street**—sto **dhromo**; **across the street**—
  sto **dhromo** ahpe**nandee**
  "Oh-**dhohs**" is the formal word for "street" that is used in
  addresses; "dhromos" (which also means "road") is used when
  referring to the street itself.

strike, a (the) work stoppage—**mia** (ee) ahper**gheea**

string—**spahng**gos; **guitar, etc. string**—**mia** hor-**dhee**

strong—dhee**natos** (m), dhee**natee** (f), dhee**nato** (n)

stuck (adj).—kolee**meno**

student, a (the)—**en**as (oh) mathi**tees** (m), **mia** (ee) mathee**tria** (f);
  (pl. ee mathi**tess**, ee mathee**triess**)

stupid—**vla**kas

sty, a—**ena** krith**aree**
  The Greeks say that if you have a sty, it is because a pregnant
  woman (other than your wife) desires you. Doctors say it's because
  you're overtired...

style, the (fashion)—ee mo-**dha**

styptic pencil, a—**ena** steep**tikoh**

subway, the—oh ee**lektrikos**

success—epi**tikheea**; **Good success!**—**Kahlee** epi**tikheea!**

sue (to)—na **kahno** mee**nisee**; **I'm going to sue**—Tha **kahno**
  mee**nisee**

suede—soo-**ehd**

sugar—**zakh**aree

suggest (I)—Proteeno; **What do you suggest?**—Tee proteenees?

suit, a (the) clothing—ena (toh) kostoomee

suitcase, a (the)—mia (ee) valeetsa (pl. valeetsess)

sum, the—ee sooma or toh seenolo

summer, summertime, the—toh kalokayree; **this summer**—aftoh toh kalokayree; **last (next) summer**—toh perasmeno (toh ahlo) kalokayree

summons, a—mia kleesee

sun, the—oh eelios; **sunbath**—eeliotherapeea; **sunburn, a**—eeliako engavma: **sunburned**—kahmenos ahpo ton eelio: **sunflower, a**—enas eelios: **sunflower seeds**—eeliohsporee; **sunglasses**—yaliah eeleeoo; **sunrise**—ee anatolee tou eeleeoo; **sunset**—eelio-vaseelema; **suntan, a (the)**—ena (toh) mahvrisma ahpo ton eelio

sunstroke, a—mia eeleeasee

supermarket, a (the)—ena (toh) sooperh market

superstition, a (the)—mia (ee) proleepsee

suppository, a—ena eepothetoh

> If you have a son anywhere between 4 and 14 years old, you will find a strong resistance among Greeks to giving him medication in the form of a supppository. This is because of a wide-spread belief that such treatment could turn him into a homosexual.

sure—seegooro or vevayo; **Sure!**—Vevaya!

surname, a (the)—ena (toh) ehponimo

surprise, a (the)—mia (ee) ekpleeksee; **What a surprise!**—Tee ekpleeksee!

suspenders—teerahndess

swallow (I)—Katapeeno; **I swallowed**—Katahpia

sweater, a (the)—ena (toh) poolohvehr or mia (ee) fahnella

Swedish (adj.)—Swee-dhìkoh; **language**—Swee-dhika; **a Swedish man**—enas Swee-dhohs; **a Swedish woman**—mia Swee-dheza

sweep (to)—na skoopeeso

sweet, a (the)—ena (toh) gleekoh (pl. gleeka); **sweet (adj.)**—gleekos (m), gleekiah (f), gleekoh (n)

swelling (It's)—Preezeteh

swim, a—ena koleembee; **I'm going for a swim**—Pao koleembee; **Let's go for a swim**—Pahmeh koleembee; **I can't swim**—Dhen boroh na koleembeeso; **I have been swimming**—Koleemboosa; **swimming pool, a** (the)—mia (ee) peeseena

Swiss (adj.)—Elvetikoh; **a Swiss man**—enas Elvetohs: **a Swiss female**—mia Elvetee-dha

switch, a (the)—enas (oh) dheeakoptees

sympathy—seempathia; **My sympathies**—Ta seelipiteeriah mou

symphony, a (the)—mia (ee) seemfoneea

Symposium, the (Plato's)—Toh Seembosio tou **Plah**-tonos

synthetic—seenthetikos (m), seentehtikee (f), seenthetikoh (n)

system, a (the)—ena (toh) seestima

T

table, a (the)—ena (toh) trah**peh**zee (pl. ta trah**peh**zia)
Not to be confused with "**trah**pehza," the Greek word for bank. The similarity derives from the fact that the first Greek banking businesses were conducted at tables set up in public places.

tablet, a—mia ta**blet**ta (pl. tab**let**tess)

tack, a (the)—mia pee**neh**za (pl. pee**neh**zess)

tackle (fishing)—ee-dhee psari**kees**

tag, a (the) label—mia (ee) eti**ket**ta (pl. ee eti**ket**tess)

take (to)—na **pah**ro; **Can I take this?**—Boroh na toh **pah**ro?; **I'll take it**—Tha toh **pah**ro; **I'll take it back**—Tha toh **pah**ro pee**so**; **Can you take me?**—Borees na meh **pah**rees?; **Take your time**—Meh teen eeseek**hee**a sou; **I want it to take out**—Thelo na toh **pah**ro mahzee mou. I took—**Pee**ra; You took—**Pee**ress; He (she) took—**Pee**reh

talcum powder—**tahlk**

talented—meh tah**len**toh

talk (to)—na mee**lee**so

tall—pseelohs (m), pseelee (f), pseeloh (n); **the tall one**—oh pseelohs

tampons—tahmpon

tan, a (the) sun—ena (toh) mah**vris**ma; **tanned**—mahvrismenos (m), mahvrismenee (f), mahhvrismeno (n)

tank, a (the) wàter, gas etc.—ena (toh) dhe**poz**itoh

tape—taynеea; **cassette tape, a**—mia casetta; **recording tape**—magneetoh-tayneea; **a tape recording** mia eeh-hograh**fis**ee; **tape** recorder, a (the)—ena (toh) magneetohfono; Scotch tape—selotayp; surgical tape—lefkoplahst; tape measure, a (tailor's)—mia mezoora; (carpenter's)—mia cordella; video tape—veedio casetta; to tape (record)—na kahno mia engrafee; I would like to tape this—Tha eethela na kahno mia engrafee.

taste, a (the)—mia (ee) yevsee; tasty—nostimo; good taste—kalo goostoh; to taste—na dhohkimahso; Can I taste it?—Boroh na toh dhohkimahso?

taverna, a (the)—mia (ee) tavehrna

tax, a (the)—enas (oh) foros; tax stamp, a (the)—ena (toh) har-tohseemo

taxi, a (the)—ena (toh) taksee

tea—tsah-ee; a cup of tea—ena fleetzahnee tsah-ee; with milk (sugar/lemon)—meh gahla (zahkaree/lemohnee); iced tea—non-existent except in places like the Athens Hilton.

teach (to)—na dhee-**dhah**-kso; I'll teach you—Tha seh dhee-**dhah**-kso; Will you teach me?—Tha meh dhee-**dhah**-ksees?; teacher, a (the)—enas (oh) **dhah**skalos (m), mia (ee) dhahs**kala**

tear, a (rip)—ena skheesimo

tear, a (crying)—ena dhahkree (pl. dhahkria); in tears—dhakris-menos (m), dhakrismenee (f), dhakrismeno (n)

technique, a (the)—mia (ee) teknikee

telegram, a (the)—ena (toh) teelehgrahfeema

telephone, a (the)—ena (toh) teelehfono; directory—enas kah-tahlogos

television—teeleh-orasee; I want to watch television—Thelo na dhoh teeleh-orasee

tell (to)—na poh; I want to tell you something—Thelo na sou poh kahtee; I told you—Sou eepa; I told him (her)—Tou (tees) eepa; She (he) told me—Mou eepeh; Tell me—Pehs mou

temper; a (bad)—enas theemohs

temperature, a (fever)—enas peeretohs; I have a temperature—Eh-ho peeretoh; He (she) has a temperature—Eh-hee peeretoh

temperature, the—ee thermokraseea

temple, a (the)—enas (oh) naohs; the Temple of Poseidon—oh Naohs tou Posee-dhohnos tennis—tennees; **tennis ball, a**—mia **bah**la tou **tennees**

tent, a (the)—mia (ee) skeenee (pl. ee skeeness); **tent pegs**—pah-salohs ya skeenee; **tent pole, a**—enas orthstatees skeenees

terrace, a (the)—mia (ee) tehrahtsa

terrible (fearful, awful)—foveros (m), foveree (f), fovero (n)

test, a (the)—mia (ee) eksetasee

testicles, the—ee orkhees; **slang**—ta ahmeletita ("the unmentionables") or ta arkhee-dhia ("balls")

than—ahpo (also means "from")

thank (to)—na efhariteeso; **I want to thank him (her)**—Thelo na ton (teen) efhariteeso; **Thank you**—Efharistoh (**You're welcome**—Parakalo)

that (pronoun)—ekeenos (m), ekeenee (f), ekeeno (n); **That man**—Ekeenos oh ahnthropos; **That bottle**—Ekeeno toh boukahlee; **I want that**—Ekeeno thelo

that (relative pronoun)—poo; **The man that did it**—Oh ahnthropos poo toh ekaneh

the (masc. singular)—oh (pl. ee); **feminine sing.**—ee (pl. ee); **neuter sing.**—toh (pl. ta)

theater, a (the)—ena (toh) theh-atro (pl. theh-atra)

theft, a (the)—mia (ee) klepseea

their—tous (m. *or* pl.); **fem. *or* pl.**—tees; **Their clothes**—ta roukha tous; **their dresses**—ta foostahnia tees

them (object of a verb)—tous (m. *or* mixed), tees (f), ta (n); **I want them**—Ta (tous, tees) thelo

them (object of a preposition)—aftous (m. *or* mixed), aftess (f), afta (n); **for them**—ya aftous (aftess, afta)

then—tohteh

there—ehkee; **over there**—ehkee pehra; **There is** (*or* "**Is there?**")—Eeparkhee; **There are**—Eeparkhoon; **There!**—Na!; **therefore**—etsee

thermometer, a (the)—ena (toh) thermometro

thermos, a (the)—ena (toh) thehrmo

these—aftee (m), aftess (f), afta (n)

they—aftee (m), aftess (f), afta (n); **They are**—Eenay; **They were**—Eetahn; **They will be**—Tha eenay; **They have**—Eh-hoon; **They had**—Ee-hahn

thick (as in a liquid)—peek**toh**; as in wood, etc.—hond**hroh**

thief, a (the)—**en**as (oh) **klef**tees (pl. ee **klef**tess)

thimble, a (the) sewing—**mia** (ee) dhakti**lee**thra

thin (a person)—ah-**dhee**natos (m), ah-**dhee**nate (f), ah-**dhee**natoh (n); **thin** (paper, etc.)—lep**toh**

thing, a (the)—**en**a (toh) **prahg**ma (pl. ta **prahg**mata); **my things**—ta prahg**ma**ta mou

think (I) believe—No**mee**zo *or* Pees**te**vo; **What do you think?**—Tee no**mee**zees (pees**te**vees)?; **I am thinking**—Skep**to**may; **I want to think about it**—**The**lo na toh skep**thoh**; **What are you thinking about?**—Tee skep**te**say?; **thought (I)**—Skef**ti**ka; **I thought that**—Skef**ti**ka oh**tee**; **I've thought about it**—Toh eh-ho skef**thee**

thirsty (I am)—Dheep**so**; **Are you thirsty?**—Dheep**sahs**?; **She (he) is thirsty**—Dheep**sa**ee

this (pronoun)—af**tohs** (m), af**tee** (f), af**toh** (n); **I want this**—Af**toh the**lo; **This bottle**—af**toh** toh bouka**hlee**

this (adj.)—**toh**so; **this big**—**toh**so me**gah**lo; **this much**—**toh**so po**lee**

thorn, a (the)—**en**a (toh) ahn**gah**thee

those—e**kee**nee (m), e**kee**ness (f), e**kee**na (n); **I want those**—e**kee**na **the**lo; **those bottles**—e**kee**na ta bouka**hlia**

thought, a (the)—**mia** (ee) **skep**see (pl. ee **skep**sees)

thread, a (the) sewing—**mia** (ee) **klos**tee (pl. **klos**tess); **of a screw**—ta spee**ro**mata

throat, the—oh lay**mohs**

throw out (to)—na pe**tah**kso

thumbtacks—pee**ne**zess

thunder, the—ee vron**dee**

tick, a (the) insect—**en**a (toh) tseem**boo**ree (pl. ta tseem**boo**ria); **tick collar, a**—**en**a ko**lah**ro ya tseem**boo**ria

ticket, a (the)—**en**a (toh) eesi**tee**rio (pl. eesi**tee**ria); **ticket agency, a (the)**—**en**a (toh) prakto**ree**o taksi-**dhee**on; **I want two tickets for...**—**The**lo **dhee**o eesei**tee**ria ya...; **1st class**—pro**tee** theh**see**; **2nd class**—dhef**te**ree theh**see**; **3rd class**—tree**tee** theh**see**; **tourist class**—toori**sti**kee theh**see**; **deck class**—kata**stro**ma; **roundtrip**—met'epistro**feess**; **I don't have a ticket**—Dhen eh-ho eesiteerio; **I lost my ticket**—**Eh-**hasa toh eesit**eer**ioh mou. **Airplane tickets** for interior Olympic flights may be bought at the airport, but it is advisable to buy them beforehand at the local Olympic agency, because it is often impossible to get tickets at the last moment, particularly during the summertime. **Train tickets** can be purchased either at travel agencies, at the station or on the train.

tickles (It)—Gargalaee; **I'm ticklish**—Gargal**ie**may

tide, the—ee pahl**ee**ria

tie, a (the) neck—**mia** (ee) grah**vah**ta (pl. grah**vah**tess) tie up **(to)**—na **dheh**so

tight—sf**eek**toh

tile, a (the) enameled—**ena** (toh) plah**kah**kee (pl. plah**kah**kia); **mosaic tiles**—mosa-ee**ka**; **clay tiles**—keramee-**dhia**

time, a (the)—ee ora; **What time is it?**—Tee ora eenay?; **It's eight o'clock**—Eenay ohk**toh** ee ora; **What time does it leave (come)?**—Tee ora f**ev**ghee (**thar**thee)?

time (a period of)—**ena**s kay**ros**; **I don't have time**—Dhen **eh-**ho **kay**ro; **a long time**—po**lees** kay**ros**; **a moment of time**—mia **fora**; **many times**—po**less** f**oress**; **on time**—steen ora tou; **timetable, a (the)**—**ena** (toh) dhromolo**hgh**io

tin can, a (the)—**ena** (toh) kou**tee** teneke-**dhen**io; **a large tin**—**ena**s tene**kess**

tip, a (the) waiter, etc.—**ena** poorbou**ar**

tired (fatigued)—kouras**menos** (m), kouras**menee** (f), kouras**meno** (n);. **I'm getting tired**—Kou**rah**zomay; **tiring**—kouras**tikoh**

tisane, a—**ena** ts**ah**-ee tou voo**noo**

to (preposition)—**ston** (m), **stee** or **steen** (f), **sto** (n)

The gender of the noun following "to" determines which form of the preposition is used, with "steen" often but not always being employed when the first letter of the feminine noun is a vowel. In addition, the article as such is never used, being incorporated into the preposition: I'm going to the beach—Pao stee pla**hz**.

to (in forming the infinitive)—**na**; **in order to**—ya na

toast, a (drinking)—**mia** propo**sees**

toast (bread)—freegani**ah**; **a toasted sandwich**—**ena** toh**st**

tobacco—kah**pnohs**; **a tobacconist's**—**ena** kapnopol**ee**oh today—seemera

together—mahzee; all together—ohlee (m or mixed) or ohless (f)
or ohla (n) mahzee

toilet, a (the)—mia (ee) tooahletta or enas (oh) kabiness or ena
(toh) mehros (lit "the place"); toilet paper—hartee eegheeahs
(written as: LADIES—ΓΥΝΑΙΚΟΝ; MEN—ΑΝΔΡΟΝ)
Even the smallest cafés and tavernas are required by law to have a
toilet in or near the establishment. If it's outside, it's often necessary to get the key first from the owner. It is rare to find toilet
paper (or for that matter, a toilet seat) in any but the most luxu-
rious establishments, so it is advisable to always carry a packet of
Kleenex.

tomato, a (the)—mia (ee) tomahta (pl. tomahtess); sliced tomatoes—koftee tamahta; tomato juice—tomatohzoomo

tomb, a (the)—enas (oh) tahfos; the tomb of Agamemnon—oh
tahfos tou Ahgamemnonos

tomorrow—ahvrio; tomorrow morning (afternoon/ evening/
night)—ahvrio toh proee (toh ahpoyevma/toh vrah-dhee/tee
neekta); the day after tomorrow—meth'ahvrio

tonight—ahpohpseh or seemera toh vrah-dhee

too (also)—ehpeesees; you, too—ehpeesees; too (very)—polee or
pahra polee; It's too hot—Eenay polee zestee; It's too much—
Eenay pahra polee

tool, a (the)—ena (toh) ehrgaleeo (pl. ta ehrgaleea)

torch, a (the) electric—enas (oh) fahkos

torn—skeesmeno

total, the—ee sooma

touch, a (the)—mia (ee) ahfee; your touch—ee ahfee sou; to
touch—na ahngheeso

tour, a (the)—mia (ee) pehrio-dheea or ena (toh) tour

tourist, a (the)—enas (oh) toureestas (m), mia (ee) toureestria (f),
(pl. ee toureestess); tourism—oh tourismos; tourist class—
touristikee thehsee; tourist visa, a—mia touristikee ahdhia;
touristic—touristikoh

tourist bureau, a (the)—ena (toh) grahfeeo tourismoo

tourist police, the—ee touristikee astinomeea (written as:
ΤΟΥΡΙΣΤΙΚΗ ΑΣΤΥΝΟΜΙΑ)

tow, a—mia reemoulkisee

towel, a (the)—mia (ee) petsetta (pl. petsettess)

town, a (the)—mia (ee) polees or mia hora (both also meaning "city")

toy, a (the)—ena (toh) payknee-dhee (pl. ta payknee-dhia)

tradition, a (the)—mia (ee) para-dhosee (pl. ee para-dhosess); traditional—paradhosiakohs; traditionally—kahtah para-dhosee

traffic, the—ee keekloforeea; traffic lights, the—ta fahnaria

tragedy, a (the)—mia (ee) trahgo-dheea; tragic—trahghikoh

The word derives from a combination of the ancient Greek words "**tragos**" (meaning "goat") and "**oi-dha**" meaning "song," because the sung ceremonies that preceded drama as we know it were at one point performed by men wearing goat's skins.

trailer, a (the) mobile home—ena (toh) trokhospeetoh

train, a (the)—ena (toh) trayno

tranquilizer, a (the)—ena (toh) katapra-eendikoh (pl. katapra-eendika)

transformer, a (the)—enas (oh) metahsk-heematistee

transistor radio, a (the)—ena (toh) transeestor

translate (to)—na metafrahso; translator, a (the)—enas (oh) metafrastees

transport (for luggage, furniture, etc.)—metafora

trap, a (mouse, etc.)—mia fahka

travel (to)—na taksi-dhepso; I want to travel to...—Thelo na taksi-dhepso stee...; I am traveling—Taksi-dhevo; travel agency, a (the)—ena (toh) praktoreeo taksi-dheeon; travel agent, a (the)—enas (oh) prahktor taksi-dheeon; traveller's check, a—ena travelers tsehk

treat, a—ena kehrasma; It's my treat—Eenay kehrasma mou; to treat—na kehrahso; What can I offer you?—Tee na seh kehrahso?

tree, a (the)—ena (toh) dhentro (pl. ta dhentra)

tricycle, a (the)—ena (toh) treekiklo

trip, a (the)—ena (toh) taksee-dhee; Have a nice trip—Kalo taksee-dhee; to take a trip—na taksi-dhevo

tripod, a (the)—ena (toh) treepodhoh

Trojan Horse, the—oh dhoorios Eepos; **the Trojan War**—oh Tro-eekos Poleemos

trolly bus, a (the)—**en**a (toh) troleh-ee

trouble, the—ee enokleesee

trousers—pantalonee

truck, a (the)—**en**a (toh) kahmeeohnee *or* fortigo ahmahksee

trust—peestees; **I trust you (her/him)**—Seh (teen/ton) embeestevomay; **Trust me**—Embeestepsou mou; **Do (don't) you trust me?**—(Dhen) meh em beestevesay?

truth, the—ee ahleethia; **It's the truth**—Eenay ahleethia

trying (I am)—Prospatho; **I'll try**—Tha prospatheeso; **I tried**—Prospathisa; **to try on** (clothes)—na pro**va**ro *or* na dhoki**mah**so; **Can I try it on?**—Boroh na toh pro**va**ro?

T-shirt, a (the)—**mi**a (ee) fanella

tube, the (subway)—oh eelektrikos

Tuesday—Treetee

tuna fish—tonnos; **a can of tuna**—**en**a koutee tonnos

tunic, a (the)—**en**a (toh) heetonio

Turkey—ee Tounkeea; **a Turk**—**en**as Tourkos (m), **mi**a Tourkala (f); **Turkish** (adj.)—Tourkikoh; **language**—Tourkika; **a Turkish coffee**—**en**as kafess; **a Turkish delight**—**en**a lookoomee (pl. lookoomia)

The ill will that perists between the Greeks and the Turks boils just beneath the surface and could erupt with at almost any moment with an intensity that would rival if not dwarf that that recently displayed between the Sebs and the Croats. Therefore it is perhaps needless to say that the adjective "Turkish" applied to anything which the Greeks prefer to consider Greek—like their coffee—will not be greatly appreciated. On the other hand, it should also be noted that the Greeks do, sometimes, have a sense of humor about it.

turn, a (the)—**mi**a (ee) strofee; **to turn**—na **stree**pso; **Turn right (left)**—**Stree**pseh dheksiah (ahreest**er**a); **Where do I turn?**—Poo streevo?; **Turn around**—Yeeriseh peeso

turpentine—neftee

turtle-necked sweater, a (the)—**en**a (toh) zeevahngo

tweezers—tseembee-dha
twice—dheeo foress
twins—dhee-dhimee
typewriter, a (the)—mia (ee) grafomeekhanee
typical—teepikos (m), teepikee (f), teepikoh (n)

U

ugly—ahskimos (m), ahskimee (f), ahskimo (n)
Ulysses—Oh Odheeseh-ahs
umbrella, a (the)—mia (ee) ombrella (pl. ombrelless)
uncle, a (the)—enas (oh) theeohs
uncomfortable—ahvolo
Unction, Extreme—efhelayon seh etimo-thanatoh
under—kahtoh ahpo; under the table—kahtoh ahpo toh trahpe-
    hzee
underground, the—oh eelektrikos
understand (I)—Katalavayno; I don't understand—Dhen kata-
    lavayno; Do you understand?—Katalavaynees?; I under-
    stood—Katalava; Did you understand?—Katalavess?
underwear—ehso-rookha
undress (to)—na ksedeeno; I'm going to get undressed—Tha
    ksedeetho; Shall we get undressed?—Na ksedeethoomeh?
unfaithful—ahpistos (m), ahpistee (f)
unfortunately—dheestikhos
unhappy—dheestikheesmenos (m), dheestikheesmenee
unhealthy—anthi-ghee-eeno
United Nations, the—Ta Enamena Ethnee
university, a (the)—ena itoh) pahneh-pisteemio
unlucky—ahtikhos (m), ahtikhee (f), ahtikho (n)
unnecessary—peritoh
unpack (to)—na ah-dhiahso; I have to unpack—Prepee na ah-dhi-
    ahso tees valeetsess
unscrew (to)—na ksevi-dhohso
untie (to)—na leeso
until—mehkree; until now—mehkree torah; until tomorrow—
    mehkree ahvrio

up—ehpahno; **up there**—ehpahno ehkee; **It's up to you**—Eksartahtay ahpo sena.

upside-down—ahno-kahtoh *or* ahnahpo-dha

urinate (to)—na ooreeso *or* na **kah**no peepee

urn, an (the)—mia (ee) ee-**dhreea**

us—mahs; **for us**—ya mahs: **with us**—mahzee mahs

use, the (noun)—ee **hree**see; **used**—metaheeris**me**no; **useful**—hreesimo

use (to)—na hreesimopee-**ee**so; **Can I use it?**—Boroh na toh hreesimopee-**ee**so?

usually—seenee**e**thos

V

vacant—ah-dhio (lit. "empty"); **a vacant room**—ena **ah**-dhio dhoh**mah**tio

vacation, the—ee dheeako**pess**; **I'm taking a vacation**—**Kah**no dheeako**pess**

vaccination, a (the)—ena (toh) em**vo**lio

No vaccinations are required when entering Greece, although if you are planning to hike through the countryside, a tetanus booster shot would be wise. Vaccinations or booster shots for children can be found virtually everywhere there's a doctor, even on the smallest islands.

vagina, the—oh **kol**pos; **vaginal**—kolpi**koh**; **vulgar slang**—toh moo**nee** (not to be used jokingly, but can be used lovingly)

valise, a (the)—mia (ee) va**leet**sa (pl. ee va**leet**sess)

valuable (adj)—po**lee**timo; **my valuables**—ta teemal**fee** mou

valve, a (the)—ee valvee-**dha** (pl. ee val**vee**-dhess)

vanilla—va**nee**lia

variety, a—mia peeki**lee**a

varnish—vehr**nee**kee

vase, a (the)—**en**a (toh) **vah**zo

Vaseline—Vahse**lee**nee

vegetable, a (the)—**en**a (toh) lakhani**koh** (pl. ta lakha**ni**ka)

vegetarian, a—**en**as horto**fah**gohs

veil, a (the)—**en**a (toh) **ve**llo

Venetian—Enetikos (m), Enetikee (f), Enetikoh (n)

very—poh**lee**

vest, a (the)—e**na** (toh) yee**le**ko

veteran, a (of a war)—e**nas** palay-**ma**khos

veterinarian, a (the)—e**nas** (oh) ktinee**a**tros

via—dhee**ah** (written as: Διά)

vice-versa—kay tah**nah**paleen

video—**vee**dio; **video cassette (tape)**—**vee**dio ka**set**ta (tay**nee**a); **VCR**—**vee**dio case**toh**fono

Note the Greeks use the European PAL or other video systems. Thus be sure when you buy tapes that they will be playable in the U.S.

view, the—ee **theh**-ah

villa, a (the)—**mia** (ee) **vee**la

village, a (the)—e**na** (toh) **ho**rioh; **a villager**—e**nas** hori**ah**tees (m), **mia** hori**ah**tisa (f).

vine, a (the)—e**na** (toh) **klee**ma (pl. ta **klee**mata); **vineyard, a (the)**—e**na** (toh) am**bel**lee

vinegar—ksee-**dhee**

virgin, a (the)—**mia** (ee) par**theh**na

visa, a (the)—**mia** (ee) theh-o**ri**sees *or* **mia** (ee) **vee**za but usually referred to as "**mia** (ee) **ah**dhia paramo**nees**," which means "residence permit."

visit, a—**mia** epee**skep**see; **to visit**—na epis**kef**thoh; **I want to visit...**—**The**lo na epis**kef**thoh...; **I'm going to visit (stay with)...**—Tha epis**kef**thoh...

vitamins—veeta**mee**ness; **A**—**al**fa; **B**—beh; **C**—seh; **D**—deh; **E**—**ep**silon; **multi-vitamins**—**mool**tee veeta**mee**ness

volcano, a (the)—e**na** (toh) ee**fes**tio

volt, a—e**na** volt (pl. volt); **How many volts?**—**Po**sa volt?

In Greece, the current is 220 V, A.C.

vomit (noun)—e**me**toh; **I vomited**—**Kseh**rasa (*or* **Eh**kana) e**me**toh; **He (she) vomited**—**Kseh**raseh (**Eh**kaneh) e**me**toh.

voyage, a (the)—e**na** (toh) tak**see**-dhee

W

wage, the—toh mero**kah**matoh

wagon-lit—vah**gon**-lee

waist, the—ee **meh**see; **waistcoat, a (the)**—**ena** (toh) yee**leko**

wait (to)—na peri**meno**; **I'll wait**—Tha peri**meno**; **Will you wait?**—Tha perime**nees**?; **I waited**—Peh**ree**mena; **Have you waited long?**—Peh**ree**meness polee ora?; **Wait!**—Peh**ree**meneh!

waiter, a (the)—**enas** (oh) sehr**vit**oros *or* ena (toh) gar**sonee**

wake (to)—na ksee**pneeso**; **I want to wake at...**—**Thelo** na kseep**neeso** stees...; **Wake me**—**Kseep**na meh; **I'm going to wake her (him) up**—**Pao** ya na teen (ton) kseep**neeso**

walk, a (the)—mia (ee) **volta**: **Let's take a walk**—**Pah**meh ya volta; **I'm going for a walk**—**Pao** ya volta; **to walk**—na pehr**pateeso**; **I want to walk**—**Thelo** na pehr**pateeso**; **I'll walk**—Tha pehr**pateeso**; **I walked**—Pehr**pateesa**

wall, a (the)—**enas** (oh) **teek**-hos (pl. ee **teek**-hee)

wallet, a (the)—**ena** (toh) porto**folee** (pl. ta porto**folia**) See, if necessary, either **lose**, *or* **steal**.

want (I)—**Thelo**; **I want to**—**Thelo** na; **I want that**—**Aftoh thelo**; **What do you want?**—Tee **thelees**?; **She (he) wants**—**Thelee**; **We want**—**Theloomeh**; **I wanted**—**Eethela**; **I would like**—Tha **eethela**

war, a (the)—**enas** (oh) **polemos**; **the First (Second) World War**—Oh **Protos** (**Dhefteros**) Pan**gosmios Polemos**

warm—**zestoh** (also means "hot")

wash, (to) clothes, dishes, etc.—na **pleeno**; **to wash one's self**—na plee**tho**

wasp, a (the)—mia (ee) **sfeega** (pl. ee **sfeeghess**)

watch, a (the)—**ena** (toh) **rolloy**; **is broken**—**eenay** spah**smeno**; **doesn't work**—dhen dhoo**levee**; **watchband, (the)**—**ena** (toh) **brahseleh**; **watchmaker, a (the)**—**enas** (oh) rolo**gahs**

watch (to)—na para**tireeso**; **Watch out!**—Prose**kheh**!

water—**nehro**; **drinkable water**—**posimo** nehro; **mineral water**—meta**likoh** nehro; **water colors**—nehro**booyess**; **waterfront, the**—ee para**leea**; **waterproof**—ah-dhiah-**vrokho**; **watermelon**—kar**poozee**; **waterski, a (the)**—**ena** (toh) tha**lasio** skee (pl. tha**lasia** skee); **to waterski**—na **kahno** thalasio skee

watts—vaht

wave, a (the)—**en**a (toh) **kee**ma (pl. ta **kee**mata)

wax—keh**ree** (also means "candle")

way, the—oh dhroh**mos** (lit. "the road"); **Which way?**—Ahpo pioh dhromo?: **This (that) way**—Prohs ta dhoh eh**kee**; **by way of**—**dhee**a mes**soo**

we—em**mees**; **We are**—Ee**mas**teh; **We were**—Ee**mas**tan; **We have**—Eh-**hoo**meh; **We had**—Eek-**ham**eh; **We want**—The**loo**meh; **We went**—Pee**gam**eh; **We ate**—**Fah**gameh

weak—ah-**dhee**natos (m) ah-**dhee**natee (f), ah-**dhee**natoh (n) **wealthy**—**ploo**sios (m), **ploo**sia (f)

wear (to)—na fo**res**so; **What shall I wear?**—Tee tha fo**res**so?

weather, the—oh **kay**ros

wedding, a (the)—**en**as (oh) **gah**mos

Wednesday—Te**tar**tee

week, a (the)—**mi**a (ee) ev**dhoh**ma-dha; **the weekend**—toh Savatokee**riak**o; **weekly**—ev-dhohma-**dhee**-ayo

weigh (to)—na zee**ghee**so; **Can you weigh it?** Bo**rees** na toh zee**ghee**sees?; **How much does it weigh?**—**Po**so zee**ghee**zee?; **the weight**—toh **vah**ros; **Welcome/Welcome back**—Kaloso**ri**sess; **You're welcome**—Paraka**lo**

well (healthy)—**ee**ghi-**ees** (m. & f); **well (adv.)**—ka**la**; **She does it well**—Toh **kah**nee ka**la**; **Very well, thank you**—Po**lee** ka**la**, efhari**stoh**

well, a (the)—**en**a (toh) pee**gah**-dhee

west—dhee**ti**koh; **the West**—ee **dhee**see

wet—ee**gro** or **vreg**meno; **soaking**—moos**keme**no; **rainy**—**vrokhe**ros

what—tee; **What?**—Tee?; **What for?**—Ya tee?; **What is that?**—Tee **ee**nay aftoh?

wheel, a (the)—**mi**a (ee) ro-dha

when—po**teh** or oh**tahn**; **When?**—Po**teh**?; **When are we leaving?**—Po**teh** tha fee**go**meh?; **When we leave....**— Oh**tahn** fee**goo**meh...; **When I was...**— Oh**tahn** ee**moo**nah...

"Poteh" is a question word, while "**oh**tahn" introduces clauses of time.

whenever—ohpoteh-**dhee**poteh

where—poo; **Where are we going?**—Poo pah**meh?;Wherever you want**—Oh**poo the**lees

which—pee**ohs** (m), peeah (f), peeoh (n)

while—enno; **for a while**—ya leego kayro

white—ahspro *or* lefko (the latter being a bit formal)

who—pee**ohs** (m), peeah (f), peeoh (n)

whole (complete)—oh**lo**klero

whore, a (the)—mia (ee) poo**tah**na; **whorehouse, a (-the)**—ena (toh) bor**del**lo

whose—pee**ah**noo

why—ya**tee; Why not?**—Yatee oh-hee?

wick, a (the)—na (toh) fee**teel**ee (can be bought in grocery stores or kiosks)

wide—far-**dhee; width, the**—toh far-**dhohs**

widow, a (the)—mia (ee) **hee**ra; **widower**—enas (oh) **hee**ros

wife, a (the)—mia (ee) yee**nay**ka *or* mia (ee) **see**zigos (lit. "spouse"); **my wife**—ee yee**nay**ka (**see**zigos) mou

wig, a (the)—mia (ee) peh**roo**ka

wild—**ah**grios (m), ahgria (f), **ah**grio (n)

will (future aux.)—tha; **I will do it**—Tha toh **kah**no

win (I)—Nee**koh; You win**—Nee**kahs; She (he) wins**—Nee**kah; I won**—Ennee**kis**a; **You won**—Ennee**kis**ess; **He (she) won**—Ennee**kis**eh

wind, a (the)—enas (oh) ah-**eh**ras *or* enas (oh) **ah**nemos; **east wind, the**—anatoli**kos; north wind, the**—vori**ahs** (*or*, in summer, toh mel**te**mee); **south wind, the**—noti**ahs; west wind, the**—dheeti**kohs**

windmill, a (the)—enas (oh) ahnemo**mee**los (pl. ee ahnemo**mee**lee)

window, a (the)—ena (toh) parah**thee**ro (pl. ta parah**thee**ra); **window pane, a (the)**—ena (toh) **tzah**mee (pl. ta tzah**mia**)

wine—krah**see; wineglass, a (the)**—ena (toh) kraso**pot**eero (pl. kraso**pot**eera)

winter, the—oh hee**mo**nahs

wire—**seer**ma; **the wires**—ta **seer**mata

wish, a (the)—mia (ee) ef**khee** (pl. ee ef**khess**); **I wish**—Ef-**ho**meh; **to make a wish**—na **kah**no mia ef-**hee**

with—meh (used as in English)

witness, a (the)—enas (oh) martiras (pl. ee martiress)

woman, a (the)—mia (ee) yeenayka (pl. ee yeenaykess)

wonder (I)—Meepos; I wonder if you have...?—Meepos eh-heteh...?

wonderful—thavmahsios (m), thavmahsia (f) thavmahsio (n)

wood—kseelo; wooden—kseelino

wool—mahlee; woolen—mahlino; rough, natural wool—feesiko mahlee

word, a (the)—mia (ee) leksee (pl. ee leksess); What is the word for...?—Tee eenay ee leksee ya...? (or What do you call that?—Pohs toh leneh?); I give you my word—Sou dheeno toh lohgo mou

WORK, a (the)—mia (ee) dhooliah

world, the—oh kosmos

worry, a—mia stenohoria (pl. stenohoriess); worried—stenohori-menos (m), stenohonmenee (f); worry (I)—Stenohoriemay; Don't worry—Mee stenohoriesay

worse than—heerotero ahpo; It's worse—Eenay heerotero; the worst—oh heeroteros

worth (it's)—Ee ahkseea toy eenay; How much is it worth—Poso ahkseezee?

woven—eefantoh; by hand—heeropee-eetoh

wrap (to)—na teeleekso; Could you wrap it, please?—Boreeteh na toh teeleekseteh, parakalo?; wrapping paper—hartee pentileegmatos

wrench, a—ena galikoh klee-dhee

write (to)—na grahpso; I'll write—Tha grahpso; Write me—Grahpseh mou; I wrote—Ehgrapsa; She (he) wrote—Ehgrapseh

writer, a (the)—enas (oh) singrafeh-ahs (m), mia (ee) singrafeh-ahs (f)

wrong (incorrect)—lathemenos (m) lathemenee (f) lathemeno (n); mistake—lathos; I'm wrong—Dhen eh-ho dheekayo (lit. "I don't have right."); You're wrong—Dhen eh-hees dheekayo

Y

yacht, a (the)—**en**a (toh) **ko**tero (pl. ta **ko**tera)

year, a (the)—**en**as (oh) **hro**nos (pl. **hro**nia); **last year**—peh**ri**see; **next year**—tou hro**noo**; **this year**—eh**fe**tos

yes—nay *or* mah**lee**sta (the latter being both more formal and more emphatic) and ah**meh** (colloquial and very affirmative)

yesterday—ek**thess**; **yesterday morning**—ek**thess** toh **pro**ee; **yesterday afternoon**—ek**thess** toh ahpo**yev**ma; **yesterday evening**—ek**thess** toh **vrah**-dhee; **the day before yesterday**—prok**thess**

yet—ah**ko**mee; **not yet**—**oh**-hee ah**ko**mee; **still**—ah**ko**mee

Y.M.C.A.—**Hahn** (written on signs as: X.A.N.) **Y.W.C.A.**—**Hehn** (written on signs as X.E.N.)

Most large cities and towns have either these or youth hostels, the addresses of which can be obtained from the local tourist bureau or police.

Y.H.H.A and **Y.W.H.A.**—There are none at the moment, but there is, in Athens, a Jewish Community Center at 8 Melidoni Street, telephone 325-2823.

yogurt—yaoor**tee** (**with honey**—meh **mel**lee); **thick**—peek**toh** yaoor**tee**; **loose**—**hee**ma yaoor**tee**; **strained**—straghis**me**no

Yom Kippur—**Ee**mehra Eksilas**moo**

you (subject of verb)—e**see** (sing.), e**sees** (pl. *or* sing. formal); **object of a preposition**—**se**na (sing.), sahs (pl.); **direct object, verb**—seh (sing.), sahs (pl.); **indirect object, verb**—sou (sing.), sahs (pl.)

young—neh-os (m), neh-a (f), neh-o (n)

your—sou (sing.), sahs (pl.) *or* dhee**koh** sou and dhee**koh** sahs; **your sweater**—toh pul**loh**ver sou; **It's yours**—**Ee**nay dhee**koh** sou

youth hostel, a (the)—**en**as (oh) **kse**nonas neh-**oh**titos (written on signs as: ΞΕΝΩΝΑΣ ΝΕΟΤΗΤΟΣ)

These are privately-run establishments that can be found everywhere where the tourist influx is sufficient enough to justify their existence. The living conditions and house rules depend on the individual owners. The address can be obtained from the local tourist bureau or police.

Z

Zeus—Oh Zefs

zipper, a (the)—**en**a (toh) fermoo**ahr**

zodiac, the—oh zodhee**akos keek**los; **Aquarius**—Eedhroh-ho-os;
   Aries—**Ah**rees; **Cancer**—Kar**kee**nos; **Capricorn**—Ayg-
   yohkeros; **Gemini**—**Dhee**-dheemee; **Leo**—**Leh**-ohn; **Libra**—
   Zee**gohs**; **Pisces**—Eekh-**thees**; **Sagittarius**—Toks**o**tees;
   Scorpio—Skorpi**ohs**; **Taurus**—**Tah**vros; **Virgo**—Par**thehn**os

zoo, a (the)—**en**as (oh) zo-olog-yi**kos kee**pos

Part 3
SPECIAL CATEGORIES

ADULTERY—meekheeah****

As common in Greece as elsewhere and usually thought of as the sole prerogative of the male, who operates under that enduring dictum, "My wife's married but I'm not." Freedom to have sex whenever and with whomever he wishes is almost considered a Greek man's birthright, as essential to his well-being as breathing, and is tolerated by most members of the community, even the women. On the other hand, should a married woman be caught doing the same, she is considered little better than a whore, and the courts, particularly in places like Crete, would be predisposed towards the husband even if, to punish her, he slit her throat. Nevertheless, Greek women are more often than not as lusty and enthusiastic as their men about having an extra-marital fling, so don't let those black outfits fool you. But do be careful! Greek men can be murderously possessive.

Tourist girls having affairs with married Greeks should be wary of falling into the trap of thinking they might leave their wives. If the wife is a patient, forbearing woman and takes care of him and his house and children the way she should, a Greek husband would no more think of parting from her than renouncing his mother. And the wife knows this. So...

AFTERNOON, the—toh a**poy**evma**

The Greek concept of what constitutes the "afternoon" is much different from ours. In general, it means anytime from the end of the siesta period (which ends anytime between 3:30 and 4:30, depending on the place and the time of year) and sunset. Therefore, if Greeks say they'll see you in the afternoon, try to pin them down to an approximate hour otherwise you could be into dinner by the time they arrive.

AIRPORT, a (the)—ena (toh) ah-ero-**dhro**mio**

At Athens, there are two airports, the Olympic and the multi-line international one. Both have common runways and are on the coast about a 20-minute drive from the city center.

The Olympic is known as the Old (Pahli**oh**) or West (dheeti**koh**) airport, written on signs as: **ΔΥΤΙΚΟΣ ΑΕΡΟΛΙΜΗ**. The international one is known as the New (kay-**noo**rio) or East (anatoli**koh**) airport, written on signs as: **ΑΝΑΤΟΛΙΚΟΣ ΑΕΡΟΛΙΜΗ**.

ANTIQUITIES—arhay-oh**titess**

Greek law defines antiquities as anything dating before 1821 (the year the Greeks began their struggle for independence from Turkey) and deems them "national treasures." This does not preclude foreigners from purchasing any items not destined for museums, but it does prohibit taking them out of the country without a special permit—something that can often take years, if ever, to obtain. Therefore, when buying (or finding) anything which you suspect might come under this law, it would be prudent not to try to take it out of the country without the above-mentioned permit. Otherwise, if discovered, there is a strong possibility you could end up in jail. The Greek authorities, with a great deal of justification, are now quite paranoid about their country being plundered of its past and don't regard any kind of smuggling, no matter how "amateurish," as a joke. So, if you wish to take something back home and are buying it from an antique dealer, have him obtain the necessary papers for it before paying him anything (except, perhaps, a small "deposit" to induce him to hurry things up). If you have found something or bought, say, an amphora from a fisherman, you must obtain the papers yourself. This involves having it certified first by the appropriate museum curator and then by the Archeological Council of Greece—a very time-and nerve-consuming process that often has the desired effect of convincing foreigners that, instead of keeping the object for themselves, it would be better to make a generous gift of it to the people of Greece.

AUTOMOBILE, an (the)—**en**a (toh) afto**kee**nitoh

Although the Greek people adore foreign-made objects, their government has a phobia about them, particularly automobiles, and specifically a fear that once in the country they will be sold to a Greek without the import duty being paid—the tax usually amounts to 100% of the value of the car when new. Therefore, when you enter the country, the car will be stamped into your passport and you will be given a "free use" permit of six months or so. This can be renewed up to a period of one year at the nearest customs authority, but the process sometimes (although not always; it depends on the mood of the local customs official) involves having a third party, a Greek, guaranteeing that he will pay all the duties and taxes should your car "disappear," i.e. be sold by you without your paying taxes. After a year, all sorts of other provisions go into effect, depending on your country of origin.

Normally you will not be allowed to leave the country without your car and, since it is stamped in your passport, it is virtually impossible to do so. However, in extenuating circumstances—if, for instance, you should suddenly have to fly home because of a death in the family—you can arrange with the customs authorities at the airport or elsewhere to store the car, often at an exorbitant fee, until you return and to give you the necessary papers allowing you to leave. An International Driving License is required for all foreigners driving in Greece (with the exception of those in E.C. and certain other countries.) If you do not have an international license, it can easily be obtained from the local Greek Automobile and Touring Club within Greece. The customs authorities will let you through on the promise that you do so immediately. All that is required is your national driving license, two small photos, and your passport. The fee is nominal. Green cards for international insurance are not compulsory, but it would be prudent to have one anyway. If you wish to be covered during your stay in Greece, either go to or telephone the Motor Insurance Bureau in Athens or elsewhere. You can get the number from any local Greek National Tourist Organization (**EOT**).

The Automobile and Touring Club of Greece, ELPA (written in Greek as **ΕΛΠΑ** and pronounced **el**pa), offers innumerable services to foreign motorists, most particularly the issuance of required International Driving Licenses and, in the areas of Athens, Salonika, Larissa, and the island of Crete, a road patrol service in case of breakdowns and other problems and emergencies. In these areas, one telephones: **104**. For ELPA telephone numbers in other areas, please inquire at the local Greek National Tourist Organization (E.O.T.) office or the Tourist Police. ELPA's patrol cars are yellow and clearly marked with the club's initials. In addition, the organization can supply you with road maps, itineraries, insurance information, free legal advice, and hotel reservations.

Car rental agencies are to be found all over Greece, ranging in size from Hertz and Avis to small, individually-owned concerns. The latter are usually a bit cheaper and it is sometimes possible to bargain with them a little. Beware of the copious hidden charges, such as taxes, insurance, extra mileage, etc., which can sometimes increase the cost about 30% over what is listed in the lovely little catalogue. Therefore, in order to avoid a shock at the end, it is wise to have the total possible cost (toh **seen**olon) computed before you decide whether or not to rent the car.

Greek traffic regulations are in accord with those used throughout Europe and America. One drives on the right and passes on the left. Cars approaching intersections and traffic circles from the right have the right of way. Pedestrians are a constant danger, since most Greeks seem to prefer walking in the street rather than on the sidewalk. Motorcycles, the apogee of machismo for Greek males, are another hazard and even though most Greek highways have a side lane reserved strictly for them, their drivers often seem compelled to pass you in the middle of the road. On the other hand, Greek automobile drivers, are, for the most part, considerably more sensible than the rest of their Mediterranean counterparts. The exception is Athenian motorists, who are driven by relentless traffic jams into death-defying acts on the city's streets. Speed limits vary from 60-75 m.p.h. on roads and highways to 25-40 m.p.h. within city and town limits. One should always be on the lookout, particularly in rural areas, for goats, sheep, chickens, donkeys and little children, all of which have priority everywhere. Repairs should be done, if possible, with the help of ELPA (see previous page). However, if you must place the fate of your car in the hands of a local mechanic, you will find them, if not very well-equipped and up-to-date, at least, like most other Greeks, willing and eager to help. They are used to improvising with whatever means might be at hand and should be able to jury rig something that will enable you to reach a better-equipped garage and mechanic. My experience is that they are usually quite honest in their dealings with foreigners and often, out of sympathy for your helplessness in a strange country, tend to under- rather than over-charge. However, if you feel you have been cheated, your best recourse is to ask for an itemized bill (**enas** analiti**kos** logarias**mos**), take it to the local Tourist Police and let them handle it.

I want help.—**Thel**o voee**thia.**
My car had a breakdown (accident).—Toh aftokini**toh** mou **ee**-heh mia **vlah**vee (**ena** dhis**teek**hima).
Can you fix it?—**Boree**teh na ton episkeva**sete**h?
Who can fix it?—**Piohs** bo**ree** na ton episkeva**si**?
Where?—Poo?
How long will it take?—**Poso** kay**ro** tha kria**stee**?
How much will it cost?—**Poso** tha cost**ee**si?

PARTS AND TERMS
accelerator—toh **gah**zee
accident—ena dhis-**tee**-heema
adjust (to)—na rithmi**stee**
air—ah-**eh**ras
alignment—efthi**grah**misees
anti-freeze—anti-pseekti**koh**
automatic—af**toh**matoh
axle—oh **ahk**sonas
battery—ee batta**ree**o
    (to charge)—na for**tee**see
bearing—toh roule**mahn**
blow-out—klata**ris**ma
body—ee karose**ree**
bolt—ee **vee**dha (*also means"screw"*)
brake (drum)—toh **teem**pano tou **freh**noo
    (foot)—toh **freh**no
    (hand)—toh heero**freh**no
    (lining)—toh fermoo**eet**
    (shoes)—ee siago**ness** ton **freh**non
breakdown—mia **vlah**vee
brushes—ee **pseek**tress

cable—toh kalodhio; (jumper)—kalodhio meh tsimbeedhess
camshaft—oh ekentroforos
carburetor—toh karbiratehr
change (to)—na alahksi
chassis—toh sahsee
choke—toh tsohk
clean (to)—na kathareesi
clutch—toh ambrag-yahz or oh simblektees
cooling system—toh seestima pseekseh-ohs
combustion—ee kahfsee
compression—ee simbee-esis
crankcase—toh kartehr
crankshaft—oh strofalos
cylinder—oh keelindhros
cylinder block—toh blohk
diesel—deezel
differential—toh dhee-aforikoh
dipstick—oh deektees
distilled water—eegro battareeas
distributor—toh deestribitehr or oh dhee-anomeh-as
driver—oh odhigos
driver's license—toh dheeploma
drive shaft—oh kendrikos ahksonas
dynamo—toh dheenamoh
engine—ee meekhanee
exhaust (pipe)—ee eksahtmisi
fan—toh ventilatehr
    (belt)—toh looree
filter—toh feeltro
fuel—kafsima
funnel—toh hohnee
fuse—ee asfahlia
garage—toh garahz
gasket—ee flahndza or tsimoukha
gasoline—venzeenee
    (diesel)—petrelayo meekhanee
    (regular)—kanonikee venzeenee

(super)—soupehr
gas station—venzinah-dhiko
gas tank—toh depozitoh
gauge, the—oh metritees
gears, the—ee takheetitess *or*
   (toothed wheels) ta granazia
   (1st)—ee protee takheetita
   (2nd)—ee dhefteree
   (3rd)—ee treetee
   (4th)—ee tetartee
   (reverse)—ohpisthen
gear box—toh sahzmahn *or* toh kivotio takhiteeton
   (shift)—oh mohklos takhiteeton *or* oh leviess takhiteeton
generator—ee yenneetria
grease—grahso
Green Card—ee prahsinee karta
ground (elec.)—ee yeeosis
hood—toh kapo
horn—toh klakson
hydraulic—eedhravlikoh
idle (to)—na dhoulevee sto relandee
ignition—toh dhiakoptee
   (key—toh klee-dhee)
indicator light—toh flahs
inner tube—ee sambrella
insurance—ee asfahlia
jack—oh greelos
jumper cable—kalo-dhio meh tsimbee-dhess
key—toh klee-dhee
knock (engine)—oh kteepos
lead (elec.)—toh kalo-dhio
leak—mia treepa (*lit. "a hole"*)
leaking (It's)—Trehee.
liability—ee eftheenee
license (driver's)—toh dheeploma
   (plate)—ee pinakee-dha
lights (head)—ta fanaria

(signal)—toh flahs

(tail)—ta **pee**so **f**ota

(traffic)—ta f**a**naria *or* f**o**ta keeklof**o**reeas

liter, a—**e**na l**ee**tro (pl. l**ee**tra)

loose—hal**a**ro

lubrication—gras**a**risma

(system)—s**ee**stima lip**a**nsehohs

manifold—ee polap**lee**

mechanic, a (the)—**e**nas (oh) meekhan**i**kos

muffler—toh seelansi**eh**

nut—toh paks**i**ma-dhee

(lug) toh bool**o**hni (pl. bool**o**hnia)

oil—l**a**-dhee

(high-pressure)—valvol**ee**ni

overheating (It's)—Eeper-ther**may**netay.

pedal—toh petah**lee** *or* pend**a**hl

piston—toh **e**mvolo *or* pist**o**hnee

(pl. ta **emvola *or* pist**o**hnia);

ring—oh dhak**tee**lios emvol**o**u

points—ee plat**ee**ness

pressure—ee **pee**-esis

pump—ee ahnd**lee**a

punctured—klataris**me**no *or* treep**i**meno

radiator—toh pseeg-y**ee**oh

repair (to)—na episkev**a**hsi

rod—ee **ra**v-dhos

screw (to)—na vee-**dho**si

(unscrew)—na ksevi-**dho**si

screwdriver—**e**na katsav**ee**-dhee

shock absorber—toh amorti**sehr**

spare parts—andal**a**kti**k**a

spark plug—toh b**oo**zee (pl. ta booz**iah**)

speed, the—ee takh**ee**tita

speedometer—toh kont**ehr**

spring (coil)—toh elat**ee**rio (pl. ta elat**ee**ria)

(leaf)—ee s**oos**ta (pl. ee s**oos**tess)

start (It doesn't)—dhen **pehr**nee brohs ee meekhan**ee**

starter, the—ee **mee**za

steering, the—toh see**sti**ma dhee-ef**theen**seh-os

steering wheel—toh tee**moh**nee

suspension—toh sispansio**hn**

system—toh see**sti**ma

tire—toh **las**tikho (pl. ta **las**tikha).

    (pressure)—ee **pee**-esis sta **las**tikha

    (spare)—ee reh**ser**va

thermostat—oh thermo**sta**tees

throttle—toh **tsohk** ah-**eh**ra

top-up (to)—na ye**mee**si

tow, a—mia rimoul**ki**sees

tow truck, a—enas ye**ra**nos

transmission—toh sah**zmahn** *or* toh ki**vo**tio takhi**tee**ton

trunk—toh port-ba**gahz**

tune-up, a—mia **reeth**misi

valve—ee val**vee**-dha (pl. val**vee**-dhess)

vibrating (It's)—Treh**mee**

warranty—ee eng-**yee**-see

washer—ee ro-**del**la

water—**neh**ro

    (distilled)—**eeg**ro batta**ree**eas

wheel—oh **tro**hos; (pl. ee **tro**hee)

    (front/rear)—brosti**nos**/pi**sinos**

windshield—toh pahr-**breez**

    (wiper)—oh yalo-katharis**tee**ras

work (It doesn't)—Dhen dhou**le**vee.

wrench (open-end)—ena ga**li**ko klee-**dhee**

    (box-end)—ena klee-**dhee zee**ta

    (lug)—ena stasta**vros** klee-**dhee**

    (offset)—ena kari-**dha**ki spas**toh**

    (socket)—ena boozoklee-**dhoh**

TIRE PRESSURE

pressure, the—ee **pee**-esee

    front/rear—embrohs/pee**so**

    a little more (less)—**lee**go periso**te**ro (leego**te**ro)

lbs. = kgs.	lbs. = kgs.
18 = 1.3	26 = 1.8
20 = 1.4	27 = 1.9
21 = 1.5	28 = 2.0
23 = 1.6	30 = 2.1
24 = 1.7	33 = 2.3

BABY, a (the)—**en**a (toh) mo**roh** *or* e**nas** (oh) **beh**bis (m), **mia** (ee) **beh**ba (f); **my (our) baby**—toh mo**roh** mou (mas); **your baby**—toh mo**roh** sahs; **How many months (years)?**—**Poh**so mee**non** (hro**non**)?

To the Greeks, there seems to be nothing in life more precious than a baby or young child, and nowhere have I seen them more pampered, clucked-over and revered than here. So, if you are traveling with children, you will find yourself virtually holding the keys to the city of the Greek soul. Nothing (not even a seat on a crowded Athens bus) will be denied you if you ask for it in the name of your child. Conversely, you will also be inundated with endless (and usually critical) advice about how to take care of it, as if only the Greeks know how to properly bathe, feed and clothe an infant and to protect it from the vagaries of life.

A very polite Greek phrase to be used in connection with other people's children is:

May the child (children) live for you.—Na sas **zee**si (**zee**soun). Which is to say, may it bring you joy and happiness and also, if necessary, may it provide for you in your old age. If a Greek says this to you, the proper reply is simply:

Thank you.—Efharis**toh**.

Needless to say, should you be introduced to or even shown a photograph of a Greek's child, a "Na sas **zee**si" on your part will be much appreciated.

Occasionally, after having cooed and clucked over your child and having told you how beautiful it is, a Greek may suddenly turn and spit on the ground. Don't be offended. This is done to ward off the evil eye.

baby bottle, a—**en**a beebe**ron**; **baby food**—paydhi**kess** tro**fess**;

baby oil—pay-dhiko **lah**-dhee; **baby powder**—pay-**dhikee poo**-dhra.

Baby supplies of all types and brands, international and Greek, can be found practically everywhere in Greece; in fact, the country seems to be littered with them. They can be bought in grocery stores, doctor's offices, confectionery stores, cosmetic shops, and pharmacies. In emergencies, there is always by law at least one pharmacy open 24 hours a day, seven days a week.

baby sitter, a—**mia bay**bee **sitter**

I would like a babysitter for three hours—Tha **ee**thela **mia bay**bee **see**tehr ya trees **o**ress.

In remoter areas where the word "baby sitter" may not be understood, one can say :

I would like a woman to sit with the baby—Tha **ee**thela **mia yinay**ka ya na **kaht**si meh toh **mo**roh.

There are baby sitting agencies in Athens. Consult the English-language blue pages of the telephone directory.

BANK, a (the)—**mia** (ee) **trah**peza (written as: ΤΡΑΠΕΖΑ).
 Where is the bank?—Poo **ee**nay ee **trah**peza?
 Are the banks open?—**Ee**nay a**neek**tess ee **trah**pezess?
 I want to change money—**The**lo na a**lahk**so **hree**mata.
 I'm waiting for money from...—Pe**ri**meno **hree**mata ah**po**...
 Has it arrived?—**Mee**pohs **eel**than?
 I want to send money to...—**The**lo na **stee**lo **hree**mata stee...
 How much is the commission? **Po**so **kah**nee ee pro**mee**thia?
 bank account, a (the)—**e**nas (oh) trape**zi**kos logarias**mos**
 check, a (the)—**e**na (toh) tsehk; **personal**—proso**pi**ko tsehk
 traveller's check—**e**na trah**ve**lehr tsehk
 letter of credit—**mia** pisto**ti**kee episto**lee**
 money—**hree**mata; **foreign**—**kse**na **hree**mata;
 money order—takhi-dhromi**kee** epita**gyee**

Although banking hours have tended to vary in the past, an attempt is now being made to bring them in line with those in Europe, i.e. a continuous day from 8 A.M. to 4 P.M. Whether the government will succeed is not yet certain. What you can count on, however, is that all banks will definitely be open Monday through Fridays from 8 A.M. to 2 P.M. On Saturday mornings during the tourist season, certain currency-exchange bureaus are kept open for the sole purpose of changing foreign money. In the remoter villages and on small islands, one or two of the local grocery stores or tourist shops usually serve as agents for a Greek bank, and these are open whenever their owners and the local laws and customs decide. In emergencies, one can always find a tourist shop or restaurant that will be willing to change one's money, although this practice is entirely against the law. When changing money at a bank, be careful to keep your receipts (usually, but not always, colored pink.) These could be very valuable, particularly if you wish to extend your visa; they are proof that the money on which you have been living has come from outside the country and not from illicit work within Greece. In addition, they are vital should you wish to change your Greek drachmas back into foreign currency before leaving. (For information on this often exhausting and complicated procedure, ask at the local branch of the National Bank of Greece—Ee Ethni**kee Trahpeza** tees Ell**ah**-dhos, written as: ΕΘΝΙΚΗ ΤΡΑΠΕΖΑ ΤΗΣ ΕΛΛΑΔΟΣ.

PASSPORTS ARE REQUIRED FOR ALL FOREIGN EXCHANGE TRANSACTIONS.

BAPTISM, a (the)—ena (toh) **vahf**tisma

Greeks customarily baptize a child 40 days after its birth. Nowadays, however, some children are not baptized until a year later. It is the godfather (oh no**nohs**) who plays the principal role in the ceremony because it is he who will be responsible for the child's religious education. The father also participates, but the mother does not—the child being both literally and symbolically taken from her and presented, for the length of the ceremony, at least, to God.

If you are invited to a baptism, it is not necessary for you as a foreigner to bring a present (you would almost be stepping out of line if you did), but if you have a camera, nothing would make the parents happier than to have photographs taken of themselves and their newly-named child.

BARBER, a (the)—enas (oh) **koureh**-ahs

barber shop—Koureeo (**KOYPEION**); **haircut, a**—ena kourema; **short**—konda; **not too short**—oh-hee polee konda;

back/sides/top—pee**so**/sta **plahya/epahno; shampoo**—sampoo**ahn; shave, a—en**a ksee**ris**ma; **manicure, a—en**a mahniki**oor**

Tipping: For the average barber, a token 50 drachmas; for those in a luxury hotel, the same as you would back home.

BARGAINING—toh pa**zah**ree

The Greeks have a Levantine addiction to bargaining and can be tempted into it even though it may involve only the price of a can of evaporated milk. Since some Greeks tend to charge more to foreigners than they would to their own countrymen, a bit of haggling on your part would not be in bad taste; it could gain you a Greek's respect.

Some rules of thumb:

1) Keep your money hidden, preferably dispersed in various pockets in small amounts, so that your entire bankroll is never seen.

2) Don't be overly aggressive and make a ridiculously low counter offer to his ridiculously high asking price. This is both an insult to his intelligence and an implication that you think he's being dishonest. It could cause him, as a matter of principle, to refuse to bargain at all.

3) Therefore, the best opening move is to look surprised, hesitate, and then, if he doesn't voluntarily lower the price, say:

No, I'm sorry, I can't.—**Oh**kee, sig**no**mee, dhen bo**roh**.

After that, if he wants to lower the price, he will. You, in turn, keep repeating "No, I'm sorry" (while perhaps even attempting to leave) until the price gets down either to where he won't go any further or to what you think the item is worth.

In other words, from a Greek's point of view, the game of bargaining is fun, but God forbid that either you or he should take it so seriously as to think he had started off by trying to cheat you. And if he lowers his price, it's simply because he realizes that you're not as rich as other foreigners—and also because he's come to like you, even if you are taking food out of his children's mouths.

BEACH, a (the)—mia (ee) pla**hz**

Sometimes called para**lee**ah ("seaside") or ah**ktee**, which is the formal Greek for beach that you will often see written on signs as: AKTH.

Where is the beach?—Poo eenay ee plahz?

Is there a beach?—Eh-hee plahz?

With good (fine) sand?—Meh kahlee (pseelee) ahmoh?

nudist beach, a (the)—mia (ee) para**lee**ah yeemniston

Until recently, nudist beaches have been extremely rare except in such exotic, sophisticated spots as Mykonos. Now however, they are being established (mostly by foreigners) in many parts of Greece even though in certain places it is entirely against the law. But if you go to an extremely isolated and hard-to-get-to spot, the police tend to turn a blind eye—unless, that is, a Greek complains and then they must act. Try to avoid the temptation to sunbathe nude on or anywhere near a public beach. You will not be liberating the Greeks, just insulting them.

BEARD, a (the)—ena (toh) **moosee**

Beards have a special significance in Greece. Aside from being traditionally worn by priests, they are also grown as a sign of mourning. Therefore, should a normally clean-shaven Greek acquaintance of yours suddenly appear sporting a scruffy, unattractive growth on his face, it is best not to joke about it; his father, mother, brother or other beloved members of his family could have died since you last saw him. Conversely, to say "**moosee**" to someone is to call him a liar.

BEAUFORT SCALE, the—ee kleemaks Bo**for**

A scale for measuring wind force which the Greeks use particularly for determining whether or not boats and ships will be allowed to sail. A little understanding of it will help you to know what kind of seas to expect when taking a ship.

How many Beauforts?—Posa Bofor?

Eight Beaufort—Awktoh Bofor

Beaufort

No.	M.P.H	Description
O	0-1	Total calm.

1-4	1-18	Light to moderate breezes.
5	19-24	Strong breeze.
6	25-31	Strong breeze, moderate swells.
7	32-38	Near gale, high swells.
8	39-46	Gale, strong seas, small craft warnings.
9	47-54	Strong gale, very rough seas, most ships forbidden to sail.
10	55-63	Total gale; all ships forbidden to sail.
11	64-72	Violent storm, rarely occurs in Greece.
12	76-136	Hurricane; has never occurred in Greece

As a somewhat comforting footnote, it should be remarked that winds very rarely reach as high as 10 Beaufort in the summer. In the winter, they have only twice, in the history of recorded Greek weather reports, reached 11; the first was in 1978. The second, a by-product of a visitation of El Niño, paralyzed the country for three days in April, 1998.

BEAUTY PARLOR, a (the)—ena (toh) komo**tee**rio *or* **mi**a (ee) komo-sees (written on signs as: ΚΟΜΜΩΤΗΡΙΟΝ *or* ΚΟΜΜΩΣΕΙΣ).

bleach—ksah**neeg**ma
brush—**voort**sa
cold—**kree**oh
color rinse—hromo **sam**pooahn
  (**auburn/blond/brunette**—**pee**ro/ksantho/kastano)
comb—**hten**ee *or* tsat**sah**ra
cut—**kohp**seemo
  (**razor cut**—**kohp**seemo meh ksirahfee)
hair—**mah**liah
  (**oily**—leeparah; **normal**—nor**mahl**; **dry**—kserah)
hairset—meezam**plee**
hot—**zest**oh
manicure mahni**kioor**
page-boy—**pahz**
pedicure—pedi**kioor**
permanent—pehrma**nahnt**
rollers—**rol**ah

shampoo—sampoo**ahn**
tint—vah**fee.**
Tipping: 10-20 %, depending on the quality of the establishment.

BOATING & FISHING

Boats of varying types can be rented but only rarely without their owners. A marvelous way to spend the day is with one of the locals exploring the coastline and small beaches of the area you're in. Fishing in Greece is no longer what it used to be because of massive, unending pollution of the Mediterranean and the illegal but wanton use of dynamite but some fishermen. Using a speargun is prohibited if you are wearing any sort of underwater breathing apparatus.

BOATING TERMS

For various mechanical and engine terms, see under AUTOMOBILE. For wind forces, see BEAUFORT SCALE.

aft—**pee**so
anchor—**ahn**ghira
barometer—varometro
  falling—**pef**tee
  rising—ah**nehr**-hetay
berth (dock)—apovrathra
boat, a (the)—**mi**a (ee) **var**ka
  fishing boat—ka**ee**kee
  motor boat—venzeena**ka**tos
  rowboat—**var**ka meh koupi**ah**
  sailboat—**var**ka meh pah**nee**
  yacht—**ko**teero
boom—**pee**kee
bow—ploree
buoy—seema**dhoo**ra
cabin—ca**bee**na
Cast off!—**Lee**seh!
chart—**har**tees
charter, a—**e**na **nah**vloma
charter (to)—**nah**vlono
crew—**plee**roma

current—**rev**ma
Customs—Tel**oneeoh**
deck—**katahstroma**
dinghy—**var**kah**kee**
engine—**mee**khanee
forward—**brostah**
harbour—**limah**nee
lifebelt/jacket/saver—toh so**see**vio
moor (to)—na or**mee**so
motor (outboard)—eksol**em**vios kin**iteer**
net—**dheek**tee
oar—**kou**pee
pier (large)—lee**mah**nee
  (small)—**molos**
port—lee**mah**nee
Port Authority—Limanar**heeoh**
port (side)—ahr**isterah**
propeller—prop**ella**
rudder—teem**oh**nee
sail—**pah**nee
starboard—dhek**siah**
stern—**preem**nee
storm—foort**oona**, **thee**-ela
tide—pahl**eeria**
wave—**kee**ma (pl. **kee**mata)
weather forecast—prov**lepsis** kay**roo**
wind—ah-**eh**

FISHING TERMS
fish (to)—na psar**evo**
fishing—**psah**rema
I'd like to go fishing—Tha ee**thela** na **pao** ya **psah**rema
bait, fly—dhol**oma**
fishing boat—psar**ovarka**
fish hook—ahn**ghee**stree
fishing line—arm**eedhee**
fisherman—psar**ahs**

fish net—**dheek**tee
fishing rod—kahlahmee
spear—kamahkee
spear gun—psarontoofeko
tackle—**seen**erga psari**kees**
weight—mo**lee**evee *or* vareedhee

BOOKSTORE, a (the)—**en**a (toh) vivliopo**lee**oh; (written on signs as: ΒΙΒΛΙΟΠΩΛΕΙΟΝ).

Books in English are available virtually everywhere, although the selection is usually extremely haphazard, Unless you have a desperate craving that must be satisfied without delay no matter what the price, look around first for second-hand bargains, particularly in the lobbies of hotels and boarding houses, as well as at the local tourist bureau. In Athens, there are several second-hand bookstores in the Monastiraki Flea Market, the biggest being Vassiotis's at 24 Ifestiou St., while for new books, the largest selection is at Eleftheroudakis, on Nikis St. directly behind the American Express office overlooking Constitution Square. Other good bookstores are Compendium, 33 Nikis St.; Pantelides, 11 Amerikis St.; Kakoylides 25-29 Panepistimiou (in the stoa); Romvos, 11 Kapsali (near Kolonaki Square).

BREAD—pso**mee**; **white**—**ah**spro pso**mee**; **dark**—**mah**vro pso**mee**; **country**—horiahtiko pso**mee**; **dry, twlce-baked**—paksimah-dhee

Bread is sold by the kilo and half-kilo (**en**a kilo/mee**so** kilo), the quality and style varying considerably from baker to baker and region to region, not to mention town to town. The best and slightly more expensive is the horia**h**tiko pso**mee**. Mention perhaps should also be made of the fact that some young Greek men find it extremely amusing to send unsuspecting foreign girls to the bakery to buy a kilo of "pso**lee**"—which is extremely obscene Greek slang for "penis."

BREAKFAST, A (THE)—**en**a (toh) proeeno *or* pro-yevma

Usually cafés with signs saying WE SERVE BREAKFAST mean that they serve instant coffee, bread, marmalade or honey, and sometimes margarine or butter. Occasionally, you may find a place that will make you fried eggs (usually swimming in olive oil.) As for bacon or sausages, forget it unless you are staying in a luxury hotel.

COFFEE—kafess; **instant**—Nescafeh; **black**—sketoh; **with milk/sugar**—meh gahla/zahari; **Greek (black/med. sweet/ sweet)**—kafess (sketoh/metrio/gleekee vrastoh); **decaffeinated**—horees cafeh-eenee

BREAD—psomee; **with butter (honey/marmelade)**—meh vootiro (**melee/marmelah-dha**)

EGGS—ahvga; **fried**—ahvga **mah**tia; **boiled**—vrasta ahvga (**for 3 minutes**—ya treeah lepta); **omelet, an**—mia omeleta (pl. omeletess)

BUS, a (the)—ena (toh) leh-ohforeeoh; **bus statlon**—stathmos leh-ohforeeon; **bus stop**—ee stahsee leh-ohforeeou

Where is the bus for...?—Poo eenay toh leh-ohforeeoh ya...?
Is this the bus for...?—Aftoh eenay toh leh-ohforeeoh ya...?
When is the bus for...?—Poteh eenay toh leh-ohforeeoh ya...?
Is there a bus for...?—Eh-hee leh-ohforeeoh...?
I want to get off at...—Thelo na katevo stee...
Will you tell me where?—Tha mou peeteh pou?
Some possible replies to the above questions:
Efeegeh—It left; Seh **lee**go—In a little while; **Lee**pee—It left; Seh dheka lepta—In 10 minutes; Ekeeno—That one over **there.**
Meta apo mia ora—In one hour; Stees mia ee ora—At one o'clock; Dhen eeparhee—There isn't one.

Buses are the cheapest as well as the most reliable form of transportation in Greece, and there are usually services to and from even the remotest villages. When traveling from city and town terminals, one pays before getting on the bus. When picking up the bus in a village or at a city or town bus stop, you pay on the bus, always entering it from the rear and/or middle. In large cities, however, there is also a type of bus requiring exact change: on these, the entrance is from the front and one deposits the fare in a coin box. When purchasing a ticket either from a terminal or a conductor, you must keep it; occasionally, a controller will board the bus and ask you for it.

Intercity buses leave from terminals situated in that part of the city nearest the exit road for their destination. These terminals are called "prakto**reea**" ("agencies") and are often just a table in a café or restaurant. Tickets can and should be bought in advance, particularly in the summer.

Smoking is now forbidden on all buses.

Bus stop signs are often virtually unlocatable; they are blue, about as big as the cover of Reader's Digest and stuck on invisibly-thin poles somewhere in the approximate area of the stop. Written on them in white letters is the word: ΣΤΑΣΙΣ.

CAFÉ, a (the)—**en**a (toh) kafe**nee**oh (written as: ΚΑΦΕΝΕΙΟΝ); café owner, a (the)—**en**as (oh) cafet**zees**

Usually specializing only in coffee, soft drinks, cognac, ouzo, and occasionally whiskey, these sometimes serve **breakfast** and, particularly in rural areas where there is no local restaurant, simple one-pot dinners or quick fries of eggs, liver or fish and perhaps a salad. In addition, again in the smaller villages, they may also double as a supplementary grocery store, selling a small variety of tinned goods, bread, candies, and bottled spirits as well as, very rarely, cigarettes. Above all they are a Greek male's home-away-from-home, a refuge from his husbandly, fatherly or filial duties, and except for Sunday mornings following church or for other special feast days, one rarely sees a Greek female invading the premises.

CAIQUE, a (the)—**en**a (toh) kah-**eee**kee

These are the broad-beamed, masted fishing boats which one sees in every harbor and cove in Greece, ranging in size from about 5 to 30 meters. They can be rented for fishing trips or excursions, by the hour or by the day, the price usually being quite reasonable, but it is always wise to shop around first to get an idea of the what the going rate is. The law forbids foreigners taking these boats out their own; one must be accompanied by its its captain.

CAMPING—**kahm**ping

Organized camping sites with bathing facilities, etc. exist throughout Greece and are indicated on most local maps. Camping in areas other than these is strictly forbidden by law, but if you do not attempt to do so on or near a public beach or someone's private property, the police usually turn a blind eye unless there is a complaint by one of the locals. These restrictions are particularly overlooked in areas and times of the year when existing sleeping facilities are taxed beyond their capacity. But wherever you camp, be careful of fire, an annual nightmare in the very dry Greek summers.

Where can we camp?—Poo bor**oo**meh na **kah**noomeh **kamp**ing?

Can we camp here?—Bor**oo**meh na **kah**noomeh **kamp**ing eh**dhoh**?

Is there drinking water?—**Eh-**hee **po**simo nehro?

May we light a fire?—Ehpeetrepeteh na ah**nap**someh fotiah?

axe—tsekooree

backpack—sak**ee**dhio

bucket—koovahs

campsite—katas**kee**nosee

compass—peek**seed**ha

flashlight—fah**kos**

gas canister—feeahlee **gah**zee

rope—skeenee

sleeping bag—sleeping bag

stove—**som**ba

tent—skeenee

tent pegs—**pah**salos ya skeenee

water bottle—feeahlee nehroo

CARDS (playing)—trapoul**o**harta; **card game, a (the)**—**mia** (ee) hartopek**seea**

A Greek passion, especially among males and particularly when the tourist season is over and there is little else to do except work and be with one's family. The favorite game is kun-**kan**, a kind of gin rummy, with **po**kehr a close second. Although a considerable amount of money often passes hands, you will rarely see any on the table; the accounts are discreetly kept on pieces of paper and paid-up afterwards. I have a friend, a small-town restaurant owner, who regularly loses most of his summer profits at the rate of about $3000 a month during these "friendly" winter sessions.

CASINO, a (the)—ena (toh) kahzeeno

Although—or perhaps because—the Greeks are inveterate gamblers, there are only three proper, licensed casinos in the country: one on Mt. Parnes, about 35 km. outside of Athens. and the other two on Rhodes and Corfu. In addition, there are numerous card-playing rooms all over the country (including those of most cafés) as well as illicit but barely-concealed back room dice and poker playing establishments.

CAT, a (the)—mia (ee) **gah**tah (pl. **gah**tess); **Is that your cat?—Eenayee gah**tah sou?; **I like cats—M'ares**soon ee **gah**tess.

You will rarely hear a Greek, except those living in the larger urban areas, make the above statement. Cats (as well as dogs) are considered animals—that is, creatures without souls—and very few of them achieve the status of becoming members of the family. The concept of having pets is completely alien to the rural Greek way of life; everyone must work, including the animals, and if they don't, they are scavengers that must be driven away. Those cats which you do see living with families or hanging around tavernas without being kicked out are tolerated because of their mice-catching ability; the rest are considered fair game for little children with sticks and stones. This is not an innate sensitivity on the part of the Greeks, but simply what they believe to be a fact and necessity of life. There's nothing you can do to change this state of affairs, so just try to bear with it as much as possible.

CHEESES—teeriah; cheese, a (the)—ena (toh) tee**ree; grated—tree**meno.

The most common Greek cheeses are the following:

feta—salted, white goat's- or ewe's-milk cheese usually served on top of Greek salads. The quality varies considerably.

graviera—similar to Gruyere but rarely as good. The best is made in Crete. Very expensive.

ka**seree**—whitish-yellow, semi-soft and slightly tangy. Served as it is, or grated over pasta, or sliced and fried.

kefalo**teeri**—similar to the above kaseri but harder and tangier. Usually served grated over pasta but can be fried.

mizeethra—a white, goat's- or ewe's-milk cheese that is found in both its soft and hard forms. When soft, it resembles cottage cheese and is sometimes called **manoori**. In its hard form, it is usually eaten plain or grated over pasta and is sometimes called ant**ho**teero.
Of all of these, only **fe**ta is regularly found in restaurants.

CHURCH, a (the)—**mi**a (ee) ekli**see**a

Greece is a country of churches, their white, vaulted shapes seemingly everywhere, jutting in rough stone blocks out of the landscape-as if they had been carved there by Nature herself. Most of these are family owned, built to honor a particular saint for a particular family reason; however, because they are churches, they belong, in a sense, to all the people and thus are rarely closed. One is invited to enter and light a candle to the saint; one is also expected, but not required, to leave a few drachmas for new candles, oil and maintenance.

C.I.A.—See**ah** *or* ee See-**aee**-ay

In just as bad repute here as elsewhere, particularly because of its tacit or active support of the Colonels' junta (1967-74) and the abortive overthrow of Archbishop Makarios of Cyprus. The Greek C.I.A. is called "**Kee**p", its initials being **K.Y.Π**.)

CIGARETTE, a (the)—**en**a (toh) tsi**ga**ro (pl. tsi**ga**ra); **Do you have American (English) cigarettes?—Eh**-hees Amerikahnika (**Ahng**lika) tsi**ga**ra?

Because of licensing regulations, cigarettes are rarely sold anywhere except at sidewalk kiosks. Occasionally they can be found in cafés and grocery stores but usually only in villages which do not have kiosks. In all but the larger cities, most kiosks tend to close around midnight (and sometimes also during the afternoon siesta) so be careful to stock up beforehand. International brands can be found almost everywhere but they are relatively quite expensive. Greek cigarettes are not only much cheaper but, in the author's opinion, very good; they are mild and tasty and do not, as American cigarettes are wont to do, smoke themselves down to nothing in about 10 minutes.

CINEMA, a (the)—ena (toh) sin**ema** *or* **en**as (oh) kinemato**grah**fos

First-run films can generally be found in most of the larger cities, the greatest variety and quality being in Athens. Most cinemas do not open until the late afternoon or early evening, and it is almost impossible to find out the times without (1) telephoning the theater and (2) speaking Greek, although one can visit the theatre and look at the schedule posted on the box office, In big-city cinemas, one is offered a program by the usherette and expected to tip her something, usually 5 to 10 drachmas. In the middle of the film there is invariably an intermission, which lasts from about 5 to 15 minutes, depending on what the camera operator has decided to do with his time. During this period, one can either buy candy and soft drinks from the usherettes or go to the lobby bar, which, aside from alcoholic drinks, may also serve a variety of edibles such as cakes, cheese pies and even shish kebabs.

In the summer, all but an infinitesimal fraction of indoor theaters are closed because of a lack of air conditioning, the owners switching to high-walled outdoor theaters, the chairs of which are usually of the iron and plastic-ribbed café type, nestled in rows on a floor of gravel. These cinemas are a delight, often charmingly landscaped with beds of flowers and eucalyptus bushes and open to a sky glittering with stars. It is advisable to bring along a light sweater as, even in the middle of the summer, it can become quite chilly sitting outdoors for two hours without moving. SMOKING IS PROHIBITED EXCEPT IN OUTDOOR THEATERS.

CLEANERS, the—toh pleent**eerio; dry cleaners, the—**toh steg-nokathari**steerio; pressers, the—**toh seedhero**teerio; cleaning, the—**toh kath**ar**isma

Washing, dry cleaning and pressing are usually done within the same establishment (laundromats being as rare in Greece as Turks), and the service is relatively fast, normally 2 days. However, it is almost impossible to find such places outside of the larger towns and cities. This is due both to a water supply problem and the custom of having the women of the house do all the cleaning by hand, usually out of doors on a rough stone slab. So if you are in a rural area, you must either do it all yourself or find a woman whose family is small enough to allow her the time for your clothes, too.

COLORS, a (the)—ena (toh) **hroma** (pl. ta **hroma**ta)
dark—**skoo**ro; light—ahnee**ktoh**; medium—**me**trio

color	**hro**ma
dark	**skoo**ro
light	ahnee**ktoh**
medium	**me**trio
azure	gala**nos**
black	**mah**vro
blue	bleh
brown	ka**feh**
fuchsia	**fouk**sia
gray	**gree**zo
green	**prah**sino
hazel	anee**ktoh** ka**stano**
lavender	le**vahn**da
maroon	koki**nopo**
mauve	mohv
ochre	**okh**ra
orange	porto**kah**lee
pink	**rodhi**no or roz
purple	veesi**nee**
red	**koki**no
sienna (burnt)	koki**nopo** ka**feh**
sienna (raw)	keetrinoka**feh**
umber	**ohm**bra
violet	vio**lettee**
white	**lefko** or **ahspro**
yellow	**keetri**no

COMMUNISM—komoonismos; **communist, a—en**as komoonis-
tees (pl. komoonis**tess**)

Outlawed in 1947 following a bloody civil war which often pitted members of the same family against each other, the Communist Party was again legalized in 1975 after the collapse, first, of the monarchy and then of the Colonels' junta. Although it has lost much of its former power and following, it still retains a certain militant attractiveness, particularly for those whom America so totally alienated by its support, first, of the monarchy and then of the junta.

CONFECTIONERY STORE, a (the)—ena (toh) zakharopla steeoh
(written on signs as: ΖΑΧΑΡΟΠΛΑΣΤΕΙΟΝ)

Paradises for people afflicted with a sweet tooth, the best of these
make their confections (pastries, cakes, cookies, puddings, etc.) on
the premises. Usually, but not always, they also function as cafés,
serving coffee, tea, soft drinks and a variety of alcoholic beverages,
excluding wine. (See **DESSERT**, p. 147.)

CUSTOMS, the (border)—toh telo**nee**oh.

Generally, because of government policy and the large numbers of
tourists usually arriving en masse in the summertime, one is waved
straight through customs. However, there are occasional spot checks,
particularly if you have brought along a large amount of luggage
and/or arrive by train or by automobile; for some reason, these latter
customs inspectors seem to be much stricter than those at airports. If
you bring with you such things as inflatable rubber boats, outboard
motors, and similar non-portable, non-personal items, they will be
entered in your passport and you will thus be required to have them
in your possession when you leave. This is to ensure that you do not
sell them while in the country. Personal items such as cameras, tape
recorders, typewriters, etc. are allowed into the country without
problem.

DENTIST, a (the)—enas (oh) o~ondee**a**tros
(written as: ΟΔΟΝΤΙΑΤΡΟΣ); **I want a good dentist—Thel**o
kah**l**o o-dhondee**a**troh; **With modern equipment—**meh moh-
dherna erga**l**eea; **Where is the dentist's?—**Poo **ee**nay toh o-
dhondee**a**tree**oh** ?
abscess, an—ena ah**pos**tima
bleeding—aymora**gyee**
bridge—ye**fee**ra
cap, a—mia co**ro**na
cavity—koo**fah**la
denture—o-dhondo-stik**hee**a
extraction, an—mia eksagog-**yee**
filling, a—ena sfragh**is**ma
gingivitis—oo**lee**tees

gums, the—ta oola
nerve, the—toh **neh**vro
novocaine—novoca**ee**nee
pyorrhea—pee**o**rıa
root, the—ee **ree**za
tartar—**poo**ree
temporary—proso**ri**no
tooth—**dhohn**dee (pl. **dhohn**dia)
toothache, a—**en**as pono-dhon-dos

IT HURTS!—Ponaee!

In Athens and other major cities, there are English-speaking dentists, most of whom have studied abroad and are equipped with all the latest devices and techniques. To locate one, look in either the Blue Pages of the telephone directory or in the English-language Athenian newspapers, where they advertise in the personal section. If you are visiting an island or any other out-of-the-way place, it is advisable to take an analgesic rather than visit the local dentist; not only are their equipment and techniques usually quite primitive but they tend to extract teeth rather than bother to deal with them.

DESSERT, a (the)—**en**a epi**dhor**pio (pl. ta epi**dhor**pia)
Desserts, with the exception of fruit and sometimes yogurt and honey, are rarely, if ever, served in tavernas and restaurants. Instead, if you wish a properly caloric after-dinner dessert, you must go to a confectionery store called a zakharoplas**tee**oh. Listed below are some of the enormous variety of sweets obtainable in such places.
cake, a—**en**a keh-ik (pl. keh-ik)
chocolate pudding—**krem**a soko**lah**ta
cookies—bees**kot**ta
   almond—ahmig-dha**lo**ta; **butter**—koulou**rah**kia; **coconut**—ahmig-dha**lo**ta ah**po** karee-dhia; **powdered, crescent-shaped**—kourambee**eh**-dhess
custard, a—mia **krem**a (pl. **krem**ess)
   vanilla—mia **krem**a; **crème caramel**—**krem**a kara**mel**eh; **rice pudding**—reezo**gal**lo

fruit desserts—epi-**dhorpia** ahpo **froota**
  apple pie—meelopita; **cherry tart**—tarteleta kerahsi; **fruit compôte**—kombosta froota; **glazed fruit**—frooee glahseh; **orange tart**—tarteleta nerandzi
halva—halvahs
  plain—**sket**oh; **pistachio**—fisteekee; **vanilla**—vahneel-ya
ice cream—pagotoh
  bowl, a—**ena** bowlahki; **cone**—**ena** honahki; **cup**—**ena** keepelahki; **on a stick**—**ena** ksilahki; **chocolate**—sokolahta: **pistachio**—fisteekee; **strawberry**—fraoola; **vanilla**—vahneel-ya.
galaktoboureko—gahlaktobooreko
  Baked, milk-custard "pie" lined with thin pastry over which syrup is poured.
pastries—**pahs**tess *or* gleeka tahpsioo
  baklava—bahklavah: Layers of thin pastry and nuts soaked in syrup or honey.
  kataifi—kandaeefee: Rolls of shredded pastry filled with chopped nuts and soaked in syrup.
  puffs—soee
  loukoumades—loukou**mah**-dhess: Deep-fried, leavened balls sprinkled with honey and cinammon.
vanilla taffy—**mi**a vah**neel**-ya *or* **ena** eepovreekhio: Served in a spoon dipped in a glass of cold water.

DIARRHEA—dheeahria

Often a problem in Greece, but nowhere near on the scale and intensity of Mexico's famous "Montezuma's revenge." Usually results from eating unwashed fruit and vegetables, as Greece's drinking water is generally quite pure. The most popular remedy among Europeans is boiled rice with lemon juice, something that is almost impossible to find in Greek restaurants. The remedy sworn to by Greek fishermen is grated, dried squid bone mixed in a little water, and they definitely have modern medical science on their side, since squid bones are composed almost entirely of kaolin, an absorbent, chalky substance that is the basis of most pharmaceutical preparations for diarrhea. So, if the thought of swallowing grated squid bone doesn't quite appeal to you, go to a pharmacy and ask for something containing kaolin (kah-oleenee), one brand name of which is "Kaomycin."

DOCTOR, a (the)—en**as** (oh) yia**tros** (written as: ΙΑΤΡΟΣ or ΓΙΑΤΡΟΣ)

Most of the doctors in the major cities and larger islands have been educated at one time or another abroad and speak either English, French, German or a smattering of all three; whether or not they are abreast of the latest techniques depends both upon their age and their personal initiative, the younger ones usually being a bit better informed, but the older ones having the benefit of years of practical experience.

In the more remote areas, the doctors are either quite old and ill-informed or very young and extremely inexperienced, the latter having been most likely assigned to the area as part of their military service. I would therefore advise viewing any diagnosis or medicines offered by either of these types with a great deal of caution; better to head for Athens or any other large city as soon as possible if the malady seems to warrant it. For instance, a friend of mine's heart attack (quite serious) was diagnosed by both the young and old doctor on a small island as "nothing but stomach trouble." Fortunately, we were able to hire a caique and sail him to a larger island's hospital just in time to save his life.

BASIC PHRASES
EMERGENCY—ah**nang**hee
"Help!"—**"Voeethia!"**
24-hr. Police Emergency Telephone—100 or 171
Army helicopter—(01) 166 (available only through
a Greek doctor)

EMERGENCY TERMS:

accident	dhis**teek**hima
car	afto**keen**itoh
ambulance	astheno**for**o
artificial respiration	tek**ni**tee anapnoee
baby	**mor**oh

child	pay-**dhee**
bleeding	aymora**gyee**a
broken	spas**me**no
choking	pneeg-**yeteh**
food	faghee**toh**
drowning	pneeg-**yeteh**
sea	**thal**assa
dying	pe**thay**nee
fire	foti**ah**
first aid	**pro**tess vo**eethi**ess
heart attack	em**frag**ma
oxygen	ok**si**gono
tank	fee**ah**lee
police	astino**mee**a
snake bite	**dhah**goma fee**dhi**oo
stretcher	fo**ree**oh
tourniquet	aymostati**kos epee**-dhesmos
Call a doctor.	Teelehfo**nee**steh **yia**tro.
Call an ambulance.	Teelehfo**nee**steh ahsthenofo**ro**.
It's an emergency!	**Ee**nay ah**nan**ghee!
I'm sick. (male/female)	**Ee**may ah**ros**tos/ ah**ros**tee.
I'm not feeling well.	Dhen ays**thah**nomay kah**lah**.
I ate....	E**fa**gah...
I drank...	**Ee**pia...
I took...	**Pee**rah...
It hurts (here).	Poh**nae**e (eh**dho**).
I want a (good) doctor	**The**lo **e**na (**kah**lo) **yia**tro
I need a doctor	**Pre**pee na **eh**-ho **yia**tro.
Where is the doctor?	Poo **ee**nay oh **ya**tros?
Where is the doctor's office (clinic/hospital)?	Poo **ee**nay toh **yat**reeoh (tee klini**kee**/ toh nosokomee-oh)?
Is there a doctor near here?	**Eh**-hee **ya**tros kon**da**?
Where is the pharmacy?	Poo **ee**nay toh farma**kee**o?
May I see a female doctor?	**Bo**roh na dhoh **mee**a yia**tros**?
I have medical insurance.	**Eh**-ho ahs**fa**lia eegyee**ahs**.

TYPES OF DOCTORS:

CARDIOLOGIST—cardhiologos
CHIROPRACTOR—heeropraktor
DERMATOLOGIST—dher-matologos
DIAGNOSTIC CENTER—dhee-ahgnostikoh kentron
EAR-NOSE-&-THROAT—otorino-laringologos
GYNECOLOGIST—yeenaykologos
HOMEOPATH—omeopathikos
MICRO-BIOLOGIST—meekrovee-ologos
NEUROLOGIST—nevrologos
OPHTHALMOLOGIST—off-thalmologos
OSTEOPATH—osteopathitikos
PATHOLOGIST—pah-thologos
PEDIATRICIAN—pay-dheeatros
PSYCHIATRIST—pseekheeatros
RADIOLOGIST—ahktinologos
SPECIALIST—enas ee-dheekos
SURGEON—heeroorgos
UROLOGIST—oorologos

Diagnosticians *per se* do not exist in Greece as this is what all doctors are theoretically supposed to be anyway. Therefore, one either goes to a diagnostic center or says:

I want a doctor who is good in diagnostics—Thelo ena yiatro poo eenay kalos stee dhee-ahgnosee.

SYMPTOMS

I'm not feeling well.	Dhen aysthanomay kahla.
It hurts here.	Ponaee eh-dho.
I have been vomiting.	Ehkana emetoh.
I feel dizzy.	Zaleesomay.
I can't eat.	Dhen boroh na fao.
I can't sleep.	Dhen boroh na keemitho.
I feel worse.	Aysthanomay heerotera.
I feel better.	Aysthanomay kaleetera.

I am...	Eemay...
Are you...?	Eesteh...
diabetic	dheeahveetikos
epileptic	epileeptikos
asthmatic	ahs-thmatikos
I'm pregnant.	Eemay **eng**-eeohs.
I have...	Eh-ho...
You have...	Eh-heteh...
a temperature	peeretoh
an allergy	ah-lehr-**ghee**a
an infection	moleensi
an itch	**mee**a fagoora
fever	peeretoh
I have a cold.	Eh-ho kree-oh-**lo**-yima.
I have a cough.	Eh-ho **vee**ha.
I have a headache.	Eh-ho ponokefalo.
I have toothache.	Eh-ho ponodondos.
I have a sore throat.	Eh-ho ponolaymos.
I have a stomachache.	Eh-ho stoma**ho**ponos.
I have a fever.	Eh-ho peeretoh.
I have backache.	Ponaee ee **plah**tee mou.
I have constipation.	Eh-ho dhees-kee-liohtees.
I have diarrhea.	Eh-ho dhee**ah**ria.
I have a heart condition.	Eh-ho teen kar-dhiah mou.
I have a pain in my heart.	Ponaee stee kar-**dhee**ah mou.

MEDICAL TERMS

AIDS	Ayds
alcoholic	alco-oli**kos**
alcoholism	alco-olis**mos**
anemia	ahnay**mee**a
amputation	ahkroteeriasmos
anesthetic	ah-nays-theetiko
anesthetist	ah-nays-theesiologos

antibiotic	ahn-dee-viotiko
antiseptic	ahn-dee-seeptiko
blood	**ay**ma
blood group	oh**mas ay**matos
blood pressure:	**pee**-esees **ay**matos
low blood pressure	epotasi
high blood pressure	epehr-tasi
blood transfusion	meta**hn**-yeesees **ay**matos
bone	**ko**kalo
cancer	ka**kee**nos
cholera	hole**hr**a
clinic	kleeni**kee**
dentist	oh-dhon-**dhee**-yatros
epidemic	epi-dhee-**mee**a
fever	**pee**retoh
flu	**gree**pee
fracture	**kah**tagma
germs	meekrovia
heart attack	**em**fragma
hepatitis	eepa**tee**tees
hygiene	ee-yee-**ee**nee
indigestion	dhees-**pep**seea
infection	**mo**leensi
influenza	**gree**pee
limb	**ah**kro
needle	ve**lo**nee
nurse	noso**ko**ma
operation	eng**hee**risees
oxygen	ok**see**gono
pain	**po**nos
physiotherapy	feesiothera**pee**a
pins and needles	mou-dhee-**ah**-zo
rabies	**lee**sa
snake bite	**dha**-goma fee-dhee-**oo**
stethoscope	steetho**sko**pio
stomachache	stoma**ho**ponos
surgeon	heero**lo**gos

(act of) surgery	en**ghee**risees
syringe	**see**ringa
thermometer	thehr-**mo**metro
toothache	pono-**dhon**-dos

MEDICATION

dosage, the	ee **dhoh**see
What is the dosage?	Tee **ee**nay ee **dhoh**see?
After (before) each meal	Meta (preen) **ka**theh **yev**ma
At night	Toh **vrah**-dhee
In the morning	Toh pro-**ee**
How many drops (pills/caspules)?	**Po**sess **sta**goness (**hah**pia/kap**sool**ess)?
teaspoon, a	**e**na kouta**la**ki (pl. koutala**ki**a)
tablespoon, a	**e**na kou**tah**li tees **sou**pas (pl. kou**tah**lia)
How many times a day?	**Po**sess **fo**ress teen ee **meh**ra?
prescription, a (the)	mia (ee) seenta**gyee**
side effects	pare**nerg**-yiess
countraindications	ahnten**dheek**sees
precautions	profee**lak**sees
I take this medication.	**Pehr**no aftoh toh far**ma**ko.
I need medication for...	**The**lo far**ma**ko ya...
What type of medication is this?	Tee **ee**-dhos far**ma**ko **Ee**nay **ah**ftoh?
How many times a day must l take it?	**Po**sess **fo**ress teen ee**meh**ra **pre**pee na toh **pah**ro?
When should I stop?	**Po**teh **pre**pee na stama**tee**so?
I'm on antibiotics.	**Pehr**no andivee-**oh**tika.
I'm allergic to ...	**Ee**may ah-lehr-**ghi**kos...
antibiotics	sta ahn-dee-vio**ti**ka.
penicillin	steen peniki**lee**nee.

I have been vaccinated.	Eh-ho kanee emvolio.
I have my own syringe.	Eh-ho teen dheekee mou seeringa.
Is it possible for me to travel?	Boroh na taksidhepso?

antibiotic	ahn-dee-viotiko
antidote	ahndeedhohtoh
antihistamine	andeestaminikoh
antiseptic	ahndisiptiko
antitoxin	ahnditokseenee
aspirins	ahspireeness
bandage, a	enas epee-dhesmos
bandaid	hansaplast or lefkoplast
codeine	codeh-eenee
cortisone	kortizohnee
cream	alifee or krema
drug	farmako
expectorant	apok-hreptikoh
gauze	gahza
hypodermic	eepo-dhorio
insulin	insouleenee
iodine	eeoh-dhio
kaolin	kah-oleenee
laxative	kathartikoh
lotion	lohseeohn
lozenges	pasteel-yes
medicine	pharmaka
mercurochrome	merkoorohrohm
milk of magnesia	gahla magniseeas
morphine	morfeenee
nose drops	stagoness ya tee meetee
nose spray	spray ya tee meetee
ointment	alifee
penicillin	penikileenee
sedative	katapra-eendikoh
sleeping pills	eepnotika hahpia
sling	koonia

splint	**nar**theeks
swabs	k**ses**tra
syringe	see**rin**ga
syrup	see**ro**pee
cough	see**ro**pee ya toh **veek**ha
tablet	tah**ble**ta
terramycin	terami**kee**nee
tetanus (anti-injection)	ahndiftetani**kee enes**ee
thermometer	the**hr**mometro
tranquillizer	eeremisti**ko far**mako

DOG, a (the)—**en**as (oh) **skee**los (pl. ee **skee**lee); **bitch, a (the)**—**mi**a (ee) **skee**la (pl. ee **skee**less)

dog food—fah**ghi**toh ya **skee**lo; **leash**—ena loo**ree** ya **skee**lo. **Can I have the bones for my dog?**—**Bo**roh na **eh**-ho ta ko**ka**la ya ton **skee**lo mou? **Does it bite?**—Dhah**go**nee?; **Don't be afraid. It doesn't bite**—Mee fo**vah**seh. Dhen dhah**go**nee.

Unfortunately, most Greeks actively dislike dogs, or are afraid or contemptuous of them—or a combination of all three. For the reasons behind this, please see my entry under CAT above. See also KENNEL below.

DOWRY, a (the)—**mi**a (ee) **preek**a

Dowries still have a great deal of importance in Greece, although in Athens and other large cities, progressive thinking and/or economic reality have all but eliminated the custom. In rural areas, however, it continues to weigh like a chain around the necks of both a prospective bride and her family, all of whom must often work like slaves to provide a dowry (usually a fully-furnished house and its plot of land) acceptable to the groom and his family. I knew of one girl, the daughter of a sheepherder on a small island, who was then (1980) in her fourth year of waiting for her father and three brothers to accumulate the money just to begin building her house, while inflation continually pushed the possibility out of their reach. One can only contemplate with horror the fate that befalls a man with five daughters and no sons...

DRINK, a (the)—ena (toh) pot**oh** (pl. pot**a**) *or* **ena** (toh) piot**oh** (pl. piot**a**)

beer	beer**a**
brandy	kon**yak**
coffee	kaf**ess**
Greek:	Eleeniko:
black, a	**ena skeh**toh kaf**eh**
medium-sweet	**ena meh**trio
sweet	**ena** glik**eev**rasto
iced	Nescaf**eh** frap**eh**
instant	**Nes**cafeh
with milk	meh **gah**la
with sugar	meh **zakh**aree
cognac	kon**yak**
juice	hee**mos**
apricot	ver**ee**koko
orange	portokal**ah**-dha
peach	ro-**dhah**-kinou
pineapple	**ah**nana
tomato	tomah**tohz**oumo
lemonade	lemon**ah**-dha
milk	**gah**la
orangeade	portokal**ah**-dha
ouzo	**oo**zo
soda water	**so**-dha
soft drink	anapsiktik**oh**
tea	**tsah**-ee
chamomile	hamom**ee**lee
tonic water	**tohn**eek.
water	**neh**ro
mineral water	metaliko **neh**ro
whiskey	oo-**ees**ki
wine	krah**see**
red	**mah**vro *or* **ko**kino
retsina	ret**see**na
rose	roz**eh**
white	**ah**spro

dry	broosko
sweet	gleekoh
barreled	heema krahsee

Note: Barreled wine is sold by the kilo (or half- or quarter-kilo), a kilo being approximately 1 quart.

TOASTS:

Birthday, Name Day	**Hron**ia pola! ("Many years!")
Bottoms up!	**Ah**spro **pah**toh!
Cheers!	**Veev**a! *or* Eh**veev**a!
To us!	**Ya**mas!
To your health!	Eesi**ghee**a!

ENGAGEMENT, an (the)—**en**as (oh) aravohnas; **engagement ring, an (the)**—**mi**a (ee) **veh**ra (worn on the left hand).

Greek engagements, particuly in rural areas, tend to last an inordinately long time, from one to even three or five years. This is partly due to the difficulties in getting together a dowry (see above) as well as the sensible, old-fashioned idea that people should find out how well they get along together before locking themselves into a marriage. See also MARRIAGE.

FACT, a (the)—**en**a (toh) yego**nos**; **Is that a fact?**—Ee**nay** yego**nos**?

In Greece, anything that is stated as a "fact" (such as bus and boat schedules, etc.) should be confirmed by at least two other people, preferably more. Facts in Greece are rarely simple, straightforward, objective truths. They change in accordance with both the knowledge of the person being questioned and with what he thinks you might want the answer to be. This is not lying; it is simply stretching the truth a little so that the person stating the "fact" doesn't have to lose face by admitting that he doesn't exactly know, and so that you will be as pleased as possible with his reply. So, don't believe anything you hear, particularly when you know it's what you want to hear.

FARM, a (the)—mia (ee) **farm**a; **farmer, a (the)—en**as (oh) yeh-**orgos**

Do not hesitate, if you are traveling through the countryside, to ask farmers if you can buy some of their produce; they will be most happy to sell it to you (and will probably give you some, anyway, before you ask). Aside from agricultural products, they may also have yogurt, cheeses, honey and wine for sale. And, if you come during the grape and olive picking seasons, you can probably find work if you need it. See HARVEST below.

FISH (to)—na **psar**evo; **fishing—psar**ema

I'd like to go fishing—Tha **ee**thela na **pao** ya **psar**ema; **Are you going fishing tonight?—**Tha pahs ya **psar**ema apopseh?

bait or fly	**dhol**oma
fishing boat	**psarovarka**
fish hook	ahn**ghee**stree
fishing line	ar**meedhee**
fisherman, a (the)	**en**as (oh) psa**rahs**
fish net	**dheek**tee
fishing rod	kah**lahmee**
spear	ka**mahkee**
spear gun	psaro**toofeko**
tackle	ta **seen**erga psari**kees**
weight	mo**leevee** *or* va**ree-**dhee

Fishing in Greece is no longer what it used to be, specifically because of the massive, unending pollution of the Mediterranean as a whole. Nevertheless, there are still some spectacular catches to be made. Fishing with a speargun is prohibited if one wears any sort of underwater breathing apparatus.

FOREIGNER, a (the)—enas (oh) **ksen**os (m), **mi**a (ee) **ksen**ee (f); (pl. ee **ksen**ee)

"Ksenos" not only means "foreigner" or "stranger," it also means, with equal emphasis, "guest"—which is why the state-owned tourist hotels are called the "Xenia" and why you will find yourself, sooner or later, inundated with offers of hospitality (drinks, flowers, food, etc.) as you travel through the country. For more on this, see HOSPI-TALITY below.

FRIEND, a (the)—**en**as (oh) **fee**los (m), **mia** (ee) **fee**lee (f) *or* **en**as (oh) **gnos**tos (m), **mia** (ee) **gnos**tee (f)

Since "feelos" and "feelee" can also mean "boy friend" and "girl friend, it is best—if you want to make it perfectly clear the person is just a friend and not a lover—to use the terms "gnostee" and "gnostos", which are comparable to the English word "acquaintance". Further confusion can result from the spoken, plural form of the masculine noun, which sounds exactly like the singular female:

my friend (f)—ee **fee**lee (**gnos**tee) mou (pl. ee **fee**less *or* **gnos**tess); **my friends** (m)—ee **fee**lee (**gnos**tee) mou

In addition, a mixed company of male and female friends is also referred to as "ee feelee (gnostee) mou." The only way of clearing up this confusion is to speak of the person or persons by name.

FRUIT—**froo**ta; **fruit juice**—**hee**mos **froo**ton; **canned**—com**pos**ta; **fresh**—**fres**ka; **a serving of (melon)**—**mia** mer**ee**dha (pep**on**ee)

apple	**en**a **mee**lo (pl. **mee**la)
apricot	**en**a ver**ee**koko (pl. ver**ee**koka)
fig	**en**a **see**ko (pl. **see**ka)
dried	**kse**ra **see**ka
grapes	sta**fee**lia
lemon	**en**a le**mon**ee (pl. le**mon**ia)
melon	**en**a pep**on**ee (pl. pep**on**ia)
orange	**en**a porto**kah**lee (pl. porto**kah**lia)
peach	ro-**dhah**kino (pl. ro-**dhah**kina)
pear	**en**a ah**klah**dhee (pl. ah**klah**dhia)
plum	**en**a dhamas**ki**no (pl. dhamas**ki**na)
pomegranate	**en**a ro-**dhee** (pl. ro-**dhi**a)
quince	**en**a kee-**dhoh**nee (pl. kee-**dhoh**nia)
raisins	sta**fee**-dhess
tangerine	**en**a manda**ree**nee (pl. manda**ree**nia)
watermelon	**en**a kar**poo**zee

FUNERAL, a (the)—mia kee-**dhee**a

Having an aversion to funerals, I have never gone to one in Greece. They have, however, come to me, passing by in the street on their way to the church or the cemetery, the coffin more often than not open. The Greeks have an extraordinary awareness and acceptance of death; they do not attempt to hide or ignore it as we are wont to do in most Western countries. It is, for them, very much a part and parcel of life. However, if you are in a shop or café and the owner starts closing the shutters and doors, you will know that a funeral procession is approaching. This is done out of respect for, not fear of, the dead. After the procession passes, business resumes as usual, the Greeks also being fully aware, again perhaps more than we, that life does still go on.

GAMBLING—tzohgohs

Gambling, except for that which is done on the premises of licensed casinos, is strictly illegal. However, in one form or another (dice, cards, backgammon), it is practiced in practically every café and back room in Greece and is such a deeply-rooted national addiction that the police, for the most part, wisely tend to turn their heads the other way, realizing that to attempt to stamp out gambling would be as politically idiotic as trying to prohibit the drinking of ouzo. The players, in turn, reciprocate by keeping all money discreetly off the table, the accounts being kept on pieces of paper and cardboard and paid up later.

Backroom dice games, however, are another story, and being caught in one of these can result in the confiscation of all the money in your possession as well as a 3-to-6 month jail sentence and/or a stiff fine for every day of said sentence. See also CARDS.

GAS (cooking)—**gah**zee; **gas cooker, a (the)—mi**a (ee) koo**zee**na (also the word for "kitchen"); **a bottle of gas—mi**a feeahlee **gah**zee

All stoves in Greece work either on electricity or bottled gas; only in certain parts of Athens is gas piped directly into the house. Therefore, if you are renting a place with a gas stove and a relatively absent landlord, you yourself will have to deal with the problem of getting a new bottle of gas. In cities and most large towns, the dealers both deliver and install the bottles; in villages and islands, it will usually be up to you to do this. The color of the. bottles determines which dealer they belong to. When buying a bottle for the first time, you must pay a huge deposit on it; this will subsequently be returned to you when you return the bottle for the last time.

GAS STATION, a (the)—ena (toh) venzi**nah**-dhiko; **Where is the gas station?**—Poo **ee**nay toh venzi**nah**-dhiko?

In the larger cities and islands, gas stations look just like gas stations and/or garages and are rarely located anywhere but on the main routes to and from the city. In remoter areas, if you don't see a gas station, don't despair; they are often cleverly disguised as something else, such as a stable, storage depot or home garage; on islands, they are usually located somewhere near the waterfront to service caiques. So ask:

Where can I buy some gasoline?—Poo bo**roh** na ago**rah**so ven**zee**nee?; **My tank is almost empty**—Toh teposi**toh** mou **ee**nay ske-**dhon ah**-dheeoh.

GIFT, a (the)—ena (toh) **dhor**o (pl. **dhor**a); **a gift for you—en**a **dhor**o ya sena; **a gift for me?—en**a **dhor**o ya mena?

That old cautionary phrase "Beware of Greeks bearing gifts" has virtually no validity nowadays nor, probably, has it ever had except in the case of that famous "gift" of a wooden horse to the Trojans. Greeks are by instinct extremely hospitable to foreigners and they tend to express this by giving gifts of anything that might be at hand at the moment: flowers, drinks, fruits, candy for the children and, quite often, the food off their own plates. There is nothing you can do about this except to graciously accept it; to attempt to reciprocate can often be taken as a kind of insult or, if not that, then such an embarrassment to your host that he or she will be compelled to overcome it by giving you even more in return.

GREETINGS & GOODBYES

In Greece, it is both the time of day and one's familiarity with the person spoken to which determine the type of greeting or goodbye to be used:

In the Morning (until about 11:30 A.M.):

Good morning	Kahlee mehra
Hello! (familiar)	Yasoo!; (formal or plural)—Yasahs!
Goodbye (general)	Ahndeeo
(familiar)	Yasoo
(form. or pl.)	Yasahs

In the Afternoon (from about 11:30 A.M. until 7:00 P.M. or sunset):

Good afternoon (formal)	Hayreteh
Hello and Goodbye	same as in the morning

In the Evening (from about 7:00 or sunset until one goes to bed):

Good evening	Kahlee spehra
Hello and Goodbye	same as in the morning and afternoon
Good night	Kahlee neekta
Sleep well	Kahlo eepno
Sweet dreams!	Ohneera gleeka!

Introductions:

Pleased to meet you	Hayro pohlee
Pleased to have met you	Hahrika pohlee

And finally:

Tell him (her) greetings from me Pehs tou (tees) hayreteesmata ahpo mena

Au revoir (see you again) Kahlee ahndamosee

GUEST, a (the)—enas (oh) ksenos (m), mia (ee) ksenee *or* episkeptees (m), episkeptria (f); **the guests** (subject)—ee ksenee; (object)—ksenoos; **I'm expecting guests**—Perimeno ksenoos.

Note that the word for "foreigner" or "stranger" is also ksenos. This reflects what Lawrence Durrell so aptly calls "the iron law of hospitality" that exists in Greece: all foreigners are to be welcomed as guests and treated with the utmost deference, no matter what their personality or politics may be like, and no matter how grumpy or tired you, their Greek host, may feel at the moment.

GYNECOLOGIST, a (the)—enas (oh) yeenay-ko**logos**

The names, addresses and phone numbers of English speaking gynecologists can be found in the Blue Pages of the telephone directories of most large cities and islands. Otherwise, inquire at the office of the local Tourist Police. In addition, it is also wise to ask for recommendations among the local inhabitants; gynecologists, being considered extremely important members of the community, are thoroughly scrutinized, and the people will not hesitate to tell you who is considered good and who bad:

Who is the best gynecologist?—Peeohs eenay oh kal**ee**teros yeenay-ko**logos?**

Self-administering pregnancy tests are now available at most pharmacies, being sold under the brand name GYNOTEST, which certain pharmacists may pronounce "**yee**notest" or "**ghee**notest".

HANGOVER, a—enas pono**kef**alos ah**po** me**thee**si (lit. "a headache from drinking").

Strangely enough, the Greeks have no word at all to describe that more general malaise so common in the West when one feels as though death is creeping like a fungus throughout one's nervous system. And, in fact, none of the Greeks I have met while living there for 22 years has ever seemed to suffer in this manner, although many of them have consumed, in an evening, considerably more alcohol than I. Some people attribute this to the Greek habit of always eating while drinking. I personally suspect it has something to do with the Greek god Bacchus protecting his own while leaving us foreigners cruelly out in the elements.

HARVEST, the—oh therismos; **harvest season, the—toh theh**ros;
   When is the harvest season?—Poteh ee**nay toh theh**ros?

During the harvest seasons (particularly for grapes and olives), work is quite often available to young foreigners wishing to earn some travel money. You should be aware, however,that it is completely illegal and that if the local police decide to act (which they rarely do, as the work is so backbreaking and basically unrewarding that it is almost impossible for farmers to find enough Greeks to do it), this could result in a fine and/or expulsion from the country.

HASHISH—hahseesee

This is the most prevalent form of hemp available in Greece, quite a bit of it home-grown and smoked by more Greeks than you might imagine. However, inasmuch as several of my acquaintances, including a charming, intelligent, well-bred 45-year-old American woman, have spent a minimum of 2 years in a Greek jail and then been permanently expelled for having been busted smoking it, I would suggest that it's not worth taking the risk—particularly if it's offered to you by a charming young Greek. He could be a cop.

HELICOPTER, a (the)—**en**a (toh) elikoptero

Theoretically, military helicopters are available to fly emergency cases from remote areas to the nearest hospital. However, because most rural doctors are loathe to assume the heavy responsibility of requesting one from Athens, often the only recourse is to hire one from Olympic Airways, which can be prohibitively expensive. As a friend of mine who had just suffered a severe heart attack said when I told him the price, "I'd rather die." So we rented a caique instead—and saved his life.

HOME—**speet**ee; **my home**—toh **speet**ee mou; **your home**—toh **speet**ee sou; **I'm going home**—**Pa**o sto **speet**ee mou; **I'll be at heme**—Tha **ee**may sto **speet**ee.

"Speetee" also means "house", and therefore some confusion may arise. In other words, a person's "home" could be either a house or an apartment, whereas the house he is referring to may not be his home—if you can follow that. In addition, there is another, formal word for "home" which you may come across on business cards and in telephone directories. It is usually used to indicate the home phone number as separate from the business one and is written as **OIKIA** *or* Οικία.

HOMOSEXUAL, a (the)—**en**as (oh) omofilofilos (m), **mia** (ee) omofilofilee (f); **homosexuality**—omofilofileea; **slang**—teeootos ("gay"); **en**as bee**ness** ("a faggot"); **en**as **poos**tees ("a fag"); and terms like **seek**a ("fig"), ahdhel**fee** ("sister"), and dhespee**nees** ("Miss").

In Greece, homosexuality does and does not have the same stigma attached to it as in America and other Western countries. One must first remember that homosexuality was a completely-accepted social practice in classical Greece and that today it is as equally accepted in many countries of the Levant—an area as well as state-of-mind in which Greece, irrespective of its Orthodox Christianity and increasing ties with Europe, is deeply rooted. Second, there still exists in many parts of Greece, as in the Levant, a socially-rigorous separation of the sexes before marriage (although this is rapidly being eroded by "liberated" Western ideas) that places a great deal of emphasis on the virginity of the bride and thus virtually forces males (and sometimes females) to seek outlets with members of their own sex. So in Greece today, one finds a dual attitude towards homosexuality: as in the West, it is looked down upon as an aberration, while at the same time, as in the Levant and classical Greece, it is widely and usually unashamedly practiced, often by heterosexuals. Most of the latter do not think of themselves, and are not thought of by others, as homosexuals; they are merely doing what they need to do until the time and opportunity comes for them to marry, after which they rarely have a homosexual relationship again—although it should also be noted that most Greek men very much prefer the company of other males and are not at all shy about demonstrating deep affection for members of their own sex.

As for truly gay Greeks, they exist in no greater proportion in Greece than elsewhere, and are made just as much fun of by the "straight" world. On the other hand, when the laughter has died down, I have often seen its object trotting off home to bed with one of the butch types that's been teasing him—sex in Greece being sex, and sometimes seeming much less complicated with a **poostee** than with, say, a young girl intent on marriage or a married woman whose husband may be intent on revenge.

HOSPITAL, a (the)—ena (toh) nosokom**ee**o (written as: ΝΟΣΟΚΟΜΕΙΟΝ); **Where is the hospital (clinic)?**—Poo eenay toh nosok**amee**o (ee klin**ikee**)?

I have included "clinic" in the above question for two reasons. First, because there are more clinics than hospitals in Greece, and second because there is an important distinction between the two that should be understood by the tourist.

All hospitals are state-owned and provide either free or extremely-inexpensive medical services, even for foreigners, the cost depending on the type of care and medicines required. Clinics, on the other hand, are much more expensive, even though some of them may be the only kind of "hospital" available, say, on an island and may not even offer the type of specialized services that one usually associates with the name. However, in areas where both clinics and hospitals are available, it is the clinics which usually provide the best medical care.

So, if you have the money and want the best, go to a clinic in a large city. Otherwise, Greek hospitals are a good bet; although they sometimes appear a bit run down and may often be crowded, the staff are usually quite attentive and polite, the care is more than adequate, and you should be able to leave without having paid—or lost—an arm and a leg.

HOSPITALITY—filok**seneea**; **Thank you for your hospitality**—
Efhari**stoh** ya tee filok**seneea** sahs.

Although Lawrence Durrell calls Greek hospitality an "iron law," meaning one that is to be adhered to even in the worst of times or political enmities, it also seems to be second nature to the Greeks, a product of their insatiable curiosity about all things foreign and a fierce pride in their own self-sufficiency, in their ability to give without expecting anything in return, which is coupled with, on the other side of that coin, an almost child-like need to be thought well of. So, when you find yourself the object of a Greek's hospitality—and you will—the most you can do is just to accept it without trying to reciprocate and beat the Greeks at their own game. You won't win, and you could end up insulting their pride.

HOTEL, a (the)—**en**a (toh) kseno-dhok**hee**o
(written as: **XENOΔOXEION**).

All hotels except those in the luxury class are price controlled according to their assigned category. These prices are required to be posted inside the door of the room, and if you find you have been overcharged and the hotel manager refuses to back down, your best resort is to go to the local tourist police and let them handle it.

If you are one person and find yourself given a double room, ask if you are paying for the entire room or just the bed; certain hotels in the cheaper categories tend to rent beds, not rooms, and you could wake up in the middle of the night to find yourself sharing your room with a stranger; on the other hand, if you don't mind this, you can save yourself some money by making it clear that you want just the bed, not the room (see the vocabulary below).

Greek hotels no longer pay any attention to whether foreign couples are married or not, but they will want to keep one or both of your passports. This is to register you, as required by law, with the local police; it is also to ensure that you do not skip out without paying the bill.

In hotels with the bath down the hall, hot showers often cost extra, and one must arrange with the manager beforehand to have the water heater turned on.

a single room	**ena** moh**nok**leeno
a double room	**ena dhee**kleeno
a single bed	**ena** mohno kreva**htee**
a double bed	**ena** dheeplo kreva**htee**
with bath	meh **bahn**-yo
without bath	ho**rees bahn**-yo
with hot water	meh zestoh nehro
with breakfast	meh proee**noh**
for one night (week)	ya **mia neek**ta (ev-dhoh**mah**-dha)
for two or three nights	ya **dhee**o ee trees **neek**tess
I don't know yet	Dhen k**seh**ro ah**ko**ma
Am I paying for the bed or the room?	Pli**ro**no ya toh kreva**htee** ee toh dho**mah**tio?
I want the entire room only for myself	**Thelo ohlo** toh dho**mah**tio **mohno** ya **mena.**
I only want to pay for the bed	**Thelo** na pli**roso mohno** ya toh kreva**htee.**

HOUSE, a (the)—**ena** (toh) **speetee** (pl. **speeti**a); **a 2- or 3-story house**—**ena**s **peergos** (lit. "tower"); **an apartment house**—**mia** pohlikahti**kee**a

Since **spee**tee also means "home," please also see the entry under HOME.

Buying a house in Greece can be a joy and can also become one of the most hideously-complicated legal nightmares of one's entire life. (The author speaks from personal experience, having partaken equally of both the joy and the nightmare—but I wouldn't have missed it for anything.) The source of the joy is obvious; the nightmare evolves principally from the difficulties of acquiring a clear, unequivocal title to the land. Because of Greece's dowry and inheritance systems, an abandoned farmhouse with one acre of land may have 22 different owners living in 22 different cities and/or countries, all of whom must agree to the sale because none of them own any specific, designated piece of the land. (It took me 18 months to find all of them, during which time two died, spawning four more heirs.)

The point is, one needs to acquire both a locally-born lawyer who is acquainted with the property and families involved, as well as an impartial big-city lawyer who knows all the intricacies of Greek law and who will protect your interests against those of the locals. The rule of thumb in this case is to trust everyone openly and implicitly (for the sake of your relations with the community) but to trust absolutely no one (except—perhaps—your own lawyer) for the sake of both your legal security and precious sanity. It should also be noted that it is absolutely illegal for any foreigner (except E.C. members) to own property anywhere on Greece's frontiers. These include not only the northern borders with Albania, Yugoslavia and Bulgaria, but also the island frontiers such as the Ionian Islands, the Dodecanese, Samos, Lesvos, Chios, Corfu, and Crete. There are, of course, loopholes—namely, having a Greek friend buy the house for you in his name or forming a "land development corporation" with a Greek as majority stockholder—but such loopholes can quickly turn into pitfalls, particularly in Greece. What, for instance, might happen should your Greek friend or partner suddenly die? How attractive would your lovely house look to his heirs, who could take it without even a legal whimper on your part? And another example—one which I have seen much too often to ignore—what do you think would happen if you and your Greek friend had a sudden falling-out, perhaps precipitated by his equally sudden realization of the value of the property that's in his name? This is human nature and these are the chances that one must take with it. So...

ICON, a (the)—mia (ee) eeko**na** (pl. eeko**ness**)

Most of the moderately-priced icons that one sees in souvenir shops are merely cheap color reproductions pasted on wood and then "antiqued." Genuine icons are worth their weight in gold and priced accordingly. However, in order to export one painted before 1821, one needs a special and difficult-to-get permit. On the other hand, there are many hand-painted reproductions of ancient icons on the market that are often fine works of art in themselves and, although sometimes a bit expensive, are definitely worth the money. The best are to be found in Athens and Crete, particularly the latter, where icon painting and reproduction is a long and honored tradition.

JUKE BOX, a (the)—ena (toh) juke box; **too loud—polee** dheena**tah**

As you will soon discover, Greeks like their music at the highest possible decibel level, and it is for this reason that they are second to none, not even Americans, in their affection for monstrous, brain-shattering jukeboxes. You can request that the owner turn the music down, and he usually will—but then, everything being relative, the noise level will probably still be ear-splitting. Therefore, you can (1) leave or (2) keep drinking wine or ouzo; eventually, believe me, you will become acclimatized.

JUNTA, a (the)—mia (ee) **hoon**da

It may surprise many foreigners to learn that the infamous Colonels' junta (1967-74) was not the first in modern Greece, that, in fact, juntas have been more the rule than the exception in this cherished "cradle of democracy" during the 20th century. It may also surprise many Americans to learn that the Greek people consider the United States solely responsible for putting and keeping the Colonel's junta in power.

KENNEL a (the)—ena (toh) spee**tah**kee skee**lou** (lit. "a little dog house")

There are boarding kennels for dogs, cats and other animals in Athens, usually run by veterinarians. Check in the English-language Blue Pages of the telephone directory, or telephone the Hellenic Animal Welfare Society—(01)-643-5391—for all kinds of valuable English-spoken information regarding pets.

LESBIAN, a—mia lesveea

Although the name derives from the island of Lesbos, birthplace of the ancient and reputedly lesbian Greek poetess, Sappho, female homosexuality seems to be a rather isolated phenomenon in modern Greece, particularly when compared to the rather large amount of homosexual relations that happen among males (see HOMOSEXU-ALITY). But then, in the male-dominated Greek social system, sexual expression of any kind among females has until recently been strictly confined to the beds and needs only of their husbands—at least theoretically.

LESSON, a (the)—ena (toh) matheema (pl. ta matheemata); I want to take some lessons—Thelo na kahno matheemata; I want to give English lessons—Thelo na para-dhee-dhoh Ahnglika matheemata.

I GIVE ENGLISH LESSONS:
ΠΑΡΑΔΙΔΩ ΑΓΓΛΙΚΑ ΜΑΘΗΜΑΤΑ

The giving of English lessons is strictly forbidden without a work permit. However, this is a most difficult "crime" to detect and in small communities and islands without private tutoring schools, the police tend to look the other way if it is not done too blatantly. In fact, I know of one American on a small island who earned a living by teaching the police themselves.

LIBRARY, a (the)—mia (ee) vivliotheekee

It is useful (and economical) to know that most cities and towns and some islands have a fair proportion of English-language books in their libraries, quite a few of which have been left behind by tourists (meaning that there are usually many current popular novels available and not just dusty, scholarly tomes). The trust with which the librarians allow foreigners to borrow their books is astonishing; one usually needs to leave only one's name and address, with no deposit being required. How they still have any books left on their shelves, only God knows. Perhaps the Golden Rule does still operate—in libraries anyway.

LOST (adj.)—hah**men**o; **I lost**—**Eh**-hasa; **I lost my wallet (passport)** **Eh**-hasa toh portfolee (dheeahvateeri**oh**) mou; **The Bureau of Lost Property**—Toh Grafee**on** Apoles**then**don Ahndiki**men**on.

All losses should be reported as soon as possible to either the regular or tourist police, because, surprisingly enough, most lost property, even wallets with money in them, eventually finds its way to the proper authorities. Most Greeks are incredibly honest about this; one is always reading in Greek newspapers about envelopes containing hundreds of thousands of drachmas (Greeks do not trust checks and do most of their business with cash in hand) being dutifully turned over to the police.

It is customary, particularly if money is lost, to offer a small reward to the finder, say about 10%. Sometimes it will be accepted, sometimes not. If not, then, depending on the person, buy them a drink or candies or a toy.

LOVE (n)—ah**gah**pee; **My love**—Ah**gah**pee mou; **I love**—Ah**gah**poh; **I love you**—S'ah**gah**poh; **Do you love me?**—M' ahga**pahs**?; **I love him (her)**—Ton (teen) ah**gah**poh; **I'm in love with...**—Eemay erotev**men**os (m), erotev**men**ee (f) meh...; **I'm falling in love with you (him/her)**—Erotevomay meh **sen**a (af**toh**/af**teen**); **He (she) loves you**—S'ah**gah**pa**ee**; **Do you love her (him)?**—Teen (ton) ahga**pahs**; **a love affair**—**mi**a eroti**kee** sk**hes**see.

To make love—na **kah**no eh**ro**ta; **I want to make love to you**—**The**lo na **kah**noomeh eh**ro**ta (lit. "I want us to make love."); **I like making love to you**—M'ah**re**see na **kah**noumeh eh**ro**ta.

Love is often not a word to be used lightly with Greek men, particularly at the beginning of a relationship except, perhaps, when you are obviously under the influence of too much Greek sun, moon, music and/or wine; then its utterance can be considered excusable.

However, in more sober moments, the words "I love you" might tend to fill most Greek men with such an overwhelming sense of responsibility that it could send them scurrying off in search of someone much less complicated. Conversely, should a Greek man whisper "S'ahga**poh**" sweetly in your ear, take it with about a bottle of salt, because he, like most Mediterranean males, has probably learned very early in life to say the things he thinks female tourists think they want to hear. In other words, play it cool and perhaps something genuine will eventually develop. On the other hand, if it should, please see my entries under MARRIAGE and WOMAN below before you go any further.

Falling in love or having an affair with a young and unmarried Greek girl is something to be approached with caution, as well as, I would advise, apprehension. In fact, in all but the largest cities and everywhere in Crete, I would advise avoiding it altogether. Greek families still place a great deal of value on the virginity of a girl at the time of her marriage, and said families are usually quite large (and often well-armed) with countless brothers, and/or male cousins, in-laws, godfathers, etc. who are on a constant state of alert to deal with interlopers, particularly non-Greeks. They will not look lightly on your playing around with the reputations and possibly bodies of their cherished young ladies, and the consequences, particularly in places like Crete, could be severe. So the word to the wise is: forget it. However, with the advent of television, discotheques, and various other Western influences, things are gradually changing, and in the anonymity of Athens and Thessaloniki it is now possible to have the same kind of relationship, casual or serious, that one would expect to find at home. However, you should always be aware that there is still, somewhere, that family lurking (and ready to pounce) in the background.

Greek women, on the other hand, married, divorced, or past what is considered the best marriageable age (13 to 22), are fair and lovely game—except, that is, in small communities where everyone knows everyone else and strangers aren't allowed to. As for the relative merits of Greek women and men as lovers, the range of opinion is as varied as the individuals involved. It is generally agreed that Greek men are classic male chauvinist pigs but on a lesser scale than their self-preening Italian counterparts. Before marriage, they are usually quite attentive, although, when among a group of other men, they quickly show a girl her place, which is somewhere outside the circle. As for their abilities in bed, I have heard certain foreign girls describe them as being abrupt and concerned only with achieving their own orgasm, while other girls swear that Greek men are the gentlest and most considerate lovers they have ever been with. As for Greek women, I have been told by many Greek men that they are about as active and interesting as mattresses (this said while explaining why they, the Greek men, seek out foreign girls.) My own experience has been exactly the opposite: Greek women are wonderful, passionate and loving.

MARKET, a (the)—mia (ee) ahgora; **street market, a (the)**—mia (ee) laee**kee** ahgora; **Where is the market?**—Poo ee**nay** ee ahgora?

Markets—permanent and roving—are one of the most delightful aspects of Greek life, as they are, of course, in most countries. The sellers are usually specialized: one for vegetables, another for grocery items, another for meat, and so on, supermarkets being a relative rarity except in the larger cities. Street markets usually operate in a specific area on only one morning a week; one should ask the tourist police where and when; in Athens you can also check the city's excellent English-language magazine, The Athenian, for the days and locations of the various markets.

Shopping hours vary from place to place, and can be quite maddening to figure out. In Athens, again, check The Athenian.

MARRIAGE, a (the)—enas (oh) **gah**mos; **a church (civil) marriage**—enas eklisiastikos (politikos) **gah**mos; **marriage certificate (license), a**—ena pistopee-eetiko (mia ah-dheea) **gah**mou; **marry (to)**—na pahn**dre**vomay; **I want to marry you**—**The**lo na seh pahn**dref**toh; **Will you marry me?**—Tha meh pahn**dref**tees?; **married (I am)**—Eemay pahndreh**men**os (m), pahndreh**men**ee (f); **Are you married?**—Eesay pahndreh**men**os (pahndreh**men**ee)?

In Greece, marriage is still regarded as a rather serious and responsible institution—particularly (or at least) as far as the wife and children are concerned—and divorces (the Orthodox Church allows each person three) are relatively rare except among the better educated, faster-living upper and upper-middle classes. Preparations for a marriage can be highly ritualized, complicated affairs and are often arranged more by the parents than by the prospective bride and groom. The settlement of a proper dowry sometimes involves prolonged negotiations, and it is not unusual for engagements to last a year or more—both for this reason and also to allow the families to get to know one another and assess their prospects together. In fact, it could be said that, in Greece, it is the families as well as the children which marry.

Marriages between Greek girls and foreign men are extremely rare, unless the man happens to be of Greek extraction. The Greeks, after having been continuously occupied by foreign powers for almost 2000 years, are very sensitive about preserving the purity of their blood, particularly through the matriarchal side. This is probably one of the biggest reasons why, against virtually all odds, they continue to survive as a people and a nation.

Marriages between Greek men and foreign girls are common, but in such a union there is very little blending of the two cultures: it is the girl, not the man, who must adapt; she must, as far as possible, eliminate her foreign notions and live and raise her children as a Greek.

Therefore, if a foreign girl is considering marriage to a Greek man, she should first look around at the married women in the city, town or village in which her prospective husband lives—if she can find them. Usually one cannot. Because, except for brief, food shopping forays, they are usually in the house cooking, cleaning, taking care of the children and washing their husband's clothes—while the husband, when not working (or even while working) is usually out on the town, sitting in some café sipping coffee, playing cards or backgammon and/or talking either with other men or with a few of the latest crop of pretty young tourist girls. To see a Greek man sitting with his wife in a café is about as rare in this country as snow in July or finding a Turk on Crete.

So, a woman's place is very definitely in the home, and if a foreign girl agrees with this point of view, she can find herself very happily married. But she should never make the mistake of thinking, even for a second, that she will be able to change her husband or that he, because he's been so attentive and "liberated" during their courtship, will turn out to be any different from other Greek men. A patriarchal system that has endured for more than 3000 years is not so easily brushed aside, and Greek men, no matter how progressive they might seem to be at moments, love it. They have been coddled in it particularly by the women in their family) since birth, and they are not about to give up any of its freedoms and privileges. Nor will the other men (and women) in the community let them. The pressure on a Greek man and his foreign bride to conform is enormous and sooner or later she will find herself relegated with the other women to the home while her husband picks up where he left off out with the boys and/or with those fascinating (because they're "free") tourist girls. Of course, times are changing—and rapidly so in Greece; since the fall of the Colonels' junta, the country has been moving increasingly closer to the West, and this growing exposure to Western ideas through TV, films, magazines and the continual presence of record numbers of tourists is particularly evident among younger Greeks, whose modes of dress and action would have been unthinkable before 1974, except perhaps in Athens: more and more women, even married ones, are working outside the home; young girls wearing jeans and slacks can be seen unchaperoned, even by a girl friend, in discotheques or sitting with their boy friends in modern cafés opened by young entrepreneurs to cater specifically to people of their age group or younger; and finally, there seems to be an increasingly casual attitude towards pre-marital sex, an astonishing development in a country where it was quite recently (and perhaps still is in certain areas) a wedding night custom for the groom to display a blood-stained sheet outside of the bedroom window as proof of his bride's virginity. Nevertheless, these old customs, linked with closely-knit, patriarchal family units, have served Greece as a bastion against foreign influences for centuries, and one doubts that even this current wave of Western liberalism will ever be able to completely breach their fortifications.

MENU, a (the)—ena (toh) menoo *or* **en**as (oh) kah**tah**logos

Greek menus are extremely unreliable, most of them being standard forms on which more than half the items listed are probably unavailable in that particular restaurant; in addition, some of the best dishes of the day may not be listed at all. So it is always best to follow the Greek custom and go into the kitchen to have a look for yourself. Most items on most menus have English translations. Therefore in the interests of space, the dishes listed here will be those that are the most uniquely Greek.

ORDERING & PAYING

waiter, a (the)—enas (oh) sehrvito**ros** *or* **en**a (toh) gar**sohn**
Waiter!—Garsohn!

Aside from yelling, another more effective way of gaining a waiter's attention, but one which is very difficult for non-Greeks to perform because it seems so imperious, is to clap your hands once or twice, loudly, in the manner of an oil-rich Arabian sheikh. Either that, or to bang on the side of a glass (if he's brought you one) with a fork or spoon (if he's brought you any). These work, if anything does, but usually, anything doesn't. My advice, having worked in a Greek restaurant, is to depend on the waiter as little as possible. When ordering, go into the kitchen yourself, find someone who looks like the boss, and point out both where you are sitting and what you want. In addition, try to secure your drinks before you get your food; otherwise, they may be brought long after you've finished eating. And if you want extra utensils, bread, napkins or more water, go and get it yourself.

When you want to pay, go in again to the boss, who is usually controlling the checks, and try to pay him on the spot.

Tipping:

For restaurant waiters the tip is usually included in the bill. This is indicated on the menu by a double list of prices, the one on the right being the cost of the food plus the tip. However, if the service has been courteous and prompt, it is customary to leave a little something extra. Give this to the waiter by hand, since any money left on the table is considered to be the property of the busboy (see below) who clears and sets the tables.

For **taverna waiters**, the tip is usually not included in the bill unless the taverna is a luxury one. Therefore, leave about 10-20%, again giving it directly to him.

For **the busboy**, one usually leaves a small tip on the table, usually under a plate.

MISCELLANEOUS ITEMS & TERMS

Waiter!	Gar**sohn**!
I want....	**Thelo**....
Please	Parakalo.
Thank you.	Efharistoh.
ashtray	ta**sah**kee
bill, the	ton logarias**mo**
bread	pso**mee**
chair	kah**rek**la
food	fahghee**toh**
Fork	peer**oo**nee
glass	po**tee**ree
knife	mak**hay**ree
lemon	le**mo**nee
mustard	moo**star**-dha
napkins	pet**set**tess
oil	**lah**-dhee
pepper	pee**peh**ree
plate	pee**ah**toh
portion of, a	**mia** meh**ree**-dha
salt	a**lah**tee
slice of, a	**mia feh**ta
table, a	**ena** trah**peh**zee
spoon	koat**ah**lee
(for soup)	(tees **soup**ahs)
straw, a	**ena** kala**mah**kee
sugar	**zak**haree
toilet, the	ee too-**ah**letta
toothpicks	odhondoh-gli**fee**-dhess
vinegar	**ksee**-dhee

water	nehro
(mineral)	metaliko nehro
wine	krahsee

The bread, knives, forks, spoons, and sometimes napkins are usually brought to the table by the waiter in a basket. The ensemble is called "**the service**"—toh sehrveetsio.

APPETIZERS	OREKTIKA or Meze-**dha**kia or Mezeh
cheese	teeree
cheese, fried	saganahkee
eggplant dip	melitzano-salata
fish-roe puree	taramosalata
meatballs	kefte-**dhah**kia
octopus	htapo-dhee
olives	eliess
smelts	maree-dhess

If these tiny fish are small enough, you can eat the whole thing, tail and all.

vine leaves, stuffed	dolma-dhess
yogurt-garlic dip	tzahtzeekee

EGGS	AVGA

Never served in restaurants and rarely in tavernas, particularly during peak hours.

SOUP	SOUPA
bean soup	fasolia soupa
egg-lemon-rice soup	avgolemono
fish soup	psarosoupa

RICE	REEZEE
rice, cooked	peelafee
with meat sauce	meh keema
with tomato sauce	meh saltsa

PASTA	ZEEMARIKA
macaroni	mahkaronia

macaroni pie	pahsteetsio
with grated cheese	meh treemeno teeree

POULTRY	POOLERIKA
chicken	kotopoulo

MEAT	**KREH-AHS**
Beef	vo-dhino
and-pasta casserole	youvetsee
stew	kokonistoh *or* stifa-dho
meatballs	kefteh-dhess
in tomato sauce	soutzoukakia
in egg-lemon sauce	youvarlakia
Goat	katseekee
Lamb	arnee
chops (large)	breezoless
(small)	paee-dhahkia
kebabs	arnee souvlahkia
(see also SOUVLAKI below)	
stew	arnee yiakhnee
Pork	Heerino
with cabbage	meh lakhano
with celery	selino
Veal	Moskharee
schnitzel	sneetzel
stew	kokinistoh moskharee
Variety Meats	Ta Sothiko
liver	seekotee
testicles	ahmeletita
	(lit. "unmentionables")

SEAFOOD	THAHLASINA
fish, a	ena psahree (pl. psahria)
shellfish	thahlasinah
baked	psahree pseetoh˙ *or* psahree plahkee
fresh	fresko
fried	teegahnitoh

frozen	kahtepsigmeno
grilled	tees **skah**ras

SAUCES:
butter-lemon	vootirole**mo**no **salt**sa
garlic puree	skordhal-**ya**
oil-lemon	ladhole**mo**no **salt**sa

bonito	pala**mee**-dha
bream, sea	fa**gree**, etc. (see **porgie** below)
cod	bahkal-**ya**ros
lobster	ahsta**kos**
mackerel	skoom**bree**
mullet (grey)	**ke**falos
(red)	bar**boo**nia
octopus	htapo-**dhee**
porgie	fa**gree**, li**three**nee, sina**gree**da, **sar**gos, tsi**poo**ra
rock fish	skor**pee**na
sea urchins	akhi**nee**
shrimp	gah**ree**-dhess
shark	gah**la**yos
smelts	mah**ree**-dhess
squid	kala**mah**ree
swordfish	ksi**fee**ahs

VEGETABLES — LAKHANIKA
beans (dried)	fasolia ksira
(fresh)	farolia **fres**ka
(dried, cooked, large)	**yee**gantess
cabbage	**lah**khano
(stuffed)	**lah**khano-dolma-**dhess**
chick peas	re**vee**thia
courgettes	koloke**ethia**
eggplant	melit**zah**ness
fried	teegani**tess**

-meat pie	moosa**kah**
greens	**hor**ta
peas, split, yellow	**fah**va
peppers, green	peeper**iess**
stuffed	yemis**tess**
potatoes	pah**tah**tess
fried	teegahni**tess**
tomatoes	to**mah**tess
stuffed	yemis**tess**
vine leaves (stuffed)	dol**ma**-dhess
zucchini	kolo**kee**thia

SALADS	SA**LAH**TESS
a salad	**mi**a sa**la**ta
Greek salad	horiahti**kee** sa**la**ta

DESSERTS   EPI-**DHOR**PIA

With the exception of fruit and (perhaps) yogurt with (perhaps) honey, desserts (and coffee) are normally not served in any Greek restaurants aside from those in the luxury, international category. One must go instead to a combination confectionary store-and-cafe called a "zakharopla**stee**oh".

SOUVLAKI   SOUV**LAH**KEE

Cubed, sliced *or* ground meat grilled on a skewer, i.e. shishke-babs, the name deriving from the Greek word **souv**la, which means "skewer" *or* "roasting spit." When the meat is ground and pressed upon a revolving skewer, it is sometimes called "**yee**ro," which means "around" or "turning". Thus the name "gyro" in English.

These are sold either as main courses in restaurants *or* from side-walk shops as fast-food snacks. The latter are almost a national pas-time, as popular in Greece as hot dogs and hamburgers are in America. They come in various forms with various garnishings, and no two shops sell the same quality, so one must and should experi-ment. A brief lexicon:

peeta—the flat, round, unleavened bread in which the meat is wrapped.

yeero—either ground *or* sliced meat pressed into a large, conical shape and grilled electrically on a long, vertical, rotating skewer from which the portions to make a souvlaki are sliced.

kala**mah**ki—small cubes of meat (usually pork) grilled on a thin wooden skewer. Usually served with a chunk of bread, but one can ask for it with pita: "kala**mah**ki meh **pee**ta."

souv**lah**ki—the generic name for all types of souvlaki as well as the specific name of the commonest variety: cigar-shaped beef patties mixed with spices and grilled on a skewer.

one souvlaki—**en**a souv**lah**ki (pl. souv**lah**kia); **with pita**—meh **pee**ta; **with garnishings**—com**pleh** *or* meh **oh**la; **without onions**—**ho**rees **kre**mee-dhee.

(The garnishings are usually tomatoes and chopped parsley and onions, or if you're lucky, they will also include yogurt and french fries.)

MIDWIFE, a (the)—**mi**a (ee) mah**mee**

Midwives and midwifery are traditional and legitimized institutions in Greece, and it would be reasonable to estimate that well over 50% of the country's present population has been delivered by midwives alone, which is to say without the aid of a gynecologist. Although most midwives have had only minimal medical training (and some none at all), they are respected and revered by the members of their communities, the majority of whom would much prefer to have a midwife rather than a qualified doctor deliver their babies.

MOMENT, a—**mi**a **steeg**mee; **just a moment**—**mi**a **steeg**mee

You will quickly learn that moments in Greece do not pass as rapidly as they are expected to do in the rest of Western Civilization. In fact, a moment can consume as much as a half an hour, or even more, especially when you are waiting for a waiter to bring you something to eat. There is virtually nothing you can do about this except, perhaps, to make sure you always carry with you something to read while waiting. See also ah**meh**sos.

MONARCHY, the—ee mohnar**khee**a

Although the monarchy was seemingly forever abolished by popular referendum in 1974, no book about Greece and its people would be complete without an understanding of its role in the history of modern Greece and, particularly, of the often stormy attraction which it (and various forms of authoritarian government) seems to have held for the Greek people. In spite of a proud and fierce independence of spirit which allowed them to survive almost 2000 consecutive years of foreign domination—from the victory of Rome over the Achaean League in 146 B.C. to the successful revolt against the Turks in 1821—with hardly a bristle of their essential Greekness altered, the Greek people, at the same time, seem to have in their nature a need for and a fascination with the sway of a strong, domineering father-figure—whether it be in the shape of a democratically elected leader, a dictator, a monarch, or a foreign power such as, in recent years, Britain and the United States. But this is very much a love-hate relationship, a kind of schizophrenia that has kept the Greek character and the Greek nation constantly at war with itself over the last 150 years and produced the incredible upheavals listed in the chronology below. It is an era about which most of us, preferring to think of Greece only as our "cradle of democracy," are shockingly uninformed. To have some knowledge of it will not only deepen your understanding of the Greek people today but also, perhaps, of what their future may hold.

1831—The Kingdom of Greece is created by Britain, France, and Russia after the leader of Greece's post-revolutionary regime, Capodistrias, is assassinated. Otto I of Bavaria is named Greece's first king.

1843—Otto gives into demands for a constitutional monarchy after revolts in Athens.

1862-63—An internal coup brings down Otto I. After refusing to allow Queen Victoria's son, whom the Greeks voted for, to assume the throne, the British propose Prince William George of Denmark. A Greek election ratifies this choice, and he becomes King George I.

1909—A military coup forces George I to replace his premier, Mavromichalis, with Venizelos, the hero of the Cretan War of Independence.

1910—George I assassinated in Thessaloniki. Succeeded by son, Constantine I.

1911—Venizelos reforms the 1864 constitution, granting more individual freedoms as well as protections against abuses by the state.

1915—Constantine I dismisses Venizelos in a dispute over whether or not to remain neutral in World War I, Venizelos wishing to enter the war on the side of the Allies. Consequently, the Allies begin a blockade of Greece.

1916—Venizelos forms a rebel government at Thessaloniki.

1917—The Allies' blockade finally forces Constantine I to abdicate in favor of his youngest son, Alexander. Constantine goes into exile, Venizelos returns as premier, and Greece enters the war on the side of the Allies.

1920—Alexander I dies. Venizelos, campaigning to continue fighting against Turkey (with the encouragement of the Allies, who have already signed the armistice ending their part in W.W.I) is voted out of power by the war-weary Greeks. The royalists, having campaigned on a pacifist program, assume power and organize a plebiscite which returns Constantine I to the throne. They then resume the war against Turkey (again with the encouragement of the Allied powers).

1922—The massacre of the Greek army and Greek civilians by the Turks at Smyrna ends the war. A coup d'état by army officers forces Constantine I to abdicate again, this time in favor of his oldest son, who becomes King George II. Greece ruled by a Revolutionary Committee of army officers.

1923—Elections, held after months of attempts by the Revolutionary Committee to reconcile royalists and Venizelists, are won by the Venizelists. George II quickly leaves Greece. Admiral Coundouriotis becomes regent in his absence.

1924—After a series of parliamentary struggles, Venizelos cedes power to the republicans, who proclaim Greece, after 93 years as a monarchy, a republic again. The regent, Coundouriotis, is named President.

1925—The constitution is overthrown as a military coup d'état establishes General Pangalos as dictator.

1926—Another military coup re-establishes the constitution.

1928—Venizelos, winning the general elections, begins 4 years as premier.

1933—A rapid succession of weak parliamentary governments provokes another military coup on the eve of the 1933 elections. An attempt to assassinate Venizelos fails.

1935—A revolt organized by Venizelos in Athens, Macedonia, and Crete is put down by General Condylis, who, as Venizelos flees to France, ousts the current premier and organizes a plebiscite which restores the monarchy and brings George II back to Greece.

1936—Venizelos dies in exile. General Metaxas, named premier by the king, abolishes the constitution and becomes, with the full accord of George II, dictator of Greece. All political opposition is suppressed, as is anything that reeks of democratic ideas, such as Sophocles's Antigone and Pericles's Funeral Oration.

1938—Metaxas named premier for life.

1941—Metaxas dies. As Hitler's armies invade Greece, George II and his government flee to Cairo, establishing a government-in-exile there for most of the war.

1943—While still fighting the Axis occupation, Greek royalist, communist, and republican resistance groups also start fighting each other.

1944 (Oct.)—The British army enters Athens, followed a few days later by the Greek government-in-exile, although George II remains in London pending another plebiscite.

1944 (Dec.)—Communist resistance groups refuse a British order to turn in their arms and fighting breaks out in the streets of Athens between the communists and British and Greek government troops.

1946—As full civil war erupts in Greece, a plebiscite organized by the royalist government returns George II to the throne.

1947—George II dies and is succeeded by his brother, Paul I. The Truman Doctrine is proclaimed and $ 300 million in aid as well as U.S. military advisers are sent to Greece.

1949—The Civil War ends as the communists are defeated following Tito's break with Moscow. Severe curtailment of civil liberties as the government temporarily reverts to the 1911 Constitution. Communist party outlawed. The U.S. replaces Britain as the principle foreign influence in Greece.

1952—The rightist "Greek Rally" party wins elections under a new electoral system devised with the aid of the American ambassador and, with close royalist ties, begins an uninterrupted 14 years in power.

1963—Grigoris Lambrakis (the subject of the novel and film, "**Z**") a deputy of the far left EDA party, is murdered by extreme rightists. Suspicion that this was done with the tacit complicity of the police and the government is one of the factors that causes the premier, Constantine Caramanlis, to step down and call for new elections. Caramanlis loses elections and goes into exile in Paris.

1964—The Center Union Party, led by George Papandreou, is voted into power and succeeds in forming a government, thus breaking the rightists' 14-year reign. Paul I dies and is succeeded by his son, Constantine II. However, it is generally conceded that the real power is held by his mother, Queen Frederika.

1965—After carrying out a series of somewhat progressive reforms, Papandreou is forced to resign as premier when Constantine II refuses to sign his directives aimed at purging the army.

1967 (April)—Several attempts by the Royalists to form a government having failed, parliament is dissolved and new elections are scheduled for May 28th, elections which Papandreou's party seems certain to win. A coup d'état planned by army generals to preempt the elections is itself preempted by another coup organized by army colonels. Colonel Papadopoulos emerges as the head of the new military junta.

Constantine II and his family flee to Rome after failing to rouse the people's support in an ineptly-conceived attempt at a counter-coup.

1973—A plebiscite organized by the junta abolishes the monarchy by an overwhelming and scarcely-believable majority. A "republic" is proclaimed with Papadopoulos as its president.

(Nov.-Dec.) A student revolt at Athens Polytechnic, brutally and bloodily put down by the army, forces Papadopoulos to resign. Ghizikis, a moderate, is named president, but the real power is held by General Ioannides, head of the Greek Secret Police.

1974 (July 24)—Ioannides and the junta collapse after their abortive attempt to assassinate Archbishop Makarios and seize power in Cyprus. Former premier Caramanlis is called back from exile to head a new government. War with Turkey is barely avoided.

(Dec.) A plebiscite organized by the new government again overwhelmingly abolishes the monarchy, but this time by a much more believable margin. Constantine II, in Rome, declares that he accepts the people's decision.

1975—A new constitution modeled after De Gaulle's 5th Republic is adopted. In the subsequent general elect ions, Caramanlis's right-of-center party wins by an overwhelming majority.

1977—Caramanlis's majority is considerably decreased as PASOK, the Socialist party of Andreas Papandreou, son of the former prime minister, doubles its gains.

1980—Caramanlis is elected president, being succeeded as prime minister by George Rallis.

1981—Queen Frederika dies in exile but the Greek government allows her to be buried at the former palace of Tatoi, north of Athens, provoking a storm of protest.

The Socialist Party wins a clear majority in new elections. Papandreou becomes prime minister while Caramanlis continues as president.

1996—Papandreou dies in office. Constantine II remains, as did his namesake and other monarchs before him, waiting in exile.

MONEY—hree**mata** *or* hree**ma** *or* lef**ta**; **I want to change money—Thelo na ahlahkso hreemata; I don't have much (enough) money**—Dhen eh-ho pola (arketa) hree**mata; Do you have any money?**—Eh-hees lef**ta?**

one drachma—**mi**a dhrahk**mee** (pl. dhrahk**mess**).

Greek money comes in bills of 50, 100, 500, 1000, 5000 and 10,000 drachma denominations, while coins come in pieces of 1, 2, 5, 10, 20, 50 and 100 drachmas.

Colloquial Expressions:
1 drachma—**en**a fran**ko**; 2 drachmas—dhee fran**ko**; 5 drachmas—**en**a tah**leero** (because 5 drachmas were once worth one dollar); 10 drachmas—**en**a dhekar**iko**; 20 drachmas—**en**a eekosar**iko**; 50 drachmas—**en**a peneendar**iko**; 100 drachmas—**en**a ekatostar**iko**; 1000 drachmas—**en**a heeliar**iko**; 5000 drachmas—**en**a pende-heeliar**o**; 10,000 drachmas—**en**a dekheeli**aro**

MONEY ORDER, a (the)—mia—(ee) takhi-dhromikee **epitagyee; I want to send a money order to...—Thel**o **na steel**o **mia** takhidhromi**kee** epitag**yee** sto...; **I'm waiting for a money order—Perimen**o epitag**yee**.

Money orders within Greece may be sent either by post or telegraph or from bank to bank. The fastest way seems to be by telegraph (which is sent from and received at the post, not the telegraph, office), the money often arriving the next day whereas with the other two systems (post or bank), it takes at least a week and sometimes two. However, you should be warned that all three systems are fraught, more often than not, with mysterious and agonizing delays, the money seemingly disappearing en route as though the system itself were trying to clutch it to its bosom as long as possible before coughing it up, which is not a far-fetched idea considering the perennial shortness of the money supply in Greece.

Money orders sent from outside the country should be sent in care of your name to the National Bank of Greece in your area. These, too, are often subject to interminable delays. Keep the receipt.

MOURNING—penthos; **He (she) is in mourning—Eh-**hee **pen**thos.

The act of mourning in Greece is one that is both deeply felt and highly stylized; it is literally an "act"—a public ritual that serves as a catharsis not only for the mourner (who cold be called "the actor") but for the mourner's community of friends and acquaintances ("the audience").

Keening, wailing and weeping to an extent that would shock stiff-upper-lip Western sensibilities is carried out unashamedly in public—but only by the women of the dead person's family: it is they who are the designated "chief" mourners; the men, relegated to a secondary position on these occasions, keep a manly silence, leaving the consolation of their women to other women while looking slightly embarrassed by this excessive display of grief.

But the men, too, have their own "act". It is purely physical; a slumping of the shoulders, a slowness of step, a heaviness that weighs down every tiny gesture to such an extent that it seems as though grief has literally thickened the air around them, that they are moving through its depths the way a diver moves through the dark and heavy water on the bottom of the sea; and for a week, at least, they go unshaven so that everyone can see how little they care for worldly appearances.

But suddenly, like a cloud passing away from the sun, this opening act of the mourning ritual also passes: the women stop weeping, the men shave again, and everyone resumes, as if they had never stopped, the daily task of attending to life.

Still, the ritual is not over; it continues for at least another 40 days, the women donning black dresses, shoes, stockings, and shawls, and the men either black clothes or armbands. The length of this second act depends upon the mourners and upon the depth of their grief for the people who have died; it may last only a month or it could last a lifetime—which is why you will see, particularly in the remoter villages and islands, so many, many old women, who have lost, perhaps, both a husband and a child, draped forever in black.

Death, then, is always highly visible in Greece; you can never pretend it doesn't exist. It walks arm-in-arm with life, like a fully integrated and accepted member of society—which, of course, it must be, finally.

MUSHROOMS—mahni**ta**ria.

There are numerous varieties of wild mushrooms in Greece, quite a few of them deadly poisonous. Even the Greeks, who should know better, often don't, so it is wise not to take a chance, even when you're assured that they're perfectly harmless. As I write this, there is a man dying of mushroom poisoning in a nearby hospital; his wife and two children have already been buried; and there is a possibility that the mushrooms they ate were bought in the local market.

NEWSPAPER, a (the)—mia (ee) efime**ree**-dha (pl. efime**ree**-dhess); **American (English) newspapers**—Americani**kess** (Ahngli**kess**) efime**ree**-dhess

There are several English-language newspapers and magazines published in Athens, the majority of their news concentrating, of course, on Greek-related issues. Their chief value to tourists lies in their listings of boat schedules, shopping hours, and what's on at the cinema, theater, etc., as well as their advertisements for restaurants, doctors, dentists, hairdressers, et al, and their daily stock market and currency exchange listings.

British newspapers (a day or two late) are sold in most major cities and tourist areas, as is the International Herald Tribune (a day late), and, at newsstands in Athens' Constitution Square, one can occasionally find even the N.Y. Times (several days late.)

NICKNAME, a (the)—ena (toh) parat**sook**lee

Nicknames abound in Greece, one reason being that there are often so many people with the same given name in a particular area (due, usually, to the popularity of certain local saints and the practice of handing down family names that nicknames are the only way of distinguishing one individual from another. But there also seems to be an echo of Homeric times in this affixing of a descriptive adjective or appellation to a person's name, as in "wily Odysseus," "gray-eyed Athena," and "Hector, the slayer of men." So nowadays, you will find people called "Oh **Ko**kinohs" ("The Red One") because of their red face and high blood pressure, or "Oh Pse**los**" which means "the tall one." Other nicknames—the most colorful ones—evolve from specific instances in a person's life. I know a Cretan man who once, when he was five years old, stole some olive oil from his mother and tried to exchange it at the grocery store for candy. To this day, 45 years later, he is known to one-and-all as "Lahdho-**yan**nis"—"Oil John."

OPTICIAN, an (the)—enas (oh) opti**kos** (written as: ΟΠΤΙΚΟΣ); **eyeglasses, my—**ta yaliah mou; **sunglasses—**yaliah tou ee**li**oo; **contact lenses—**fahkoos epa**feess**; **lens, a (the)—en**as (oh) fah**kos**; **prescription, the—**ee seentagyee; **broken—**spahsmena; **lost—**hahmena; **Can you repair them (by tomorrow)?—** Bor**ee**teh na ta episke**vah**seteh (ohs **ah**vrio)?; **Can you make me new ones?—**Bor**ee**teh na mou **kah**neteh kenoo**ria**?; **When will they be ready?—**Poteh tha **ee**nay e**tee**ma?: **How much will it cost?—P**oso tha kost**ee**si?

It has been this writer's experience that most opticians in Greece work very well and quite quickly if necessary. Lenses are relatively inexpensive but frames, as everywhere, are exorbitant.

ORTHODOX CHURCH, the—Ee Ortho-dhoksos Ekleeseea

The Greek Orthodox Church is one of a number of Orthodox churches which broke away from the Roman Catholic church in 1054. The single basic difference between the Catholic and Orthodox churches is the latter's refusal to accept papal authority, while the Orthodox churches differ from Protestant ones in embracing many distinctly Catholic beliefs and practices, such as the intrinsic grace of the Sacrament and a veneration of the Virgin Mary. Finally, there is a touch of both Protestantism and Catholicism in the fact that although Orthodox parish priests are permitted to marry, the upper ranks of the clergy and its monks are not.

Apart from its religious function, the church is very much of a social and political force in Greece, and its bishops are constantly embroiling themselves in affairs which other countries have long ago decided should be left to the state. On the other hand, the parish priests are, for the most part, eminently non-authoritarian; often married and with children, they tend to share not only their community's manual labor but also a bit of its members' moral lapses; were it not for their beards and cassocks, it would sometimes be extremely difficult to tell the priest from their congregations and, occasionally, its sinners. But this is one of the most striking aspects, at least on a parish level and to a mind raised in Judeo-Christian anguish, of the Greek Orthodox Church: its tolerance of human fallibility in both its laity and its priests—and you rarely find either of them rising up in outraged condemnation of the errors of the other. There seems to be very little sense of guilt around. This is most evident in parish services: people usually stand, rather than sit, strolling in and out at their convenience while the priest is chanting the liturgy; friends gossip, children play, babies cry, and one often has the feeling that one's in a café, not a church. But the faith is there; you can feel that, too, most palpably; you can feel it being enjoyed.

PASSPORT, a (the)—ena (toh) dheeavateerio; **I've lost my pass-port**—Eh-ho hahsee toh dheeavateerioh mou; **My passport has been stolen**—Mou klepsahneh toh dheeavateerio.

Lost or stolen passports should be reported immediately to the local police and as quickly as possible to your embassy in Athens.

Your embassy will then tell you the rather complicated routine you must follow in order to obtain a new one. Expired passports can usually be renewed in a matter of hours at your embassy.

PATIENCE—eepomonee

A favorite word of the Greeks, and one that you will hear very often, for very good reasons. Patience is perhaps the single greatest virtue one can have (or learn to have) in dealing with the Greek way of life. Greeks are rarely in a hurry about anything, and nothing or no one ever seems to be on time. Therefore, my advice is to always carry something to read with you, particularly if your mission is urgent.

PEDIATRICIAN, a (the)—enas (oh) pay-dhee-ahtros (written as: ΠΑΙΔΙΑΤΡΟΣ)

Most Greek pediatricians, being Greek, are characteristically solicitous about children, gentle and thorough in their examinations, and conscientious in their training*. The ones in the major cities often speak either English, French or German, having trained abroad. To find one, check the English language Blue Pages of the local telephone directory. In addition, for people without much money, there is a state-supported organization called "**Peek**-pah" (ΠΙΚΠΑ) for which independent pediatricians supply their services 2 or 3 times a week; the care, even for foreigners, is either free or costs very little. Ask the Tourist Police in your area for the address.

*Since writing this, I have had several opinions to the contrary, people saying that I am being far too generous with Greek pediatricians. Perhaps I have been lucky; or perhaps they have been unlucky.

PHARMACY, a (the)—ena (toh) farmakeeo

(written as: ΦΑΡΜΑΚΕΙΟΝ); **Where is the pharmacy?**—Poo eenay toh farmakeeo?; **Which pharmacy is open?**—Peeoh farmakeeo eenay aneektoh?

In all cities and towns, the law requires that there be at least one pharmacy open 24 hours a day, even on Sundays, and that the address of this open pharmacy be posted in the windows of all the other pharmacies. The easiest way to find the open pharmacy is to enlist the aid of a taxi driver, particularly in a large city. In small towns and on islands, the resident doctor is usually the pharmacist, and all medicines, baby supplies, etc. can be bought in his office. Cosmetics, etc. can be found in tourist shops, kiosks, and various other, often unlikely, locations.

Prescriptions are required for certain medicines, but most can be bought over the counter, particularly if you are a foreigner and seem to know exactly what you want. Whether or not you will get it largely depends upon the pharmacist himself end his own personal set of guidelines.

PHOTOGRAPH, a (the)—mia (ee) fotografee**a** (pl. fotografee-ess); **to take a photograph—**na vgahlo mia fotografeea; **I want to take a photograph of you (it)—The**lo na sou (tou) vgahlo mia fotografeea; **Will you take a photograph of me (us)?—**Tha mou (mas) **vgah**lees **mi**a fotografeea?; **I'll send you the photographs—**Tha sou **stee**lo tees fotografee-ess; **passport photo, a—mi**a fotografeea ya dheeavateerio; **I need photographs for my passport (visa, permit)—Pre**pee na **eh**-ho fotografee-ess ya toh dheeavateerio (teen **ah**-dhia) mou; **four copies—te**sera ahn-tee**gia**fa

Automatic photo booths for Greek permit size photos are beginning to spring up around Greece. In Athens, the most centrally convenient is located in the Omonia Square subway station. In addition, there is a photography shop specializing in U.S.-size passport photos just across the side street behind the American Embassy which will develop the photos while you wait.

PHOTOGRAPHER, a (the)—enas (oh) foto**grah**fos; **photography shop, a (the)—en**a (toh) fotografee**oh**

There are photography shops all over Greece, but only those in the larger cities and islands are equipped to develop color film. In any case, if you are in a remote area, it is always best, even with black-and-white film, to curb your impatience to have it developed and wait until you reach a large city. Local photographers, although well-intentioned, often have primitive equipment and techniques, and your negative could end up badly damaged. In Athens, black-and-white film can be ready in a day or two, and color film in about a week. The Kodak laboratory there is excellent.

FILM, a (the—ena (toh) feelm; **movie**—kinimatograhfoo; **black-and-white**—ahspromahvro; **color**—enghromo; **color negative**—enghromo arneetikoh; **daylight**—ya fohs tees eemehras; **artificial light**—ya tekneetoh fohs; **instamatic**—eenstamahteek; **for prints**—ya kopiess; **for slides**—ya slaeeds; **20 (36) exposures**—eekosee (treeahnda-eksee) fotografee-ess; **This size**—aftoh toh meghethos (and then point):

120 (6x6)	127 (4x4)	135 (24 x 36)
8 mm.	Super 8	16 MM.

ASA (**Ah**sa) 64 80 100 125 200 400
DIN (**Deen**)) 19 20 21 24 25 27

DEVELOP (to)—na emfaneesees; **Can you develop this?**—Boreeteh na toh emfaneeseteh?; **How many days?**—Posess mehress?; **I want one (two) copies of each**—Thelo mia kopia (dheeoh kopiess) ahpo toh kathena; **How much for each print?**—Poso ya katheh kopia?; **This size**—Aftoh toh megethos; **glossy**—yaleestero; **mat**—maht; **negative, a (the)**—ena (toh) arneetikoh; **Can you enlarge this?**—Boreeteh na meg-yentheeneteh aftoh?; **The film is jammed (broken)**—Toh feelm eenay blegmeno (spahsmeno).

CAMERA, a (the)—mia (ee) fotografikee meekhanee; **battery, a (the)**—mia (ee) bahtareea (pl. bahtareeess); **case, a (the)**—mia (ee) theekee; **exposure counter, the**—oh metritees ton fotografeeon; **film winder, the**—toh yeerisma ya toh feelm; **filter, a (the)**—ena (toh) feeltro (ultraviolet—eeperioh-dhess); **flash bulbs**—ahmpooless ya toh flahs; **cube**—keevo flahs; **electronic**—eelectronikoh flahs; **lens, the**—oh fahkos; **lens cap, a (the)**—ena (toh) kahleema; **hood, a (the)**—ena (toh) parasoleh; **light meter, a (the)**—ena (toh) fotohmetro; **rangefinder, the**—toh teelehmetro; **shutter, the**—toh kleestro or dheeahfragma; **spool, the**—ee bobeena; **tripod, a (the)**—ena (toh)—treepo-dhoh; **view-finder, the**—toh skopeftro
It doesn't work—Dhen dholevee

POLICE, the—ee ahstino**mee**a; **policeman, a (the) en**as (oh) ahsteenomos *or* **en**as (oh) horo**feel**akas; **police station, the**—toh ahstinomi**koh tmee**ma; **Tourist Police, the**—ee Tooristi**kee** Ahstino**mee**a

As in most countries, the personality of the individual Greek policeman varies from person to person and place to place; it also depends upon the personality of his superiors and upon whether or not it was a democratic or totalitarian regime which put him there. Greek police are, by and large, quite Greek—which is to say, quite human—particularly those working in small communities, and you, as a tourist, should find them both helpful and dependable, no matter what your problem may be. Unless, of course, you've broken the law; in that case, particularly if the offense is a serious one, you will not find them sympathetic at all. It should also be noted that there are a large number of undercover policemen and police informers working assiduously to entrap drug-and-dope sellers and users; these men, usually young and handsome, are exceptionally charming and can be very helpful about telling you where to buy dope; they will also put you in the slammer without a moment's hesitation or twinge of conscience.

POLLUTION—**moh**leensees

As the Mediterranean as a whole becomes increasingly polluted, so too do the seas and shores of Greece. It is not the fault of the local Greeks, who are usually scrupulously clean. Complaints should be made to the owners of tourist cruise ships, who dump their garbage at sea, and to industrialists whose factory waters run down rivers like the Rhine into the Mediterranean. On the other hand, the credit for making Athens the most polluted city in the world can be claimed entirely by the Greeks, who continue to crowd into the city in search of "a better life", and whose various governments have done virtually nothing to reverse the process or improve the existing living conditions.

POLYTECHNIC, the—toh pohleetek**nee**on

The Athens Polytechnic is now renowned in Greece as the site of the student revolt of 1973 which eventually led to the downfall of the

Colonels' junta. It is therefore much more than a university to most Greeks; rather, it is a monument to heroism and will undoubtedly remain so for many, many years.

PORTER, a (the)—enas (oh) ahk-thof**oros**; **I want a porter, please—Thel**o **ena** ahk-thof**oro**, parakalo.

Porters in airports, train stations and ports are generally dressed in grayish khaki uniforms. They can be some of the biggest hustlers in Greece, although not that dishonest unless they think they can get away with it—which they often think they can with foreigners. On the other hand, they work hard and fast and even the oldest ones seem capable of carrying loads fit only for elephants. As for payment, it is impossible in this age of galloping inflation to indicate a fair price. I always try to work things out per piece of luggage and take into account the distance it is carried and the time consumed and then offer 75% of what I would pay back home. Greece is no longer the inexpensive economic paradise it once was—neither for the tourist nor for the inhabitants. Finally, if you have two or three porters carrying your luggage at the same time (this often happens, as they work in groups), give what you would pay one to one of them; they will split it up later. There is, in addition, a species of porter who works with a two-wheeled cart (**carots**a). He is very useful for transporting large amounts of luggage from taxis to ships or from ships to hotels. He also usually has a flat and honest fee. However, he is not allowed on board a ship; you must use the other porters for that.

POST OFFICE, a (the)—ena (toh) takhee-dhrom**eeo** (wntten on yellow signs with black letters as: *or* E~TA)

I want (to send)	**Thel**o (na **steel**o)...
address, the	ee dhee-**ef**theensee
return	oh ahposto**leh**-efs
aerogram, a	**ena** ah-ehrogr**ah**ma (pl. ah-ehrogr**ah**mata)
airmail	ah-ehropori**koh**
care of (c/o)	meh**reem**nee tou
express	ekspress
general delivery	pohst rest**ahnt**

letter, a (the)	ena (toh) **grah**ma (pl. **grah**mata)
money order	epita**gyee** (see above)
package, a (the)	ena (toh) **dhehma**
postage, the	ta takheedhromi**ka**
post card	cart pos**tahl**
Poste Restante	**Pohst** Res**tahnt**
printed matter	en**tee**pa
registered	seestime**no**
special delivery	eks**press**
stamp, a	ena grama**toh**simo (pl. grama**toh**sima)
collection	seelo**gyee**
surface mail	takti**koh** takheedhro**mee**o

Greek post offices are open Mon—Fri, although the hours differ from city to town and island to island. All are definitely open in the mornings from about 8 A.M. to noon. Afternoon hours depend on the local customs and shopping hours. Big city post offices are generally open all day long, although during the afternoon siesta hours it may be difficult to find someone to send a package or money order.

Postage stamps can be bought either at the post office or at certain sidewalk kiosks, although the owners may not necessarily know the rates for various countries. Stamps for collectors are sold at all post offices.

Post Restante (written that way on envelopes) is the general address to which all your mail can be sent, i.e. Your Name, Poste Restante, Patmos, Greece. When asking for mail, you must present your passport as identification.

Printed matter (written as ΕΝΤΥΠΑ on the envelope) is the cheapest way to send bulky printed material, such as manuscripts, abroad by air mail. It must weigh less than 2 kilos and the envelopes must not be sealed, but can be tied with a string after they are inspected (to see that they contain only printed matter and no letters) by the postal clerk.

Packages must be left open for inspection before they are sent abroad. Receiving packages (except, sometimes, very small ones) from abroad can involve one in incredibly complicated (and sometimes expensive) customs procedures, particularly in the remoter areas and small islands. Often there is no resident customs inspector and one must either wait for his weekly visit before one can take the package or, if an exorbitant amount of duty has been imposed on the contents, one must go to the place where the customs office is (sometimes 100 miles away) in order to complain. Needless to say, passports must be presented when picking up packages.

PRIDE (self-respect)—feelotimo; **conceit**—eeperoseea

Feelotimo is an extremely potent emotional force in Greece, both on an individual and a national level. Individual Greeks kill one another in order to preserve their self-respect, sometimes for reasons that to Western eyes would seem absurdly innocuous. On a national level, this sense of pride explains not only Greece's survival as a nation after almost 2000 years of foreign occupation, but also its people's current enmity towards the United States. Individual Greeks may permit themselves to like individual Americans, but it will be a long time before the Greek people as a whole ever forget the insult done to them by the U.S. government's support of the Colonels' junta or its failure to prevent or solve the Cyprus crisis.

PROSTITUTE, a (the)—**mi**a (ee) poo**tah**na (pl. poo**tah**ness)

Prostitution is legal in Greece, and prostitutes are, for the most part, accepted members of the communities in which they work, human beings like everyone else performing a necessary (if slightly disreputable) social function. The film "Never On Sunday" gives a fairly accurate portrait of this relationship, although the carefree Piraeus in which it took place has gone considerably downhill since and at times can be rather dangerous. In smaller communities, like the one in which I am now living, bordellos make a point of doing their business in the afternoons and evenings, closing before midnight so as not to tempt husbands and young men to stay out too late and offend their wives and mothers.

Most, but not all, prostitutes are police-regulated and required to have a medical check-up at least once a week. This, of course is no guarantee of anything.

QUEUE, a (the)—mia (ee) oo**rah**

Although the word exists in Greek, the basic concept does not, except perhaps in lines at supermarkets, taxi stands and sometimes banks, but even in these places one is constantly in danger of being shoved out of the way by a continuing series of late arrivals. At shop counters, bus stops, ticket offices, etc., success and survival go to the fittest and most aggressive, so don't be embarrassed about shoving anyone aside, especially little old ladies; they are, by far and from years of experience, the worst offenders.

RAILROAD, the—oh seedheero-**dhromos; railroad station, a (the)—en**as (oh) stath**mos tray**nou; **by rail**—meh tray**no; I want one (two) tickets for...—Thel**o en**a eesiteerio (dheeo eesiteeria) ya...; When does the train leave?—Pot**eh fev**ghee toh tray**no?; Which platform?—Piah apovathra?; luggage depot, the—ee ahpotheek**ee ahposkev**ohn.

There are two railroad stations in Athens,. the Stathmos Larissa (for northern Greece, Yugoslavia, Turkey, etc.) and the Stath**mos** Peloponisou (for the Peloponnese). Both are located on the opposite side of the same tracks quite near Omonia Square. There are corresponding stations in Piraeus. Tickets can be bought from numerous travel agencies throughout Athens and Piraeus, or at the station, or on the train.

RAPE—veeasmos

Relatively rare in Greece as most Greek men are still being well brought up enough to take "no" for an answer, in spite of their male-dominated society and the macho manner with which many of them come on. Basically, Greek men—underneath it all—are a lot like little boys: very careful not to offend so as not to be badly-thought-of, and therefore, relatively easy to control. However, in remoter areas and places like the wilds of Crete, not to mention Athens, it is wise not to accept rides alone with a man, particularly if he's drunk and seems to have gotten the idea that you've come to Greece to find yourself a strapping Zorba type; he might just take "no" as part of the game and you could be in trouble. It's happened before and no one should consider themselves an exception.

In such cases, one ought not to feel embarrassed (easy to say...) about going immediately to the police; all Greeks abhor this kind of stain on their community's and country's honor, and they always treat its victim with the utmost solicitude and courtesy. Besides, should the violator be left unpunished, he will undoubtedly feel free to do it again—and again...

RENT, the—toh eneekio *or* toh **neekee**; **What's the rent?**—Tee eenay toh eneekio?; **rent (to)**—na eneekiahso; **I want to rent a room (house/car). Thel**o na eneekiahso ena dhohmatio (**speetee/aftokeenitoh toh**); **for 2 days (one month)**—ya **dhee**o **mehr**ess (**ena mee**na)

When renting anything, it is always advisable to agree first upon both a price and the length of the rental period. It is also best to pay in advance and to get a receipt (**mia ahpo**-dhiksee). Prices in the summer tend to abruptly rise as soon as demand exceeds supply, and I have too often seen solid verbal agreements abrogated by the owner's sudden thirst to make some extra drachmas. In addition; if you are renting a house, find out who's paying for the gas and electricity. Usually it's you.

SCORPION, a (the)—enas (oh) skorpio**hs** (pl. skorpi-**ee**)

Scorpions are prevalent throughout Greece during the spring and summer, but are usually found only in the countryside, particularly around woodpiles. The pain of the sting is quite severe, although that is usually the worst of it. Fatalities are extremely rare. However, should stomach pains, nausea and vomiting develop, a doctor should be found as quickly as possible; this means that the person is quite sensitive to the venom and a coma and death could follow. Otherwise, for minor stings, cold applications and lotions such as Benadryl help.

SCUBA DIVING—boht**eel**yes kata-**dhee**sios

Scuba diving equipment is available throughout Greece but diving for fish using air bottles is strictly forbidden; one is only allowed to use bottles for pleasure-diving, underwater photography, etc. Of course, this particular law is easily ignored, but should a local fisherman decide to report you to the police, your equipment could be confiscated and you deported.

SEA URCHIN, a (the)—enas (oh) akhi**nohs** (pl. ee akhi**nee**)

The latter are prevalent throughout Greece, particularly near rocks and in harbors, and are quite painful if stepped on. One must, to avoid constant irritation and possible infection, pull out all of the tiny, almost invisible spines.

As hors d'oeuvres, these are considered a great delicacy by the Greeks. The five orange or reddish ovaries are eaten raw like clams; the texture is slimy, the taste pungent of sea water. A little lemon juice helps.

SEASICKNESS—nafteea; **I am seasick—Meh** pee**ah**nee ee **tha**lassa; **He (she) is seasick—Ton** (teen) pee**ah**nee ee **tha**lassa.

Dramamine (dhrama-**mee**nee) and various other remedies for seasickness are available all over Greece, often at sidewalk kiosks. The Greeks, surprisingly, seem to be the most seasick-prone people in the world and are often greenish-white even before the ship leaves the harbor. Although much of this is undoubtedly psychological, there is also good reason for their fears: the Aegean is the most unpredictable of seas and can change from beautifully calm to horribly rough in moments. So if you are prone to seasickness, it would be wise to take some Dramamine even if there isn't a swell or a puff of wind in sight. If you're caught without any medicine, an old Greek remedy advises sucking on a lemon. It would also be wise to go out on deck where you can breathe some fresh air and, most important, orient yourself with the horizon so that your inner ear can get its bearings again.

SHARK, a (the)—enas (oh) karkha**ree**as *or* **en**a (toh) skeelo**psa**ro

Sharks do exist in the Mediterranean, but they rarely, if ever, come close to the shore, preferring to stay in those parts of the shipping lanes where they are well-fed with garbage, usually several hundred yards out to sea.

SHIP, a (the)—ena (toh) **pleeoh** or **en**a (toh) kah**rah**vee (pl. ta pleeah, kah**rah**via); **shipowner, a (the)—en**as (oh) pleeok**tee**-tees; **cargo ship, a (the)—en**a (toh) for**tee**go **plee**oh.

Departure schedules for ships leaving from Piraeus to the various Greek islands are published daily in the Athenian English-language newspapers. However, one can and should consult a ticket agency before giving up one's hotel room and trekking down to Piraeus.

There is nothing less certain in Greece than ship departures. This applies particularly when leaving from islands, but it is also true of Piraeus, no matter what you may be assured to the contrary.. Therefore:

Is there a ship for...?—Eh-hee kah**rah**vee ya...?
When does it arrive (leave)?—Poteh th'ar**thee** (tha **fee**ghee)?
Will it be delayed?—Tha kathis**ter**eesee?
How many hours (days)?—Posess oress (**meh**ress)?
Are you sure?—Eesteh **see**gooros?

In the summer, the weather is usually clear and moderate and there are fortunately few delays although the intermittent north wind, called the "mel**tem**ee" can make for some rough sailing and difficult docking., particularly in the Cyclades. The biggest problem is the crush of tourists: the boats are nearly always fully-booked, and so if you want to be sure of a cabin or a 2nd-class bed, it is imperative to make a reservation as many days in advance as possible. This is also true for 3rd-and deck-class tickets, the number of passengers allowed on board being rigidly controlled. In addition, because of the crowded conditions, the exhaustion and consequent inefficiency of the crew, and the possibility of delay, one should try to bring along the following emergency supplies, most of which the ships invariably run out of: food and drink, instant coffee, cigarettes, toilet paper, soap, a hand towel, reading material, Dramamine, and a good friend.

Traveling in winter, except on the large ships going to Crete, is much more chancy, and delays because of bad weather are virtually inevitable. I was once stranded (quite happily) on the island of Santorini for 3 weeks waiting for a ship to arrive, and I have a friend who spent an entire week living on a ship in Piraeus waiting for it to depart (she was quite rightly afraid to get off, except for 15-minute food-shopping forays, out of fear that if the weather abruptly cleared, it would leave without her. Tickets are absolutely no guarantee). But my classic story is of two friends who flew from Paris to spend their 10-day Easter holiday on the island of Patmos. They arrived in Piraeus to find that the ship they had expected to catch had already left, its schedule thrown completely out of kilter by a recent spate of bad weather. Undeterred, they took a plane to Cos in order to catch the ship on its way back from Rhodes to Piraeus, via Patmos. They bought their tickets, were duly accepted on board, and then watched helplessly as the ship sailed past Patmos heading straight for Piraeus, its captain having decided that there were not enough passengers wanting to get off to justify the stop and the delay. Therefore, when my friends finally did reach Patmos a day-and-a-half later, they stayed only two days, catching the first available ship off the island in terror of never being able to get back to Paris again.

So, as they say, you pay your money and you takes your chances. Traveling by ship in Greece is invariably an adventure, most of it fun, some of it a bit harrowing, but all of it worth a good story when you finally get back home.

SHOP, a (the)—**en**a (toh) maga**zee** *or* **en**a (toh) katah**sti**ma (pl. ta maga**zi**ah, ta katah**stee**mata); **I shop (I am going shopping)**— Pso**nee**zo; **the shopping**—ta pso**ni**a.
When are the shops open?—**Pot**eh **ee**nay ahnee**kta** ta maga**zi**ah?

The above question is perhaps the most agonizing and frustrating one you will have to ask during your stay in Greece. This is because Greek stores always seem to be closed when you particularly need them open. The reason is rooted in the time-honored, virtually sacred Mediterranean tradition of the afternoon siesta. All stores are closed from about 1 P.M. until about 5 P.M. whatever the day or season, and some, depending on the day of the week, the whims of their owners, and an incredibly-complicated, staggered system of opening and closing hours, remain shut until the following morning. The concept of a 9-5 workday is anathema to the Greeks, and they have sullenly resisted, often by paralyzing the country with strikes, all efforts by a succession of governments to implement it. Even the totalitarian tactics of the Colonels' junta could not accomplish this, so stubbornly cherished is the Greeks' desire for their afternoons; and often evenings, off.

The only rule of thumb about shopping that can be applied with any certainty is that all stores are usually open in the mornings from about 8-to-1, Monday through Saturday. Figuring out the evening hours requires the services and/or memory capacity of a computer. Whether or not certain stores are open on a particular evening depends both upon the type of store and on the day of the week. It also depends on which city, town or village you are in, since opening and closing hours are regulated by local governments, not by any national or even regional scheme. In Athens and other cities, the schedule can be complicated to the point of madness. On certain evenings, butcher and poultry shops are open while fish stores are closed—and vice versa—but not, as any reasonable person would expect, on alternate evenings. And on other days, both bakeries and grocery stores are closed at the same time, thus making it impossible, three nights a week, to buy either fresh or packaged bread. Fortunately, when in Athens, one can consult the city's excellent English-language magazine, The Athenian, for a table of opening and closing hours for all shops (see also PHARMACY above). In other areas, try to do your shopping in the mornings, because there will be at least one night a week when everything is closed. In addition, there are numerous holidays, secular and religious, which either close all the stores or just some of them, depending on the type and the saint involved. For instance, December 4th is the day of St. Barbara, the patron saint of grocery stores, so all groceries are closed; fortunately, she is not also the saint of butcher shops, fish markets, bakeries, etc., so one can get something to eat. Tourist shops, on the other hand, are subject to no laws except those of economic necessity, and the chances are you will find at least one of them open, wherever you are, at least 12 hours a day, seven days a week.

There are also, in Athens, small dairy-type stores called "**Evga**" (EBΓA) which are open at hours when most other stores are closed and sell a very basic selection of groceries.

SIZE, the—toh meghethos; the size number—toh noomero
CLOTHING SIZES
Women's Suits and Dresses

American	8	10	12	14	16	18
British	10	12	14	16	18	20
French-talian	38	40	42	44	46	48
German	36	38	0	41	44	46
Greek	**44**	**46**	**48**	**50**	**52**	**54**

Men's Suits & Overcoats

American/British	36	38	40	42	44	46
Greek (Europe)	**46**	**48**	**50**	**52**	**54**	**56**

Shirts

American/British	14	14½	15	15½	16	16½	17
Greek (Europe)	**36**	**37**	**38**	**39**	**41**	**42**	**43**

Waist Sizes (Approx.)

Greek (Europe)	**36**	**38**	**40**	**42**	**44**	**46**	**48**	**50**
American/British	28¼	30	31½	33	34½	36	37½	39½

Women's Shoes

American	5	5½	6	6½	7	7½	8	8½	9
British	3½	4	4½	5	5½	6	6½	7	7½
Greek (Europe)	**35**	**35½**	**36**	**37**	**37½**	**38**	**38½**	**39**	**40**

Men's Shoes

American	7	7½	8½	9	9½	10	10½	11½	11½
British	6½	7	7½	8½	9	9½	10	10½	11
Greek (Europe)	**39**	**40**	**41**	**42**	**43**	**43½**	**44½**	**45½**	**45½**

Stockings

American/British	8	8½	9	9½	10	10½
Greek (Europe)	**O**	**1**	**2**	**3**	**4**	**5**

Socks

Amencan/Bntish	9½	10	10½	11½	12
Greek (Europe)	**38-39**	**39-40**	**40-41**	**41-42**	**42-43**

SNAKE, a (the)—ena (toh) **fee**-dhee (pl. **fee**-dhee); **viper, a (the)—mi**a (ee) ok**hee**ah; **snake bite, a (the)—en**a (toh) **dhah**goma fee-dheeoo

The viper (*Vipera berus*) is the only poisonous snake in Greece. It varies in color from gray to brown or red, has dark markings across its back, and can be as long as 2 feet. It exists virtually everywhere in the countryside, even on islands, and usually makes its home within the rough stone walls that undulate all over the Greek landscape. During the spring and summer, one should be cautious when walking near these walls; especially at midday when the snakes like to come out of their lair to take a nice sunbath on the paths between the walls. At this time they are extremely drowsy and are not likely to sense your presence until you are about to step on them. Needless to say, they don't like to be so rudely disturbed and retaliate by biting. On the other hand, don't be overly alarmed. Greece is definitely not swarming with poisonous snakes; in the 10 years I spent walking daily on the paths mentioned above, I managed to almost step on only one viper—and it was probably more frightened than I.

SPIDER, a (the)—mia (ee) ah**rahk**nee (pl. ee ah**rahk**ness)

Greek spiders are generally harmless, the exception being the black widow, which usually dwells in or around human excrement, i.e. village or country toilets without proper drainage systems. The bite of a black widow is extremely painful, producing nausea, stomach cramps, profuse sweating and difficulty in breathing; it is, however, rarely fatal—if that's any comfort.

STEAL (I)—Klevo; **My wallet has been stolen—**Mou **klep**saneh toh portofolee; **You stole—Ekl**epsess; **He (she) stole—Ekl**epseh.

Except in the larger cities, it is still rare to find a Greek that steals; therefore, the chances are that the theft has been committed by a foreigner. All thefts should be reported immediately to the local police. Stealing is a blemish on the honor of the community, and the police will do everything they can to find the thief and recover your goods. I have even known them to go so far as to telephone another island

and intercept a suspected thief (a foreigner) who had left by ship. He turned out to be guilty.

SUBWAY, the—oh eelektrikos

Since the Athens subway was built primarily to service its outlying areas there are only two stops in the center of the city, one at Monastiraki (Monastiraki), the site of the city's flea market, which is just on the edge of the old Plaka area at the foot of the Acropolis. The other stop is Omonia (Omonia) Square. Both stops are equidistant from Constitution Square, about a 10-minute walk. And it is from either of these stations that one catches the subway to Piraeus (Piray-efs), Monastiraki being one stop closer. A new system, similar to that in London, has been installed in some stations. Tickets are bought at a ticket window or from machines, the destination determining the price, so you must tell the ticket seller where you are going. Afterwards, in those stations where ticket-control gates have been installed, you must put your ticket in a slot on the near side of the machine to have it punched before the gate will open. Keep the ticket. It must be collected by a controller as you leave the station at your destination; otherwise, you pay again.

SUNSTROKE, a—Mia eeleeasee.

Sun- or heatstrokes can be quite serious and possibly fatal. The symptoms are a high temperature, an inability to sweat, dry, hot skin, a strong, rapid pulse and possibly unconsciousness. The symptoms of heat exhaustion are, by contrast, a relatively normal temperature and profuse perspiration, accompanied by headache, nausea, dizziness, possible cramps, vomiting and fainting.

Emergency first aid steps in both instances should be taken to cool off the victim by sponging him with water or alcohol. In addition, with heat exhaustion, put 1 tsp. of salt in a glass of water and have him sip it slowly for about an hour; should he vomit, however, don't give him any more liquid.

I have gone into this at such length because incidents of heatstroke or exhaustion are not uncommon among over-enthusiastic tourists during the hot Greek summer, and it is wise to be forewarned and prepared. Children and elderly or overweight people are particularly susceptible.

TAVERNA, a (the)—mia (ee) ta**vehr**na (pl. ta**vehr**ness)

Greek tavernas could be called restaurants without white table-cloths and white-jacketed waiters. Usually, they are family-run concerns with everyone from the children to the grandfather lending a hand. They are often cheaper than restaurants, but not necessarily so, particularly when they are of the type specializing in seafood and grilled meats.

TAXI, a (the)—ena (toh) tak**see** (pl. ta taksiah); **taxi driver, a (the)—enas** (oh) taksee**tzees**; **taxi stand, a (the)—mia** (ee) sta**see** tak**see**; **I want a taxi, please—Thel**o **en**a tak**see**, para**ka**lo.

There are taxis everywhere in Greece, even on the smallest islands. They are invariably colored gray and often do not have a light on top to indicate whether or not they are free; either that or the light doesn't work. Do not be deterred if there is someone sitting in the front seat with the driver; it is usually a friend going along for a ride. In addition, if there is someone in the back, you may still be able to flag the taxi down; Greeks are not adverse to sharing the cost of a ride—if the driver will let you get way with it. In Athens, as in all large cities, taxis are often difficult to find. There are innumerable taxi stands as well as taxi stations: usually a roofed metal waiting area similar to those at bus stops in which one must stand in line and wait one's turn. But during rush hours, the stands are invariably empty and the stations mobbed. In emergencies, I have found that one of the best methods of getting a taxi is to walk into a large hotel like the Hilton, turn around and walk out, and politely ask the doorman to find you one.

Telephoning for a taxi is theoretically possible in Athens (see *The Athenian* magazine's Organizer section for a list of taxi stand numbers) but there never seem to be taxis waiting there to be called. In smaller cities, villages and on islands, telephoning is often the best way to get a taxi, and any café owner will be glad to do it for you.

Once in a taxi, make sure that the driver turns on the meter—if he has one. Just say "Toh rol**loy**, parakalo". If there is no meter (which is often true on islands) ask to see the price list—"toh teem**logh**io." It will show the set fare from one place to another. At night, prices rise, so don't be surprised or angry if you find yourself paying more going home than you did going out. There is also an extra charge for a large amount of luggage.

Tips are not expected, but if you're on an island, for instance, and may want to use the same driver again, a few extra drachmas could help secure him as your personal driver throughout your stay. In addition, at Christmas and Easter, there is a required tip—a small amount called "toh **dhor**oh" (gift)—which the driver will add to the fare registered on the meter.

TELEGRAM, (the)—ena (toh) teeleh**grah**feema (pl. teele-hgra**fee**mata); **the telegraph office**—Ohteh (written in blue letters on silver metallic signs as **OTE**)

OTE is the logogram of the Telecommunications Organization of Greece, which handles both telegrams and telephone calls. **OTE** offices are theoretically open 24 hours a day, but this is true only in the larger cities and towns; on islands, they tend to close both at night and during the afternoon siesta hours. In Athens, the main **OTE** office is quite near Constitution Square.

Within Greece, it is considerably cheaper (and much less time consuming) to send a telegram rather than to telephone. Conversely, with international communications, the reverse is true: a telegram abroad, word for word; costs much more than a 3-minute phone call.

TELEPHONE, a (the)—ena (toh) teeleh**fo**no; **directory en**as kah-**tah**logos;. **Is there a telephone?—Eh**-hee teeleh**fo**no? **I want to telephone to...—The**lo na teelefo**nee**so stee...; **The number is...—**Oh ahrith**mos** ee**nay**...; **long distance—**eeperasti**koh**; **automatic—**ahf**toh**matoh; **collect—**kolekt; **busy—**vooeezee ("buzzing") or meelaee ("talking"); **doesn't answer—**dhen ahpan**da**ee; **wrong number—**lahthos; **I couldn't (can't) hear—**Dhen boroosa (**boroh**) n'ahkoo-soh.

An automatic dialing system for foreign and domestic calls has now been established virtually throughout Greece. One can telephone from either the OTE office (see under TELEGRAM, above) or from any sidewalk kiosk, café, hotel, restaurant, or shop which has an automatic counter (rol**loy**) hooked up to the telephone. One pays in terms of the number of units (mohna-dhess) that have been marked up on the counter during the call.

The **automatic area codes** for all countries and major cities within the system can be found in the front pages of all telephone directories. Collect calls must be made from the OTE office. Local calls can be made from sidewalk kiosks, telephone booths or from cafés, restaurants or shops having large red telephones equipped with a coin box. At places having normal, not red, telephones, one pays the proprietor afterwards;

Coin-operated telephones function the same way as in America: one lifts the receiver, listens for the dial tone, deposits a coin in the slot, and then dials.

In emergency situations, if the number you are trying to reach is continually busy, you may telephone the operator and ask her for priority (**mia pros**kleesee); she will then put you through even if someone is still speaking on the other end.

Charges are one-third cheaper from midnight Saturday to midnight Sunday, and from 8 P.M. to 7 A.M. on weekdays.

Useful telephone numbers to all kinds of agencies, banks, government offices, etc. in the Athens area can be found in the Organizer section of the city's excellent English-language magazine, *The Athenian*.

TEMPERATURE, the—ee thermokra**seea**; **What's the temperature today?**—Tee thermokra**seea eh-**homay **seem**era?

FAHRENHEIT—CENTIGRADE CONVERSIONS

F	C	F	C
32	0	90	32
40	4	95	35
50	10	98.4	37
55	13	100	37.8
60	15	101	38.3
65	18	102	38.9
70	21	103	39.4
75	24	104	40
80	26	105	40.6
85	29		

TESTICLES, the—ee or**khees**; **slang**—ta ahme**let**ita ("the unmentionables") *or* ta ark**hee**-dhia ("balls").

Sheep and bull testicles are considered a great culinary delicacy in Greece, and I must admit—having first eaten them without knowing what they were—that I agree. Nevertheless, I still find it a bit difficult to take that first bite. (Please also see "sta ark**hee**-dhia mou".)

TIME, a (the)—ee ora; **What time is it?**—Tee ora ee**nay**?; **It's eight o'clock**—Eenay ohk**toh** ee ora; **What time does it leave (come)?**—Tee ora **fev**ghee (**thar**thee)?

TIME EXPRESSIONS

dawn	av**ghee**
morning	pro**ee**
noon	mesee**meh**ree
afternoon	mesi**meh**ree
evening	**vra**-dhee
night	**neek**ta
midnight	mee**sa**neekta
A.M.	preen mesim**vree**as (written as: Π.Μ. *or* π.μ.)
P.M.	metah mesim**vree**as (written as: M.M. *or*: μ.μ.)
after	kay
half-past	mee**see**
before	**pah**ra
a quarter after eight	ohk**toh** kay te**tar**toh
half-past eight	ohk**toh**meesee *or* ohk**toh** kay mee**see**
a quarter to eight	ohk**toh pah**ra te**tar**toh

All times before the half-hour are spoken in terms of "kay" and all times after the half-hour in terms of "**pah**ra." Thus, one never says "Eight thirty-two", but rather **"Twenty-eight before eight"**— "Ohk**toh pah**ra **ee**kosee ohk**toh**."

TOURIST BUREAU, a (the)—ena (toh) grahfeeo tourismoo;
Where is the tourist bureau?—Poo eenay toh grafeeo
tourismoo?

All bureaus of the Greek National Tourist Organization (**EOT**—pronounced Eh-**oht**) are usually extremely well-run, their staff speaking several languages and having a definite enthusiasm for a very tiring and demanding job. They are full of information about transportation schedules, archeological sites, camping, etc. and dispense a number of free maps and brochures, the most impressive of which is an extremely informative booklet called "General Information About Greece," which is updated every year and tells you about everything from taxi fares to the monthly wind velocities in various parts of Greece. The main Athenian office is on Constitution Square. The telephone number is 322-2545, but it is best to go there in person.

TOURIST POLICE, the—ee touristi**kee** astinomeea
Where are the tourist police?—Poo eenay ee touristi**kee** astin-omeea?

As with the regular police the character of the tourist policeman vanes from individual to individual, but it can be said that they are generally more relaxed and seemingly more open-minded than normal policeman. They also can speak some English, although you will find that their counterparts in the Greek National Tourist Bureau are infinitely more fluent.

The majority of Greek tourist police are extremely helpful, and if you have a problem with anything—a need for a bed, an illness, a theft, a loss, cheating on a bill, etc.—you should go to them. On the other hand, should you run afoul of the law, your best bet is the official at the nearest tourist bureau, **EOT** (see TOURIST BUREAU above.) The Greek tourist police may be quite solicitous, but they are still policemen, and it is only the glove that is velvet.

VIRGIN, a (the)—mia (ee) par**thehn**a; **I'm a virgin—Eem**ay par**thehn**a

The virginity of a girl at the time of her marriage still carries a great deal of importance in much of Greece and until recent years it was not unusual on wedding nights for the groom to display a blood-stained sheet outside the bedroom window as proof of his bride's previously unsullied state.

The name of the Parthenon, by the way, derives not from the fact that it is a temple dedicated to Ah**thee**nah Par**theh**nos ("Athena the Virgin"), but because there was a room within it built for her maiden priestesses which was called "the room of the virgins"—ton par**theh**non—which in time came to be applied to the building as whole. Perhaps—who knows?—because the men of Athens were always talking about taking a stroll up to the virgins' room...

VISA, a (the)—**mia** (ee) theh-or**ee**ses *or* **mia** (ee) **vee**za but usually referred to as "**mia** (ee) **ah**dhiah paramo**nees**," which means "residence permit."
  My visa is up—Ee **ah**dhiah mou eh-hee teli**oh**see; **My visa will be up a few days**—Ee **ah**dhiah mou tha teli**oh**see seh **lee**ghess **meh**ress; **I want a new visa**—**Thel**o mia ken**oo**ria **ah**dhiah; **for 2 (4) months**—ya **dhee**o (tes**er**ess) **mee**ness.

Citizens of most countries in non-EC Europe and North and South America are given automatic 3-month visas upon arriving in Greece. However, because diplomatic arrangements are so subject to change, it is best to check one's current status before leaving one's country. In lieu of that, see the Greek National Tourist Organization's booklet, *General Information About Greece*, available free in several languages at all national tourist bureaus. Updated every year, it is a gold mine of information and will be of particular help in guiding you through the latest labyrinth of visa application rules.

If you wish to stay in Greece longer than your original visa permits, you must request an extension at least 20 days before it expires. This is the rule, and visa authorities reserve the right to refuse you an extension if you are late in asking for it; however, most officials take account of the impulsive, spur-of-the-moment nature of a tourist's sudden love affair with Greece and usually bend this particular rule even further than one can imagine it could go. If you have any problems in this area or if you have overstayed your visa and wish to leave the country, go as soon as possible to the Athens Aliens' Bureau; they are the central authority and are able both to override other officials' decisions as well as to process you with a minimum of delay. Attempting to leave the country without a proper visa could result in a fine on top of the visa fee and might cause you to be held up just long enough to miss your plane, ship or train.

There are two Aliens' Bureaus in Athens: one is near Omonia Square at 9 Halkokondili St., Tel. 362-8301; the other is in the suburb of Maroussi at 73 Dimitriou Gounari St., Tel. 802-4800. The visiting hours are in the mornings only from 8 A.M. to 1 P.M. There are additional Aliens' Bureaus in Piraeus (37 Vassileos Constantinou St., Tel. 417-4023) and Glyfada (1 Alsous St., Tel. 8948444), and in Thessaloniki (Tel. 521-067). In other cities, towns and islands, one goes to the local police; here, the waiting time for a new visa could be as long as a week, depending upon how distant one is from the central authority of the region.

In applying for an extension, you will need, in addition to your passport, 4 small visa photos and, perhaps, some bank receipts showing that you have exchanged foreign currency for drachmas during your stay in the country. In Athens, those photos can be gotten cheaply in an automatic photo booth in the Omonia Square subway station or, more expensively, from almost any photographer's shop, including one within the Aliens' Bureau building. Elsewhere, including islands, there always seems to be at least one` photographer specializing in these things.

When filling in the extension form, you will be asked a series of questions, the answers to most of which can be found in your passport; the exceptions are your father's name, your religion, and, perhaps, your occupation. You will then be directed to go and buy some tax stamps (hartohsima) either somewhere in the building or front another bureau or even from a local café or sidewalk kiosk. In buying these stamps, you are paying for the cost of extending your visa; the amount varies according to your nationality and to whether this is the first, second or third extension of your visa, i. e. the longer you stay in the country, the more you pay, the amount being minimal in the beginning, but then escalating dramatically. Once you have returned to the office with these tax stamps, the process of applying for a visa is complete; you will then, depending on where you are, either be given a visa immediately or asked to return to pick it up at a later date.

WEATHER, the—oh kay*ros*; **is beautiful (bad)**—**ee**nay o**ra**yos (**ka**kos); **It's cold (warm/hot)**—**Kah**nee **kree**oh (**zes**tee/po**lee zes**tee); **rainy**—vrok*heros*; **windy**—ahnemo-*dhees*; **weather forecast, the**—ee prov*lepsee* kay*roo*

One can go on forever about the weather in Greece, so I'll try not to:

In summer, it is hot (75-100° F), and virtually cloudless and rainless. There is some humidity, particularly in the larger cities and certain, but not all islands. The prevailing wind, called the mel**tem**ee, comes from the north and is a blessing; on Crete, there is a southern wind which occasionally sweeps in from the Sahara and turns the island into an oven.

In winter, the weather varies considerably. In the north and mountains, there is snow; south of Athens, in the plains, the weather rarely drops below freezing, the temperature averaging about 55° and occasionally soaring into the 70's. Rain falls, but not as constantly as most foreigners think when they refer to Greece's "rainy season". It is not monsoon time, and there are quite a few days that are as cloudless and beautiful as summer. The prevailing winds are from all directions, but the Greeks say that the worst weather comes from Italy.

In the spring and fall, the weather is superlative, ranging in temperature from 65° to 85°. Occasionally, there are some massive rainstorms. The winds vary in strength and direction.

WEDDING, a (the)—**en**as (oh) **gah**mos

Greek weddings are beautiful to watch, but interminably long, lasting about an hour. Fortunately, one can stroll in and out of the church at will without committing a *faux pas*. The party afterwards is also beautiful and often interminable. If you are invited to a wedding party, it is not necessary for you, as a foreigner, to bring a gift, but a box of candies would be much appreciated.

WINTER, the—oh hee*monahs*; **in the winter**—ton hee*monah*.

"Is the winter in Greece," foreigners ask, "cold, damp and rainy—miserable?" The answer is yes, but emphatically no. There are terrible periods, but then the weather clears and you are treated, about one day a week, to a glorious burst of spring, the sun so hot that one sits outside in a T-shirt, turns pink, and is sorely tempted to go swimming. (I have done so in December, fortified, however, by about a quart of home-made Greek wine.) It is in winter that two remarkable phenomena happen. One is the greening of Greece, the turning of those grayish-brown, bramble- and thistle-covered hills into a soft and undulating mass of green that is everywhere dotted with wild flowers. The other phenomenon is the cleansing of the air by the rain, and it is then that one is most forcibly struck by the much talked-about "Greek light." Objects miles away, tiny houses on distant hills, are defined with a stunning clarity, as though the light were somehow etching and shaping the tiniest detail; islands 40 to 90 miles across the sea, never visible in the summer, abruptly appear, leaping out at one as though they were being suddenly brought into focus through a zoom lens. There are really no words to describe the effect which this has on one's sensibilities except to say, perhaps, that it is delicious.

Winter in Greece is a quiet time, a pensive time, and a card- and backgammon-playing time; the cafés are full, day and night, with restless men waiting for the summer and its work to begin again; and with little else to do, they recklessly gamble away their profits from the previous tourist season in anticipation of the one to come. For Greek housewives, it is, as always, a time of quiet desperation, and for farmers, of waiting either for the rain to stop or the rain to come. It is a kind of limbo, the winter, but an extremely beautiful one, and I highly recommend it to anyone curious about this other side of Greek life.

WOMAN, a (the)—mia (ee) yee**nay**ka (pl. ee yee**nay**kess).

The Greek word for "wife" is also "yee**nay**ka," meaning, perhaps, that the two are synonymous and that being a woman means being a wife—but not much else. Although there is much truth in this, times in Greece are changing. Women were given the right to vote in 1952, and in 1975, a new constitution granted them, on paper at least, equal rights. In 1980, there were 11 women (including Melina Mercouri) in the 300-seat Greek parliament, a sharp contrast, at the time to the zero number of females sitting in the US Senate.

Greece is perhaps the last Western country where matrilineal and matrifocal societies survived the onslaught of wheeled patriarchal invaders from the north, persisting in Crete until the fall of the Minoan empire in the second millenium B.C. In addition, if one thinks back on Helen of Troy, Antigone, Medea, Clytaemnestra and even long-suffering Penelope, as well as the heroine of the Greek War of Independence, Bouboulina, it is clear that Greek women have always had a powerful hold on the mind and imagination of their country, not to mention its politics. One need only observe the strength and patience with which they deal with their families today to understand why.

WORK, a (the)—**mi**a (ee) dhool**iah**; **good (bad) work**—kalee (kah**kee**) dhool**iah**; **difficult work**—dhee**s**kolee dhool**iah**; **a worker**—**en**as ehrg**ah**tees (pl. ee ehrg**ah**tess); **to work**—na dhool**ep**so; **I want to work**—**Thel**o na dhool**ep**so; **I am working**—Dhool**ev**o; **Are you working?**—dhool**ev**ees?; **He (she) is working**—Dhool**ev**ee.

Greek law states that no foreigner is allowed to do work that a Greek is capable of or wants to do. Although this would seem to exclude everything, it doesn't. Greek language schools are allowed to hire one foreigner per branch, as are other companies, such as travel agencies, that deal with foreigners. In addition, there are certain jobs that Greeks don't like to do—menial, back-breaking work like gathering fruit, grapes and olives and demeaning (for Greek women) work like waitressing, house-cleaning baby-sitting, etc. So, although it is illegal to be employed in the latter type of job one can find openings if one wants them; the length of the job will depend on how soon the police either spot you or are complained to by one of the locals—and there always seems to be at least one with nothing better to do than complain. The worst that can happen to you then is that you will be thrown out of the country, the least (and most likely) is that you will be reprimanded and told to move on.

Anyone wishing to get a permit to work legally in Greece, say as a tourist guide, is required by law to apply for it from abroad, the procedure being to get a letter of intent from the company wishing to hire you and then going with it to the nearest Greek consulate or embassy in your country. You will then, probably without any trouble at all, be granted a visa and a work permit for a limited period of time, say six months to a year, after which you apply for an extension within Greece.

PART 4

COMMON GREEK EXPRESSIONS, GESTURES, AND OTHER PHENOMENA

AH**MEH**SOS—"Immediately," "Right away"

Usually uttered by waiters after receiving your order. Never to be taken seriously, particularly if you have high blood pressure. In Greece, "immediately" really means "as soon as I possibly can," which allows for an enormous amount of leeway and innumerable de tours. Don't hold your breath.

AHSTA—"Stop it!" "Forget it!" or "Leave it!"

Often heard when you (the tourist) don't have enough small change to make up the last few drachmas of a purchase in a store or when you are trying to pay your share of the bill at a café, taverna, etc. Can't be taken literally, but it is polite to protest a bit before giving in.

BOU**ZOU**KI (pl. bou**zou**kia)

A type of Greek mandolin as well as the name for night clubs which feature its music. The clubs are quite popular and usually offer high quality, professional entertainment. However, they are extremely expensive. A bottle of whiskey (the usual lubricant for a group of Greeks) costs from $60 upwards and a plate of watermelon at least $4. In addition, when one dances, it is required practice to tip the orchestra at least 100 drachmas, but often more, depending on the number of people in one's group. Frequently, the air of a bouzouki club seems to be confettied with money. God knows how the ordinary Greek gets so much, but when he has it, he certainly knows how to enjoy throwing it away.

BREAKING PLATES (and glasses, bottles, chairs, etc.)

A once-cherished Greek tradition that has, since the advent of the Colonels' junta, fallen upon hard times. Thus, in many cafés, tavernas and restaurants, you will still see signs saying **ΑΠΑΓΟΡΕΥΕΤΑΙ**

ΤΟ ΣΠΑΣΙΜΟ. (apagore**vetay** toy **spah**simo) BREAKAGE FOR-BIDDEN. The posting of this prohibition was instigated by the junta, which seems to have felt that it was ridding Greece of its most barbaric custom since the Dionysian orgies—that of expressing one's approval of another person's dancing (or one's happiness in general) by shattering plates, glasses, bottles, and sometimes chairs and tables on the dance floor. Since the fall of the Colonels, the practice has resumed (indeed, it never entirely stopped during their reign) but it seems to have lost much of its former vigor. The continuing rise of a new and self-censoring middle class may be part of the reason, as well as the fact that since its popularization in the film "Never on Sunday," the practice has been being considerably overdone, particularly by foreigners who indiscriminately and in excess tended to break things without a proper Greek reason. The proper Greek reason is "**ke**fi" (see **KE**FEE, p. 229) and even these days, if a Greek or group of them is seized by this peculiarly Greek form of happiness and starts tossing glasses and plates on the dance floor, the tradition assumes its old glory and becomes a joyous thing to watch and even participate in. But it has its own internal rhythm, and one must be aware not to push it too fast or too hard, lest it collapse into pointless, drunken chaos. One must also be aware that the owner of the establishment is carefully counting up every broken item (sometimes at double its price) and putting it on the bill. So if you think you've got **ke**fi, you should also think about whether you've got enough money to pay for it.

Mention should also be made of the fact that during the prohibition of plate breaking, flowers were tossed onto the dance floor instead. This has now taken root as a tradition of its own, and a very beautiful one at that, expressing a side of the Greek personality that is often lost under the onslaught of the Zorba stereotype, particularly since the real Zorba (and Kazanzakis' one too) was probably quite a flower tosser himself.

GREEK DANCES

There are perhaps as many kinds of these as there are Greek villages. Every community tends to develop its own special variations on the basic Greek dances, and often the steps are so transformed that they become almost unrecognizable to a Greek from another area. However, there are still certain patterns which are adhered to everywhere, and the names of the dances, at least, remain the same:

The "hasapiko" (lit. "butcher's dance")—danced in a line by two or more people, their arms around each other's shoulders. It is composed of a series of short variations which can be linked together in a virtually infinite number of combinations, the leader at the left end of the line doing the improvising and calling out each new step as it comes.

The "kalamatianos"—a simple circle dance, and the only one in this group in which women were traditionally allowed to join (although these days one will also see them dancing the hasapiko, serviko, sirtaki, tsamikos, and even the tsifteteli.). An almost genteel dance in character with the basic step never varying.

The serviko or hasaposerviko ("Serbia" or "Butchers of Serbia")—a fast and extremely lively circle dance, the basic step always remaining the same. Very, very good for sweating the wine out of your system.

The sirtaki—a bastardized (or "Westernized") version of the above hasapiko, fast and flashy, like a souped-up hot rod with lots of added chrome and very little character. Usually performed by young Greek men trying to impress all the foreign girls in the room.

The tsahmikos—performed either by two men linked by a handkerchief or by a circle of people in which the interchanging leaders are linked to the rest of the line by a handkerchief. Very acrobatic, with the leader performing flips and twirls while being supported by the person on the other end of the handkerchief. Unless you are quite strong, it is prudent to avoid being the person who does the supporting.

The tsifteteli—a kind of double belly dance performed by two men, either Turkish in origin or perhaps a Greek satirical parody of the dances of their Turkish masters during the occupation. Highly suggestive sexually (or, if you will, homosexually) but not really that way at all (at least not most of the time). These days sometimes performed by a man and a woman.

The zembekiko—a solo dance for men that is extremely introspective in character, almost contemplative, as though the dancer were alone in an empty room expressing and working out a private emotion solely for himself and not at all for the people watching him. It can be incredibly beautiful and moving but, although you are allowed to express your appreciation with applause (the Greeks often do so by tossing glasses or plates on the floor), it would be a terrible faux pas to try and join him and intrude upon his privacy.

ELLA and **ELLA DHOH**—"Come" and "Come here."

Often accompanied by a waving gesture which seems to be telling you to go away.

ENDAHKSI—"Okay".

EVIL EYE, THE—toh ka**ko mah**tee *or* ee vaskane**ea**

Belief in the power of the evil eye is still very much a part of Greek life, even among the educated middle and upper classes and even in the Orthodox Church, which officially recognizes it and has a special ceremony for exorcising its curse.

The curse comes from envy—which is to say that it is visited upon people who for some reason have caused others to become envious of them, usually because they are good-looking or wealthy or have enjoyed good health and/or good fortune.

The people who are considered most capable of having the evil eye, that is, of being able to curse someone with it, are usually women and usually those with blue eyes. Some of these people know that they possess the power (generally they are by nature spiteful and envious) and they use it at every opportunity. Others possess the power unknowingly, and unwittingly bring bad luck on people and friends by envying them for one or another reason. However, once they realize they have this power, they try to do their very best not to think evil thoughts of anyone and to use their power whenever they can to remove the spells cast by others.

There are two favored methods of warding off the evil eye. The most well-known (and commercially successful, at least as far as the tourist industry is concerned) is to wear a colored bead, usually blue, painted with an eye. The other is to pretend to spit on the ground or, in lieu of that, to say "**Ptoo-soo**"—to imitate the sound. This latter method is usually employed when you find yourself envying a friend and wish to counteract the possible consequences. Thus you spit on the ground as a kind of diversionary tactic, to show the evil spirits that you are not at all envious of your friend, but rather, downright contemptuous. This is often done when admiring another person's baby and wishing to have one as beautiful for yourself. It protects the parents and, more important, the innocent child.

Animals, too, are vulnerable to the eye, which is why you see so many horses, donkeys, mules, canary cages, etc. draped with blue beads. Pigs, however, are immune—perhaps because no one could possibly be envious of such gross, sloppy ugliness.

If one suspects one has been given the evil eye, there are, aside from consulting the church, other ways of (1) ascertaining if you really do have it and (2) exorcising it. One is to cross yourself several times and try to quickly say a certain passage of Christian liturgy. if you can't get the words right, you have the evil eye; if you do get them right, then your problem is just a normal streak of bad luck. The cure in this case is to keep crossing one's self and repeating the liturgy until one does it correctly several times in a row. If this doesn't work, then you must either go to the church or find someone outside of the church who has the power to dispel the curse. These people, usually elderly women, take their power and responsibilities quite seriously, considering themselves almost as lay priests (or, perhaps more to the point priestesses), using church liturgy and holy water and oil in their exorcisms, and because of the Christian nature of their duties, rarely if ever charging money. The ceremony is simple but impressive and—I can testify from personal experience—works.

So, just to be on the safe side during your visit to Greece, buy yourself a blue bead or two, try not to be envious of others, and don't be offended should someone spit on the ground in front of you. It's all for your own good.

FASA**REEA**—means "an argument," "fight," "loud noise," or "a bothersome and unnecessary problem" depending on the context.

GAH**MOH** TOH!—"Fuck it!"

Heard much more frequently than in English and used even by young children and sweet old ladies. Therefore not as offensive to

Greek ears as one would expect. "Gah**moh** teen Panag**yee**a mou!" is a particularly popular expansion on this theme. It means, literally translated, "I fuck my Virgin Mary!" It must be noted, however, that just as you would not appreciate a foreigner wandering around your country saying "Fuck!" all the time, so the Greeks will be offended by your using their vulgarities in the same way. In other words, don't.

GOMENA, GOMENOS—"girl friend," "boy friend"

Close enough in sound to the above "gah**moh**" so that most people think the two are etymologically related, which they aren't (the words derive from "**go**ma," a kind of brilliantine which was used by flashy, hip young men back in the 20's and 30's in imitation of Rudolf Valentino, et al.).

Nevertheless, the word now carries this connotation and thus, to call a girl or boy friend your "**go**mena" or "**go**menos" implies that they are either someone you are presently sleeping with or think you can fairly easily get into bed. Comparable to calling someone "a lay" in English.

GESTURES

Greeks are, in my opinion, the champion gesture-users of the Mediterranean. Their hands, bodies and faces are rarely in repose, and it sometimes seems possible to get the gist of a conversation by watching it from fifty feet away. (There is a marvelous book on this subject, published in Athens, called INSTANT GREEK. It is written and drawn by an excellent artist named Papas and provides one with an instant insight into the Greek character.) In lieu of that and as an adjunct to it, I offer some of my own observations on those Greek gestures most necessary for a foreigner to be able to interpret:

"**No**."—Aside from shaking their heads from side to side as we do, the Greeks have another, nearly indescribable way of replying in the negative. This is done by a lifting backwards and upwards of the entire head and/or the eyes and/or the eyebrows and accompanying or not accompanying this motion with a tongued "tsk" sound. If not accompanied by a "tsk" this movement is sometimes so quick and subtle, so imperceptible except to the trained eye (you must be able to detect even the slightest flutter of an eyelash) that one cannot be sure if the person questioned has responded at all. I have often repeated a question four times (in an increasingly loud voice) only to finally realize that the person has been replying "no" since the beginning.

"Come here."—This is indicated by a waving of the hand, a kind of pawing at the air with the fingers, palm down, that looks to the non-Greek as though the person is either waving goodbye or telling you to move back a few steps. Very confusing, because the further back you move, the more frantic the "come here" gesturing becomes.

"I want to tell you something."—Indicated by a touching or a patting of the protruded lower lip with the forefinger and thus can look as though you are being told to whisper or shush up. Often performed after the above "come here" gesture, as in "Come here, I want to tell you something."

"How are you" or **"What's up?"**—Eyebrows raised inquiringly, the questioner opens his hand, palm up, as if holding an invisible grapefruit, and rotates it slightly to the left, fingers spreading fanwise. Can also mean, if done very emphatically with the arm fully extended, "What in the hell is this?" or "Don't give me that crap!".

"Unbelievable!" "Catastrophic!" "Too much!" "Too beautiful!" "Too horrible!"—An all-purpose gesture, as you can see. Comparable, perhaps, to the Western one of bringing one's palm to the side of the face in a light slap, usually to convey disbelief. The Greeks begin the same way, with the palm open and the elbow bent so that the hand is level with the side of the face. But then, instead of slapping his cheek, the Greek rotates his hand counter-clockwise two or three times, middle and forefinger extended upwards as if stirring up a whirl pool in the air. If accompanied by the expression, "Po, po, po!", this indicates something particularly monumental.

"Relations"—Used to indicate relations of a family, business or sexual nature, although the gesture itself is, to Western eyes, inescapably salacious. The hands are placed side by side, palms down, and the forefingers are extended and rubbed together, as if they were partners in bed.

"Sex"—Obvious to anyone over 4 years old. All of the fingers of the hand are kept straight out, except the middle one, which is bent perpendicular to the others. The hand is then pumped downwards.

"**Liar!**"—Comes from the verbal expression "**Moo**see" which means both "beard" and "lie." Thus, the gesture involves either stroking a long, imaginary beard between the thumb and the other fingers or placing the back of one's hand under the chin and quickly undulating the fingers horizontally like a beard flowing in the wind. It is interesting to speculate on the fact that traditionally the only people in Greek society who wear such long beards are the priests.

"**Hunger**"—A sawing motion across the stomach with the back edge of the right hand, fingers extended, palm upwards.

"**Punishment**"—Similar to our wagging of the forefinger to reprimand someone, but done with the entire hand, the fingers extended and closed together, as in a karate chop. Can or need not be accompanied by the expression, "Tha fahs k**see**lo," which means "You'll eat wood" or, as our forefathers used to say, "You'll be taken to the woodshed."

"**To my balls!**" The literal translation of "Sta ar**khee**-dhia mou!" The gesture, often but not necessarily accompanied by the phrase, is a single, sharp, karate-chopping motion of the hand in the direction of the testicles. Very insulting. "Up yours!" would perhaps be the nearest Western equivalent.

"**Moond**za"—This is the name of a curse that is so terrible and so particularly Greek that it is impossible to translate it into English. "Go to Hell!" with all of its original force would be the closest equivalent, but is nevertheless insipid by comparison. The moondza is done by spreading the fingers and shoving one's hand, palm outwards, forcefully in the direction of the recipient, sometimes saying, "N**ah**!" ("There!") or "**Arpa**!" ("Catch!") or "**Pa**reh **mia moond**za!" ("Take a **moond**za!"). Using both hands is twice as bad and can be accompanied by the phrase "**Arpa dhek**a!" ("Catch ten!"). However, this is such an overkill that it can sometimes verge on farce. Some people, though, have been known to use both hands and both feet at the same time. It is advisable to try this only when sitting down. It is also advisable not to try it at all, not even with one hand, and not even as a joke. A Greek could take you seriously and the consequences could be quite unpleasant.

HAYRETEH—"Hello" or "Goodbye."

A polite way of greeting or saying goodbye to someone, as opposed to "**Ya**soo", which is much more casual. Usually used after the morning has gotten under way and "**Kah**lee **meh**ra" ("Good morning") is no longer appropriate. It would seem to be equivalent to our "Good afternoon" except for the fact that it can be used well into what we would call evening.

KARAGYOZEES

The name of the hero of the most popular shadow play in Greece, and also the generic name of the play itself. The character Karagozees can perhaps best be described as a combination of Mickey Mouse and Charlie Chaplin, by turns downtrodden, resourceful, naive, shrewd, idealistic, pragmatic, exploiting, and exploited—in other words, very Greek. These shadow plays travel around the country during the summer' and should one appear in your area often in the local park after sunset, admission usually free—try not to miss it. You may not be able to understand a word of the dialogue, but the beauty of the marionettes themselves and the squeals of laughter from both the children and their parents are much more than half the fun.

In Athens. it is on view every night in Lysikratous Square, Plaka, starting about 9 P.M.

KAHLEE LEFTHERIAH—"Good freedom!"

Said to pregnant women to wish them a good delivery as well as freedom from having had to carry around that growing burden for so many months.

KAMAHKI—a fishing spear; **KAH**NO KAMAHKI—to pick up a girl (or boy)

A **ka**mahki is the long-handled trident that one sees in most fishing boats. Metaphorically, therefore, when a Greek says that he or she is "spear-fishing," it means that they're trying to pick someone up.

So, if you hear a Greek say this to his friends while you're sitting with him, you'll know that's what he thinks he's doing with you.

KEFEE—"happiness" or "good spirits"

A particularly Greek phenomenon that the above phrases only approximate. "Possessed by the spirit of happiness" would perhaps be better, because **ke**fee descends upon you without warning, inflates you with joy, and then, when it has run its course, disappears, perhaps not to return again for another year or even a lifetime. It can not be summoned at will, seems only to seize one in Greece, and once you've experienced it, it's very easy to tell the difference between **ke**fee and ordinary happiness and good spirits. Like knowing the difference between champagne and soda water. The Greeks can instantly recognize if someone is possessed by **ke**fee, and while she or he has it, they are treated with a great deal of deference, being allowed to do almost anything they wish (like expressing their good feelings by tossing a chair through the window) without censure. Part of this is because the person with **ke**fee tends to touch the people around him with a little of its magic and thus, like good wine, he's to be treasured, not thrown out And perhaps the other part is some subconscious realization that **ke**fee might just be a manifestation of the ancient Greek god Dionysos, still hanging around after all these centuries and reminding us that life is for living joyfully, too. But don't try to bring him on deliberately by drinking a lot of wine and doing a lot of dancing, etc. **Ke**fee is a gift of the god and it cannot be bought or forced; if you try, he will just laugh at you and pay you back for your presumptuousness by giving you a terrible, guilt-ridden hangover the next morning.

KERAHSO—"offer," "treat"

You will probably come across this word in the following phrase: "**El**la (tee) na seh ke**rah**so?"—"Come (what) can I offer you?" The Greeks are compulsive buyers of drinks for foreigners and 99% of the time, there is no ulterior motive behind it (unless, of course, you happen to be an attractive young lady or woman, but even then, the ulterior motive is secondary to the original offer). This is because the

Greeks are by nature both hospitable and curious and, since you are a stranger, they want to make you feel welcome and to have you sit with them for a while to learn a bit about you. What they do not want is for you to buy them a drink in return. Greece is their home, not yours, and therefore, as a guest, it would be extremely impolite of you to offer to treat them.

KOMBO**LO**-EE—"worry beads"

The original function and exact origin of these is disputed, but since it is generally agreed that they came from somewhere in Asia Minor, it seems certain that they are not derived from the rosary. In fact, the opposite could quite possibly be true: that they are the progenitor of the rosary and not vice-versa. In modern, scholarly Greek they are called kombo**lohg**-yion, **kom**bos being the Greek word for "knot" and **lohg**-yion meaning "maxim," or "man of letters," which in turn derives from **lohg**os, which means "reason" or "speech." So, the word komo**lo**-ee could be freely translated as "reasoning knots," giving them a strong connection to the contemplative function of the rosary. However, these days, Greek worry beads have little to do with thinking or worrying; they are, instead, a part of a man's masculine attire, his machismo, the way a key chain was for a 1940's zoot-suiter, and one's deftness in twirling the beads has, for the young, superseded their fathers' quiet shifting, one by one, of the beads along their string. This twirling has become quite an art, and you should try to get a Greek to demonstrate its intricacies to you. And, who knows?, perhaps in handling the beads, you may discover for yourself their original, quieting meaning.

KSEELO (THA **FA**-EE)—"(He'll eat) wood."

Means "He'll be punished." See "punishment" under GESTURES above.

MA**LAH**KAS—"masturbator"

An epithet used to describe someone who is stupid, lazy, and/or self-centered—i.e. who just sits around and plays with himself. Often pejorative but not always. If you really mean it, it can be one of the worst things you can call a person, but you will hear a lot of Greeks using it jokingly among friends. They will never, however, use it jokingly with foreigners, so you, no matter how friendly you might think you have become with them, should never try to use it jokingly with them. I once did—with a Greek I had known for 6 years—and the air between us turned into ice.

MAHNGAHS—"tough guy".

Originally used to describe a particular Athenian type of hood or teddy boy, tough, swaggering and often brave. Now used for these types from all over Greece. Not very complimentary, but it can be; it can also be used jokingly.

MAHTIA MOU!—"My eyes!"

An expression of endearment, like "My darling!", meaning that you are the only one for my eyes and /or that yours are the eyes through which I view the world.

MUSICAL INSTRUMENTS

bou**zou**kee—a large long-necked type of mandolin. Singly or in groups, creates the predominant sound of Greek music.

bahgla**mah**—a small bouzoukee.

leera—a long-necked, 3-stringed type of violin, played with a bow, that is the principle solo instrument in Cretan music.

la**oo**toh—the Greek lute, used both as a solo instrument and as accompaniment.

ood—a short-necked type of mandolin with an immense "belly" and no frets. Used as accompaniment.

san**too**ree—the Greek zither, a horizontal, stringed soundbox that is, in contrast with the European zither, played with soft mallets rather than plucked and strummed.

zam**boo**na—the Greek bagpipe, made from the entire hide of a young goat. The air is blown in through one of the leg openings and pressed with an arm through a single flute pipe that is joined to another leg opening. Very primitive and quite haunting. At one point, the Colonels' junta attempted to ban it, along with plate breaking (and bikinis) as "barbaric."

NAH!—"There!", "Here!", "Take that!"

Usually uttered when employing the hand curse called a moondza In its non-exclamatory form, **na** is also used to make the infinitive, just as the word "to" is used in English: "I want to go"— **Thel**o na **pa**o.

OREESTEH—"Here you are." "Can I help you?"

The meaning depends upon the situation in which it is used. You will hear a Greek say, "O**ree**steh" when you enter his shop, when he brings you something you have ordered to eat or drink, or, sometimes, when he answers the telephone. It means, in a sense, "I am (or have been) at your service."

PAHLIKAHREE—a young warrior; a good, brave person.

A high compliment, so you should be quite pleased if a Greek says to you, "**Ee**say pahli**kah**ree."—"You're a palikahree."

PANAGYEEA—"Virgin Mary," "Madonna"

Used in various exclamations, such as "Pana**gyee**a mou!" ("My Madonna!") in much the same way that "My God!" is uttered in English, although the Greeks have an expression for that, too (see The**eh** mou! below.)

PANIGYEERI—"Saint's Day Feast"

PAREH-AH—"a group of friends," "company."

PERASTIKAH—"Get well soon."

Used for all types of illnesses, from a common cold to a broken leg.

PEREEPTERO—"kiosk."

One of the more delightful as well as essential fixtures of Greek life. These sidewalk stands seem to have stuffed into them, in a space as confined as the first astronaut's capsule, just about everything one could imagine needing when all the other stores are closed: cigarettes, lighters, fluids, gases, flints, sweets, magazines, newspapers, books, shaving creams, brushes, razors and razor blades, combs, detergents, hand soaps, colognes, postage stamps, envelopes, writing paper, postcards, sun glasses, transistor radios, batteries, pens, pencils, incense, Kleenex, deodorants, suntan lotions, bobby pins, bottle openers, prophylactics, and God and its owner know what else. In addition, the majority of them have telephones from which one can make local calls or, if a special meter has been installed, long distance or international calls on the automatic dialing system. They are open seven days a week throughout the morning, afternoon and evening. However, most (but not all) of them close around midnight, so be sure to stock up on cigarettes (or whatever else you may need for the wee hours) before then.

PIRAHZEE—"It matters," or "Does it matter?": Dhen pirahzee—"It doesn't matter."

POOSTEES—a homosexual fairy.

PSSST!—"Hey!"
     The sound a Greek makes when he wants to attract your attention. Not considered at all rude, so try not to let your hackles rise if it's directed at you.

STIGMEE, MIA—"a moment", "just a moment".
     Usually uttered by waiters and shopkeepers when they want to say they'll be right with you. Not to be taken literally.

SOUVLAHKI—See under MENU.

STO KALO—lit. "to the good".
     A way of saying goodbye to someone when they, not you, are leaving the place where you have been talking. It means, in a sense, "May you encounter, wherever you're going, something good." Comparable, perhaps, to the English expression "Be well." (Also an euphemism for "Go to hell!"—usually used by children.)

THE-EH MOU!—"My God!": Oh Theh-ohs ksehree—"God knows";
     Dhoksa toh Theh-oh—"Thanks (glory) be to God!"

TEEPOTA—"nothing" *or* "something".

Depends on the situation. If someone says "Thank you," you may reply, "**Tee**poota" ("It's nothing."). Or:

> **Do you want something?—The**lees **tee**pota?
> **Nothing, thank you—Tee**pota, efharis**toh**.

TREEKIKLO—a small, three-wheeled truck, usually green.

The indispensable Greek vehicle, a motorized version of its donkeys. Their owners will transport anything, anytime, anywhere—for a price. The price is about 3 times as expensive as it would cost to take a taxi the same distance, but on the other hand, they will go places taxis won't go, at times when most taxi drivers prefer to sleep, and, of course, they carry much more. However, they are forbidden to transport passengers within most town limits and cannot operate, without a special license, within the centers of large cities. But, on small islands where there are not enough taxis, the police generally turn their backs on the no-passenger rule, particularly when a ship is loading or unloading a large amount of passengers. If engaging a **tree**kiklo, it is wise to establish the cost in advance. Otherwise, once the work has been done, the driver will have you with your back and pocketbook up against the wall.

VOLTA, EE—"the walk."

A traditional Sunday-evening walk found in most Mediterranean countries. Originally came into being as a kind of marriage market, a formalized ritual in which families would dress in their finest Sunday clothes and stroll up and down the seafront displaying their wares, which is to say, their marriageable children. Parents would meet and talk to assess each other's worth while their carefully-chaperoned prospective brides and grooms would dutifully try to strike up a relationship. Nowadays, as these kinds of arranged marriages rapidly become a thing of the past, the **volta** survives mainly as a vestigial habit, its primary function being purely social; one rarely sees boys and girls of marriageable age strolling with their parents—usually, they are off shopping around on their own at sweet shops, cinemas and discotheques.

YA, **YA**SAHS—"Hello" *or* "Goodbye"

Ya and **ya**soo are used when greeting or saying goodbye to an individual with whom you are on familiar terms. **Ya**sahs is used either when addressing a group of people or when speaking to a single person whom you do not know very well.

In other words, **ya**sahs is either the plural or the polite form of **ya** and **ya**soo. It should be noted, however, that yasoo and yasahs are both extremely casual, similar to "Hi" and "Bye" in English, and so, if the situation calls for a certain amount of politeness, you should use **hay**reteh.

YA **HARAH**—"with joy"

Used when saying goodbye to someone or to express satisfaction when asked if something has gone well or pleased you.

YOR**TEE**—Name Day *or* Name Day party.

"Z"—the title of a well-known novel and film about the assassination of Grigoris Lambrakis, an EDA deputy during the pre-junta era. Included here because there is a popular misconception about how the title should be pronounced. Most people call it "Zed", since that is the way Europeans pronounce the last letter of the alphabet. The correct pronunciation is "Zee"—the Greek word "**Zee**" being the third person singular form of the verb "to live." In other words, the title means, "He lives."

PART 5

A GREEK FESTIVE
AND
RELIGIOUS CALENDAR

PUBLIC HOLIDAYS, RELIGIOUS FESTIVALS, AND SAINTS' AND NAME DAYS

HOLIDAY, PUBLIC, A—mia ethni**kee** yortee

Inasmuch as every day of the year is a Saint's Day, it is virtually impossible to have a secular holiday with out some religious connotations. Thus there are only three truly secular holidays throughout the year and one of them—**March 25th, Greek Independence Day**—is also the date of **the Annunciation to the Virgin Mary**, an extremely important religious event, so the two celebrations have become almost indistinguishable from one another. The other two public holidays are **May 1st**, the Greek Labor Day as well as the Spring Festival, and **October 28th**, which commemorates an important date in World War II. **Carnival** is also theoretically a secular event but since it is so inextricably bound to the coming of Lent, it cannot help having enormous religious overtones.

RELIGIOUS FESTIVAL, A—ena panig-**yee**ree

These occur on major Saint's Days, usually at or around the church named after the saint, or in villages or areas for which a particular saint has some special significance. There is much dancing, drinking and feasting, often completely or partially free of charge, and a visit to one, particularly in a small village, can provide you with a truly inside glimpse into Greek life and will certainly become one of the most cherished moments of your visit to the country. Ask the Tourist Police if there are any festivals happening in your area, but be aware that virtually all occur not on the Saint's Day itself but on the *preceding* evening.

NAME DAY, A—mia yortee; **name day party, a—mia** yortee

It is a person's Name Day rather than his birthday (**ye**neth**lia**) which is celebrated in Greece. This is because the naming of a child carries with it such a wealth of family, religious, and historical connotations that the date on which the baby is born pales by comparison. A child is named for either a grandparent or a close relative or, occasionally, a godparent, although the great majority of names come from the grandparents on both sides of the family, other names being chosen only after the number of children exceeds four. And these names, of course, are also those of their grandparents' grandparents and so on, almost ad infinitum, far back into both the family's and Greece's past. Add to this the fact that the names are either those of saints of the Orthodox Church or of Greek historical or mythological figures like Socrates, Odysseus, and Agamemnon, and one realizes that within the entire spectrum of Greek names there is embodied, in a very real sense, the soul of the nation. Those having the name of a saint celebrate on the day of that saint and those with historical or mythological names not included on the Orthodox calendar celebrate on All Saints' Day, which falls on the eighth Sunday after Easter.

Traditionally, it is the person whose name day it is who gives the party, holding open house for visitors throughout the day and often long into the night. One comes to pay one's respects and, depending on the hour, is served coffee, cakes, liqueurs, ouzo, whiskey, wine, hors d'oeuvres and sometimes, if the host is feeling particularly expansive as well as well-off financially, a full-course meal and live bouzouki music. Gifts of the kind that we give on birthdays are not expected, especially if you are a foreigner, although the bringing of flowers, sweets, wine or food (even to the extent of arriving with a live lamb or goat) is traditional. One wishes the person whose name day it is:

"Many Happy Returns!"—"**Hron**ia po**la**!"

"May you live 100 years!"—"Na ta ekato**stees**ees!"

Finally, if a person's Name Day coincides with the Saint's Day Festival of a particular village or area (see **religious festival** above), then he usually celebrates at the local feast rather than at home—although he may do both.

When there is a choice of two dates for a Name Day (certain saints are honored both on the day of their martyrdom or birthday or on the date of a particular event with which they are associated), I have, for the most part, given only the most popular one, i.e. that which a person would be most likely to celebrate. For reasons of space, only the most common Greek saints' names have been included. In addition, since it is sometimes difficult for a foreigner to distinguish between Greek male and female names, **the female names are in italics.**

JANUARY	Yanooarios
1 St. Basil	**Ah**-yos Vaseelios
New Year's Day	Proto-hroniah

Basil, Vaseelios, Vaseelees, Vasos, *Vaso*, *Vassilikee*, *Vassileea*

One of the four founding fathers of the Greek Orthodox Church, St. Basil is greatly revered and is not only the saint of New Year's Day but is also the Greek Santa Claus. Therefore, it is on this day rather than Christmas that presents are given, and the family sitting down to as magnificent a table-load of foods and sweets as possible, the more abundant, the better the prospects for the coming year.

"Happy New Year!"—"Eftikhis**men**os oh kay**noorg**-yios **hron**os!"

6 Epiphany Ta **Fo**ta ("The Lights")

Fotis, Fanos, Fanis, *Fotinee*, *Theh-ofania*, *Fahnee*

In the Orthodox Church, this commemorates not the coming of the Magi but the baptism of Christ in the Jordan. Thus, the central event of the day is the blessing of the waters, an extremely important ritual in such a sea-faring nation. All over Greece, priests and parishioners gather by the nearest body of water (the sea, a river, a lake) which the priest blesses and then into which he throws a cross. Until recently, it was the custom for young men of the area to dive into the icy water and try to be the first to retrieve the cross; this was both an honor and an extremely rewarding enterprise, the successful diver being given donations by the people of the community in return for his blessings. The practice has been discontinued, say many Greeks, because the divers in certain places were trying to eliminate their competitors by knifing them under water. Whatever, the cross is now tied to a string and retrieved by the priest himself. A national holiday.

7 St. John the Baptist **Ah-yos** Yoahnnis **Prodromos**
Yoahnis, **Yah**nis, Yoahna

8 St. Domenica **Ag-yee**ah Dhomineeka
Midwife's Day, on which women of child-bearing age visit the local midwife bringing her gifts. It is on this day alone, if a party is held, that no one can criticize a woman for drinking too much.

11 St. Theodosia **Ag-yee**ah Theoh-dho**see**a
Theh-o-**dho**sios, *Theh-o-**dho**seea*

17 St. Anthony the Great **Ah-yos** Andohnios Mega**hl**os
An**doh**nios, An**doh**nis, *Ando**nee**a, Ando**nett**a*

18 St. Athanasios **Ah-yos** Atha**na**sios
Atha**na**sios, **Tass**os, Tha**na**sis, **Than**os, **Nah**sos, Atha**na**see**a

20 St. Euthymius **Ah-yos** Ef**thee**mios
Ef**thee**mios, *Ef**thi**meea, E**fi**meea*

24 St. Polyxena **Ag-yee**a Polik**se**nee
*Polik**se**nee, **Kse**nee*

25 St. Gregory **Ah-yos** Gree**gor**ios
Gree**gor**is, *Greego**ree**a*

26 St. Xenophontos **Ah-yos** Kseng**fon**das
Kseno**fon**das, Kseno**fon**

30 The Three Hierarchs ton **Tree**on Ee-erar**khon**
The Day of the Three Hierarchs of the Greek Orthodox Church: St. Basil the Great, St. Gregory the Theologian, and St. John the Chrysostom. A big school holiday.

CARNIVAL   Ahpokriess

Traditionally, Carnival begins on the Saturday night three weeks before the beginning of Lent (a moveable date, depending upon when Easter falls, which in turn determines the beginning of Lent and thus the beginning of Carnival.). However, in most places there is little evidence of celebration before the Thursday night of the second week (see tseekno**pemp**tee below) and in certain rural and very religious communities, there is virtually no celebrating done until the final Sunday, the reason being that Carnival is considered a secular, not a religious festival.

Basically, the Carnival season falls into three weekly periods. The first is called

prophonee

from the Greek verb propho**no**, which means "to announce",—i.e. the announcing of the beginning of Carnival. It is during this week that pigs which have been being fattened since the summer are slaughtered and eaten to mark the beginning of the festivities.

The second week, called

kreh-ahtinee

is "Meat-eating Week" and is particularly celebrated on Thursday,

tseeknopemptee

the name of which is derived from the Greek word **tseek**na, which describes the smell of burning meat, and **pemp**tee, which means "Thursday" It is on this night that the real spirit of Carnival usually manifests itself for the first time as people indulge in an orgy of meat-eating both in their houses and out on the town.

The third week,

teerinee

which means "Cheese-eating" is so designated because this is the time, after the glut of meat-eating the week before; when one begins gradually preparing one's body and spirit for the Lenten deprivations that are soon to come. During this week, only dairy products are supposed to be eaten, although this custom is rarely followed.

Inasmuch as Carnival is merely tolerated and not officially recognized by the Church, the only truly religious observances during this period fall on the three Saturdays preceding Lent.

These are all called

pseeh-ho**sah**vaton

which, literally translated, means "Soul Saturday," or "All Souls' Day." These are consecrated to the dead, whose souls are said to walk among the living during this period (*Black Orpheus*, the film which takes place during the carnival in Rio, is certainly the most vivid evocation of this half-religious, half-pagan tradition). On each of these Saturdays, **ko**liva, a wheat dish commemorating the dead is prepared at home and distributed among friends and neighbors in memory of deceased relatives, visits are made to cemeteries, and church services are held.

On the last Sunday of Carnival, Cheese Sunday

teerokeeria**kee**

a Carnival parade (karna**va**los) is held if the city or town has enough money to do so (which a constantly increasing number don't) or there is just a simple frolic of costumed mummers in the town square. Afterwards, one sits down to a traditional meal of macaroni, cheese pies and a special cheese broth called

teero**zoo**mee.

The meal ends with the eating of hard-boiled eggs, a reminder that the next time eggs are eaten, they will be red ones (so-colored to symbolize the blood of Christ) that will be served on Easter Sunday morning to break the Lenten fast.

FEBRUARY   Fevrooahrios

1 St. Tryphon   **Ah-yos Tree**fon
The saint who protects the fields and vines. **Ko**liva and a specially-baked bread are generally distributed on this day by farmers to honor him.

2 Candlemas   Ee Eepapan**dee**
Commemorates Mary's bringing of the infant Jesus to the temple to be blessed. Most Greek mothers do the same 40 days after their child's birth.

3 **St.Simeon**   **Ah**-yos Seemeon
The saint of pregnant women.
4 **St. Isodore**   **Ah**-yos Eesee-dhoros
Ee**see**-dhoros, See-**dheh**rees, *Eesee-dhora*

5 **St. Agatha**   Ag-**yee**a Agathee
Agathee

10 **St. Charalampos**   **Ah**-yos Haralambos
Haralambos, Hareelaos, **Har**is, *Hareeklia*
A very popular saint, revered as Greece's protector against the plague.

11 **St. Vlameos**   **Ah**-yos **Vlam**ios
Protects against wild beasts and thus is quite popular in the north of Greece.

17 **St. Theodore**   **Ah**-yos Theh-**oh**-dhoros
Theh-**oh**-dhoros, **Theh**-oh, *Theh-oh-**dhora***

LENT   Sarakos**tee** *or* me**gah**lee
                                  sarakos**tee**

"Me**gah**lee" meaning "Great" or "large" and thus distinguishing this period, which is seven weeks or 48 days, from both the 40-day desert fast of Christ and the 40-day period of fasting observed by the Orthodox faithful before Christmas. The date of the beginning of Lent is moveable, depending upon when Easter falls in any given year.

fast, a	**mi**a nis**tee**a
fasting	nis**tee**a
Lenten food	sarakosti**ano** fahghi**toh**

Strict observance of the fasting rules of Lent is no longer practiced by the majority of Greeks living in the major cities and tourist-sophisticated islands. Therefore, during this period meat markets, etc. remain fully-stocked and do a thriving business. However, in the remoter (and thus poorer and more religious) areas, the strictures of the church are often followed to the letter, and it can consequently be very difficult to obtain any food that is prohibited during this period, i.e. all. animal products—meat, poultry, eggs, milk, and cheese—and any seafood that contains blood, which means fish of any sort but does not include lobster, shrimp, octopus and squid. There are, however, always a few frozen chickens to be found left over in some butcher's freezer, and eggs, milk and sometimes even cheese from local farmers whose chickens and cows fortunately keep on producing. Greeks are, without exception, cheerfully tolerant of the heretical eating habits of foreigners.

Aside from the first three days of Lent during which strict observers also deny themselves bread and water, Holy Week, during which wine and olive oil are also forbidden, and Good Friday, which is a day of total fasting that, for the true faithful who wish to emulate the suffering of Christ, excludes everything except water and includes the sipping of a glass of vinegar, the basic Lenten fare consists of winter vegetables lettuce, cabbage, beets, spinach, cauliflower, etc. various pastas, bread, olive oil, and protein-rich beans, lentils and chick peas: a wonderfully-balanced diet that can also be said to be, for the poor and faithful, an economic godsend.

The first day of Lent is called

Kathara dheftera

which means "Clean Monday," a reference both to the purification of the body and soul after the excesses of Carnival and to the cleaning of the kitchen and its utensils (often with ashes) to rid the house of the last traces of Carnival self-indulgence, a process that goes on throughout the week, which is called "Clean Week":

Kathara Evthoma-dha

However, since it is extremely difficult to shift so abruptly from Carnival into Lent, Clean Monday still has an extremely festive air about it and is one of the brightest and most fun-filled days of the year. Traditionally, because the kitchen has been rendered spotless, little or no cooking is done at home on this day and throughout Greece droves of people head for the countryside to eat in tavernas or to have picnics: the fare being Lenten but its abundance and the spirit and spirits with which it is eaten being definitely Carnival in character. On this day, the only bread which is baked and eaten is a flattish, unleavened loaf called "lagahna" and the national pastime is kite-flying, the skies over every unbuilt-up area in Greece a marina of flying, floating objects of all shapes, sizes and colors, the ground below them filled with fathers and their children fighting over who gets to hold the string.

Principal Lenten Days of Observance:

First Saturday:
St. Theodore   **Ah**-yos Theh-**oh**-dhoros
Theh-**oh**-dhoros, **Theh**-oh, *Theh-oh-dhora*
An All Souls' Day (see pseekno**sa**vaton above) on which the dead are remembered and **ko**liva is served.

First Sunday   tees Orthosok**see**as
Commemorates Empress Theodora's triumph over the iconoclasts and the consequent reintroduction of icons into Orthodox churches.

Palm Sunday   Keeria**kee** ton Vaeeon
Fish is permitted on this day in celebration of the entrance of Christ into Jerusalem.

Holy Week   Me**gah**lee Evthoma-dha
A week of increasingly austere fasting when wine and olive oil (a great deprivation for the Greeks) are also prohibited from the diet.

Maundy Thursday   Me**gah**lee **Pemp**tee
The beginning of preparations for the breaking of the fast on Easter Sunday. Eggs are boiled and dyed red to symbolize the blood of Christ, and the baking of Easter bread is begun.

Good Friday   Me**gah**lee Paraske**vee**
For true believers, a day of complete abstention during which nothing but water and, for those who want to really taste the sufferings of Christ, vinegar (often mixed with ashes or spider webs) is taken into the body.

Holy Saturday   Me**gah**loh **Sah**vaton
A day during which the solemnity of Lent (and particularly of Good Friday) gradually lifts as preparations for the Easter Sunday's feast gather tempo. More Easter bread is baked and

lambs and goats are slaughtered, their entrails and variety meats being delivered to the housewife for the time-consuming process of making the Easter soup with which the Lenten fast will be broken in the early hours of Easter Sunday morning following the midnight announcement of the Resurrection of Christ.

MARCH[1]   **Mar**tios
1 **St.** Eudoxia   Ag-**yee**a Ev-dhok-**hee**a
    *Ev-dhok-**hee**a, Dolly*

9 **Day of the 40 Martyrs**   ton Sa**ran**da Mar**tee**ron
    Sa**rah**ndis

16 **St. Christodoulos**   **Ah**-yos Hris**toh**-dhoulos
    Hris**toh**-dhoulos, *Hristo-**dhoulee**, Loulee*

25 **Annunciation Day**   Evangheli**smos** Theh-o**tok**hoo
    Independence Day   e**pet**ios tees aneksarti**see**as
    Evan**ghe**los, Van**ghe**lees, **Van**ghelos, *Evanghe**lee**a*
A very big national holiday combining both the Annunciation to the Virgin Mary and the day on which the Greeks began their struggle for independence from the Turks in 1821. It is the only Name Day that is celebrated during Lent, and on this day fish is allowed to be eaten, usually salt cod served with garlic sauce.

EASTER[2]   **Pask**ha *or* **Lam**bree
    Easter Sunday   Kiria**kee** tou **Ah**-yeeoo **Pask**ha
    "Happy Easter!"   "**Ka**lo **Pask**ha!"
Easter Sunday festivities begin the moment the priest announces exactly at midnight on Holy Saturday, that Christ has risen (see below.) Fireworks go off, church bells peal, and, at the end of the service, everyone quickly makes their way home or to a nearby restaurant to celebrate by breaking the Lenten fast. Traditionally, this commences with the eating of a red Easter egg (paskali**no** av**go**) just as, at the end of Carnival the last thing then eaten was an egg. The custom is to tap the pointed end of one's egg against another's while saying:

"**Christ is risen!**"   "**Hree**stos ahne**stee!**"

If your egg does not break, you are considered blessed with good luck. However, this luck must then be tested against the eggs of the others at the party, and rarely does one person's egg survive the entire round. If it should, that person's outlook for the coming year is extremely bright.

The main dish of the Easter Sunday morning feast is mag-yi**reet**sa, a traditional Easter soup made with rice, chopped lamb innards and a delicious egg-lemon broth flavored with dill. It is usually accompanied by a green salad and cheese pies. Although filling, it is not overly so, being somewhat like a tune-up for the daylong feast that is to commence almost as soon as one awakes the following morning.

The main Easter Sunday meal is a cornucopia of springtime delicacies and Easter specialties: baby lamb or goat oven- or spit-roasted with new potatoes, spring salads, cheeses, Easter bread, cakes, cookies, candies and, again, a seemingly endless supply of Easter eggs, not to mention, of course, an equally endless supply of wine.

No Greek holiday, either religious or secular, not Christmas nor Carnival, can compare with this day in the joyousness of its atmosphere and the rich freshness of its cuisine. Blessed indeed is the tourist who is visiting Greece at Easter, and particularly so if he has been invited by a Greek family to share in their festivities.

The following Name Days are celebrated on Easter:
Sunday:
Lambros, *Lambrinee˙*, Anas**ta**sios, **Tah**sos, *Anastaseea*

EASTER WEEK   ev-dho**mas** tees dhiakeni**see**mou

The entire week is devoted to celebrating Easter, Monday being a full national holiday, while on the rest of the days as little work is done as possible, particularly in the fields.

Low Sunday   Kiria**kee** tou Ag-**yee**ou Tho**mah**
Tho**mas** (th as in "thin")

The last day of the Easter festivities, also called an**dee**paskha, which, loosely translated, means "end of Easter." On the following day, everyone returns to work and the schools open.

APRIL Apreelios
6 St. Eutikios **Ah-**yos Efteekhios
Efteekhios, Fteek-ho, *Eftikheea*

23 St. George **Ah-**yos Yorgos
Yorgos, *Yorgheea*

A greatly-revered saint whose day is celebrated throughout Greece, particularly by shepherds for whom he is the patron saint. A day devoted to much feasting and thus, if it falls during the fasting week before Easter (which it often does), it is postponed until Easter Monday, when one can eat and celebrate as much as one wants.

25 St. Mark **Ah-**yos Markos
Markos

The celebration of this Saint's Day is also postponed until after Easter if it should fall during Holy Week.

MAY **Ma-**yos
1 **May Day** Protomah-**ya**

The Greek Labor Day as well as the Spring Festival, when wreaths of plants and flowers are woven and hung over the front door to welcome the season.[3]
A national holiday.

4 St. Irene Ag-**yeea** Eereenee
Eereenee, Rena, Reno

8 St. John the Theologian **Ah-**yos Yoahnis oh Theh-**logos**
Theh-ologos, *Theh-ologheea*

21 St. Constantine **Ah-**yos Konstandeenos
St. Helen Ag-**yeea** Elenee
Konstandeenos, **Kos**ta, *Konstandeena, Elenee*

A very important feast-day in memory of Constantine the Great and his mother, St. Helen, as well as, by association, Constantine Paleologos, the last Byzantine emperor. Virtually a national holiday because so many people celebrate their Name Day on this date. This is also the day when the well-known fire-walkers of northern Greece perform their yearly ritual of walking over hot coals while possessed and protected by the spirit of St. Constantine. They are called "ee Anastenari-dhess," which derives from the Greek word "to sigh," describing the sounds they make while dancing themselves into a trance before walking on the hot coals. If you are in the area and wish to visit, check with the Tourist Police for the time and place.

MOVEABLE POST-EASTER FEASTS:

Ascension Day   ee **A**nalipsees tou Hri**stou**
Celebrated 40 days after Easter.

Pentecost (Whitsunday)   Pendiko**stee**
Celebrated the 7th Sunday after Easter.

Whit-Monday   dhef**tera** tees Pendiko**stees**
The Feast of **the Holy Spirit**, Ag-**yee**oo Pn**ev**matos, and a national holiday. There are often community feasts (panag-**yee**ri) held on this day at churches bearing the name of **the Holy Trinity**—Ag-**yee**a Tree**ahss**.

All Saints' Day   Ag-**yee**on **Pan**don
Celebrated on the 8th Sunday following Easter. The day on which everyone who does not have a saint's name celebrates his Name Day, and when the May Day wreaths are traditionally burnt.

JUNE	**Yoo**nios
3 **St. Martha**	Ag-**yee**a **Mar**tha
Martha	

29 **St. Peter**	**Ah**-yos **Pe**tros
St. Paul	**Ah**-yos **Pav**los
Petros, *Petroula*, **Pav**los, *Pavleena*	

30 **Day of the 12 Apostles**	Ee Seenaksees ton **Dho**-dheka
Apos**toh**lon	Apos**toh**lees

JULY   **Yoo**lios

1 **St. Anargiros**   **Ah**-yos Anarg-**yiros**
   Arg-**yiros**, Arg-**yirees**, *Arg-yeero*, *Arg-yeeroula*

7 **St. Kiriaki**   Ag-yeea Kiria**kee**
   Kiriah**kos**, *Kiriakee*

11 **St. Euphemia**   Ag-yeea Efi**mee**a
   Efimeea

15 **St. Marina**   Ag-yeea Ma**ree**na
   Mareena

20 **St. Elijah**   **Ah**-yos Ele**eahs**
   Ele**eahs**

25 **St. Ann**   Ag-yeea **Ah**na
   Ahna

26 **St. Paraskevi**   Ag-yeea Paras**kavee**
   Paraskavee, *Paraskevoula*, **Voula**

27 **St. Panteleon**   **Ah**-yos Pandeleh-**eemon**
   Pande**lees**, *Pandeleea*

AUGUST   **Ahv**goostos

1 Beginning of the 15-day Fast of the Virgin Mary. As with Lent, the first day is devoted to cleansing the kitchen utensils, and throughout the period, the same food prohibitions apply, except on August 6th (see below.)

6 **Transfiguration Day**   Ee Metamor**phosees**
   Sotee**rees**, *Sotireea*, **Hrees**tos, *Hreesteena*, *Teena*, Emanoo**el**,
   Mano**lees**, **Mah**nos, *Emanooella*
   Although not an official holiday, it is often observed as one, especially by Greeks in rural areas. To celebrate the Transfiguration of Christ, the fasting rules, specifically with regard to fish, are lifted, and there is usually a panig-**yee**ree held the evening before.

15 Assumption Day   Ee **Kee**misis tees Theh-ot**oh**koo
   Mahnos, *Mareea*, **May**ree, Panag-yotees, *Panag-yota*, *Panag-youla*
   A very big national holiday, perhaps the second largest of the year next to Easter. There is a mass exodus from the cities, particularly to the island of Tinos, where an icon of the Virgin Mary is said to have wrought many miracles especially in curing physical ills. Religious feasts (see panig-**yee**ri) are held at or near most churches associated with the Virgin, and the few restaurants and tavernas that stay open are crowded with celebrants. It is advisable not to attempt to travel anywhere on the days surrounding this festival as all means of transportation are packed with a seething mass of humanity.

30 St. Alexander   **Ah**-yos Aleksan-dhros
   Aleksan-dhros, Alekos, Aleksees, *Aleksahn-dhra*, *Aleka*, *Aleekee*

SEPTEMBER   Septem**vrios**
5 St. Zacharias   **Ah**-yos Zakhar**ee**as
   Zakhar**ee**as

8 The Virgin's Birthday   Yenisis Theh-ot**oh**kou

14 Elevation of the Cross   **Eep**soma Tim**ee**oo Stavroo
   Stavros, *Stavroula*
   Commemorates the finding of the True Cross by St. Helen, the mother of Constantine the Great, who journeyed to Jerusalem to search for it; when found, it was raised aloft by Bishop Makharios of Jerusalem. An important feast day on which basil, which marked the spot where the cross was found, is distributed to the congregation by the priest.

17 St. Sofia   Ag-**yeea** Sof**ee**a
   St. Agape   Ag-**yeea** Ag**ah**pee
   St. Elpida   Ag-**yeea** Elpee-dha
   Sofeea, *Agahpee*, *Elpee-dha*

26 St. Eustathius   **Ah**-yos Efstathios
   Efstathios, **Stathees**, *Efstatheea*

OCTOBER	Oktoh vrios
18 St. Luke	**Ah-yos Lukas**
Lukas, *Lukeea*	

20 St. Gerasimus	**Ah-yos Yerasimos**
Yerasimos	

23 St. Jacob	**Ah-yos Yakovos**
Yakovos	

26 St. Demetrius **Ah-yos Dhimeetrios**

Dhimeetrios, Dhimeetrees, *Dhimitreea*, Dhimitroula, **Mem**is, *Memee*

A widely-celebrated feast day, especially in Thessaloniki, whose patron saint is St. Demetrius. October 23rd is also the date on which the city was liberated from the Turks in 1912.

28 "Okhee" Day

A big national holiday commemorating the day in 1940 when Gen. Metaxas, then premier of Greece, said "No!" ("Okhee") to Mussolini's demands that he grant Italian troops "right of passage" into Greece. In the subsequent fighting, the Greek army mauled the Italians—much to the world's surprise and Hitler's extreme annoyance. Lots of military parading, etc. All stores are closed.

NOVEMBER	Noemvrios
1 St. Cosmas	**Ah-yos Kosmas**
St. Damian	**Ah-yos Dhahmianos**
St. Anargyrus	**Ah-yos Anarg-**yiros
Kosmas, Dhahmia**nos**, **Anar**g-yiros, **Arg-yee**ris, **Arg-***yeero*	

8 St. Michael	**Ah-yos Meekhaeel**
St. Gabriel	**Ah-yos Gavrieel**
Meekhalis, Gavrieel, **Ang**helos, *Anghelikee*, *Angheleea*, *Strateea*, *Ehfee*	

9 St. Nektarius　　　　　　**Ah**-yos Nektarios
　Nektarios

11 St. Menas, St. Victor　　　**Ah**-yos Minas, Veektor
　Minas, **Veek**tor, *Victoreea*

13 St. John Chrysosromos　　**Ah**-yos Yoahnis Hreesostomos
　Hreesostomos

14 St. Philip　　　　　　　**Ah**-yos Feelipos
　Feelipos

15 Short Lent　　　　　　Meekree Sarakostee
　Beginning of the Fast of the Nativity which lasts until Christmas
Day. A 40-day, Lenten-type fast which is called "Short Lent" to differ-
entiate it from the longer, 48-day period before Easter. Observed only
by the very religious.

16 St. Matthew　　　　　　**Ah**-yos Mat-**thay**os
　Mat-**thay**os, **Man**thos

21 Presentation of the　　　Eeso-dhia tees Theh-otohkou
　　Virgin Mary
　Mayree, *Mareea*, Panag-**yo**tis, **Pah**nos, *Panag-yota*
　The Presentation of the Virgin Mary in the Temple in Jerusalem.
One of the Orthodox Church's most important feast days.

25 St. Catherine　　　　　Ag-**yeea** Aykatereeni
　Katereena, *Kateena*, *Katereeno*

26 St. Stylianus　　　　　**Ah**-yos Steelianos
　Steelianos, *Steelianee*

30 St. Andrew　　　　　　**Ah**-yos Ah̓n-**dhreh**-as
　Ah̓n-**dhreh**-as, *Ah̓n-dhreeahna*
　The 1st Apostle and Patron Saint of Patras.

DECEMBER   Dhekemvrios

1 St. Barbara   Ag-yeea Varvara

Varvara

The patron saint of grocery stores. Thus, all of them are closed on this day. She is also the protectress of children against smallpox.

5 St. Sabas   **Ah-yos Sahvas**

Sahvas

6 St. Nicholas   **Ah-yos Nikolaos**

Nikolas, Nikolaos, Neekos, *Nikoletta, Tetee*

Not the Greek Santa Claus (St.Basil is.). Perhaps because his martyred body was thrown into the sea after he was hanged by the Turks in 1657, he has become the patron saint of seamen. There are innumerable churches built in his honor dotting the islands and coastlines of Greece, and **ko**liva blessed in these churches is often taken on voyages to be thrown into the sea to calm it.

9 St. Anna   Ag-yeea Ahna

Ahna

10 St. Menas   **Ah-yos Minas**

Mi**nas**

12 St. Spyridon   **Ah-yos Spiree-dhon**

Spiree-dhon, Speeros, *Spiri-**dhoula***

The special saint of Corfu, wheré he was born and where his mummified body is now kept. Thus, his day is marked on Corfu by much festivity.

13 St. Eustratius   **Ah-yos Efstra**tios.

Efstratios, **Stra**tos, *Efstrateea*

15 St. Eleutherius   **Ah-yos Elef**therios

Elef**ther**ios, Lef**ter**ees, *Elef**there**ea*

17 St. Dionysius   **Ah-yos Dheeonee**sios

Dheeoneesios, **Dhen**ees, *Dheeoniseea*

18 St. Sebastianus   **Ah-yos Sevastianos**
Sevastia**nos**, *Sevastee*

24 St. Eugenia   Ag-**yeea** Ev-yeneea
Ev-**yen**ios, *Ev-yeneea*

A day of preparation for the ending of the pre-Christmas fast. Pigs or turkeys are slaughtered and the Christmas bread as well as cakes and cookies are baked, particularly to give to the children who will be visiting houses that evening singing carols (**kal**anda).

25 Christmas   Hree**stoo**yena
"Merry Christmas!"   **"Kala Hreestooyena!"**

Although a major feast day, it is of secondary importance to Easter and is generally not celebrated as elsewhere by the giving of gifts (this is done on New Year's Day). However, Western customs and commercial pressures are making constant inroads into Greek tradition, and it will not be long before Christmas in Greece becomes indistinguishable from that of all conspicuous-consumption societies. On the other hand, the most important ritual of the day—the portioning of the Christmas bread—will no doubt remain. And perhaps, but not likely, the inclusion of a dish of white beans on the Christmas table in memory of the dead.

The following Name Days can be celebrated On Christmas but this is usually done on August 6th, the Day of the Transfiguration of Christ:

Hreestos, *Hreesteena*, *Teena*, Emanooel, Manolees, **Mahnos, **
Emanooella

26 Gathering of the   Ee **Seen**aksis Theh-otohk-hou
Virgin Mary
Mahrios, *Mareea*, **May**ree

These names are also celebrated on Assumption Day, August 15; December 26th is a public holiday, like Boxing Day elsewhere.

27 St. Stepben   **Ah-yos Stefanos**
Stefanos, *Stefaneea*

31 New Year's Eve   Paramo**nee** tees Proto-hroni**ahs**

Celebrated as elsewhere but not quite so frenetically, except in the major, more "civilized" cities. On this night it is the custom of both children and grown-ups to make the rounds of peoples' houses singing carols (**ka**landa) and, in addition to the usual cakes, candies and cookies that are offered Christmas Eve carolers, one also gives coins to the children and drinks to the adults (and often to the children, too).

NOTES

[1] Any Name Day that happens to fall within the Lenten period has its celebration postponed until after Easter.

[2] The date of Easter is determined by a complicated set of calculations which require that it fall after both the first full moon following both the first day of spring <u>and</u> the Jewish Passover.

[3] Traditionally, these are then burnt on All Saints' Dáy.

PART 6
GEOGRAPHICAL PLACE NAMES

GREECE

Where is...?	Poo eenay...?
How far is...?	Poso mahkriah eenay...?
Is there a ship (train/bus) for...?	Ekhee pleeo (trayno/leh-oforeeo) ya...?

Acropolis, the	ee Ah-kropolees
Aegean, the	ee Ayg-**yay**-on
Aegina	**Ayg**yeena
Athens	Ah**thee**na
Attica	Ahti**kee**
Boetia	Vee-o**tee**a
Cephalonia	Kefaloni**ah**
Chalkidiki	Halki-dhi**kee**
Chania	Hahni**ah**
Chios	**Hee**ohs
Corfu	**Kehr**keera
Corinth	**Kor**eenthos
Crete	**Kree**tee
Cyclades	Kee**kla**-dhess
Delos	**Dhee**los
Delphi	Dhel-**fee**
Dodecanese	Dho-dheh-**kah**-neesa
Epidauros	Eh**pee**-dhavros
Epirus	**Ee**peeros
Euboea	**Ev**eea
Herakleion	Eer**ah**klio
Hydra	**Ee**-dhra
Igoumenitsa	Eegoo-me**neet**sa
Ionion Islands	Neesi**ah** tou Ee-ohnee**oo**
Ios	**Ee**ohs
Ithaca	Eeth**ah**kee
Knossos	Knos**ohs**

Lesbos	Lesvos
Macedonia	Mahke-dhoneea
Meteora	Mehteh-ora
Mt. Athos	Ahyon Oros
Mt. Lycabettus	Oros Leekaveetohs
Mt. Olympus	Oros Ohleempos
Mt. Pelion	Oros Peelion
Mycenae	Meekeenay
Mykonos	Meekonos
Mytelene	Meeteeleenee
Naupactus	Nahfpaktohs
Naxos	Nahksos
Olympia	Ohleembeea
Paros	Pahros
Parthenon	Parthenon
Patmos	Pahtmos
Patras	Pahtras
Peloponnese	Peloponisos
Phaestos	Faystos
Philippi	Feelipee
Piraeus	Peerayefs
Poros	Poros
Rethymnon	Retheemnon
Rhodes	Ro-dhohs
Samos	Sahmos
Samothrace	Samothrakee
Santorini	Santoreenee *or* Theera
Saronic Gulf	Kolpos tou Saronikou
Serifos	Sehrifos
Sifnos	Seefnos
Skiathos	Skeeahthos
Skopelos	Skopelos
Skyros	Skeeros
Souda	Soo-dha
Sounion	Soonion
Sparta	Sparti
Spetsai	Spetsess

Thasos	**Tha**sos
Thebes	**Thee**vay
Thera	**Thee**ra
Thermopylae	Thehrmo**pee**lay
Thessaloniki	Thessalo**nee**kee
Thessaly	Thessa**lee**a
Thrace	**Thra**kee
Tinos	**Tee**nos
Volos	**Vo**los
Vouliagmeni	Vooliahg**men**ee
Yannina	Yoah**nee**na
Zakynthos	**Zah**keenthos

FOREIGN

America	Ahmeri**kee**
Amsterdam	Ahmster**dahm**
Antwerp	Ahm**vehr**sa
Australia	Ahfstrah**lee**a
Austria	Ahf-**stree**a
Barcelona	Varke**lo**nee
Belgium	**Vel**ghio
Beirut	**Vee**reetos
Belgrade	Veli**grah**-dhee
Berlin	Vero**lee**no
Berne	**Vehr**nee
Brussels	Vreek**se**less
Cairo	**Kah**-eero
CapeTown	CapeTown
China	**Kee**na
Cologne	Kolo**nee**a
Copenhagen	Copen**hah**gyee
Cyprus	**Kee**pros
Denmark	Dhah**nee**a
Dublin	Dhoov**lee**no
Edinburgh	Edheen**voor**go
Egypt	**Ayg**-yeeptos

England	Ahn**glee**a
Famagusta	Ah**mok**hostos
Finland	Feenlah-**dhee**a
France	Gah**lee**a
Geneva	Ye**nev**ee
Genoa	**Yen**ova
Germany	Yehr-mah**nee**a
Gibralter	Yeevral**tar**
Glascow	Glah**skov**ee
Great Britain	Me**gah**lee Vreta**nee**a
Helsinki	El**sink**ee
Holland	Ohlahn-**dhee**a
India	Een-**dhee**a
Ireland	Eerlahn-**dhee**a
Israel	Eesrah-**eel**
Istanbul	Constandee**noo**polees
Japan	Yapo**nee**a
Jerusalem	Ee-eh-rusa**leem**
Lebanon	**Lee**vahnos
Lisbon	Leesa**vohn**
London	Lon-**dhee**no
Madrid	Mah-**dhree**tee
Marseilles	Masa**lee**a
Mediterranean the	ee Me**sohg**-yios
Milan	Mee**lah**no
Morocco	Ma**rok**oh
Munich	**Moh**nako
Naples	Neh-**ah**polees
New Zealand	**Neh**-a Zeelahn-**dhee**a
Nicosia	Lefko**see**a
Oslo	**Oh**slo
Paris	Pah**ree**see
Poland	Poloh**nee**a
Portugal	Portogah**lee**a
Rome	**Rom**ee
Rotterdam	**Roh**terdahm
Russia	Roh**see**a

South Africa	Notios Ahfrikee
Spain	Eespahneea
Stockholm	Stokholmee
Sweden	Sooee-dheea
Switzerland	Elveteea
Turkey	Tourkeea
Venice	Veneteea
Vienna	Vee-ennee
Yugoslavia	Yugoslaveea
Zurich	Zeereekhee

UNITED STATES

The United States	Ee Eenomeness Politee-ess tess Amerikees

Most U.S. place names have been phonetically transcribed in Greek exactly as they sound in English. The more important exceptions are listed below:

Baltimore	Vahltimoree
Boston	Vostohnee
Chicago	Sekahgo
Georgia	Yeh-org-yeea
Hawaii	Havaee
Honolulu	Hohnolo[o
Iowa	Ah-eeova
Los Angeles	Lohs Ahnd-zeless
Massachusetts	Mahsa-oosettee
Michigan	Meetseegahn
New Orleans	Neh-a Orleh-ahnee
New York	Neh-a Yorkee
San Francisco	Ah-yos Frangheeskos

PART 7
MAPS

ATHENS:
SINTAGMA (CONSTITUTION SQUARE)

1. Sintagma
2. To and from Piraeus and the Acropolis
3. To Plaka
4. To Plaka, Monastiraki Flea Market, subway.
5. From Monastiraki and Piraeus
6. From Omonia Square
2. To Omonia Square, subway, Piraeus
3. From Kaningos Square
9. To Kolonaki Square and Mt. Lycabettus
10. To and from: American & British Embassies, the Megaron, and the Hilton Hotel & Athens Tower

A. Parliament Building
B. Airport Bus Stop Terminal
C. Motor Insurance Bureau
D. Luggage depot, Pacific Ltd., 24 & 26 Nikis St.
F. Central Post Office
C. American Express
D. Bookstore
H. Tourist Bureau (E.O.T.)
I. Telephone & Telegraph Office
J. Bookstore
K. Book & Magazine store

PIRAEUS

1. Karaiskakis Square
2. Travel agencies, boat tickets
3 & 3a. Boats to the Aegean Islands
4. Boats to the Saronic Islands
5 & 5a. Boats to Crete
6. Foreign ships: arrivals and departures

A. Customs House
B. Subway Station to Athens; Telephone & Telegraph Office
C. Trains to the Peloponnese
D. Trains to northern Greece
E. Tourist Police, 43 Akti Miaoulis

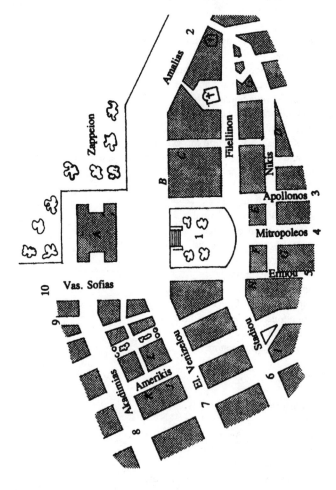

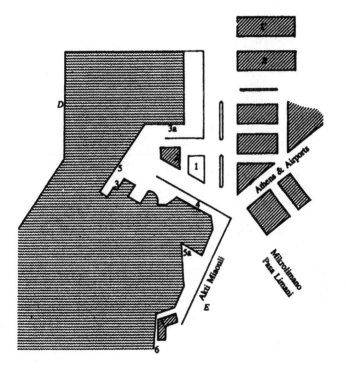

PART 8
A MINI VOCABULARY

VERBS
I am—Eemay
I am not—Dhen eemay
I was—Eemoonah
I will be—Tha eemay
I have—Eh-ho
I don't have—Dhen eh-ho
Do you have?—Eh-hees?
I need—Hreeahzomay
I want—Thelo
I don't want—Dhen thelo
I like—M'arehsee
I don't like—Dhen m'areh-see
It doesn't matter—Dhen peerahzee
I understand—Katalavayno
I don't understand—Dhen katalavayno

WORDS & EXPRESSIONS
afternoon—ahpoyevma
airport—ah-ehro-dhromio
another (one more)—ena ahlo
ashtray—tahsahkee
Athens—Ahtheena
bank, the—ee trahpeza
bed, a—ena krevahtee
bill, the—tohn logariasmo
bread—psomee
bus, a (the)—ena (toh) leh-oforeeo
chair, a—mia karekla
cigarettes—tsigahra
coffee—kafess
DOCTOR—yatros
EMERGENCY—ahnahnghee
English (lang.)—Ahngleea

food—fahghit**oh**
fork—peeroonee
glass—pot**ee**ree
help—voeethia
Greece—ee Ellah-dha
Greek (adj)—Eleeniko
Greek (lang.)—Elleenika
hot—zestoh
hotel—kseno-dhok**hee**o
How much?—Poso?
knife—mak**hay**ree
house—**spee**tee
map, a—ena har**tee**
milk—**gah**la
money—**hree**mata
napkins—petsettess
"No"—**Oh**-hee
oil—**lah**-dhee
"Okay"—En**dah**ksee
passport—dheeavateerio
pharmacy—farmak**ee**o
"Please"—Parakalo
port, the—toh leemahnee
police, the—ee astinomeea
restaurant—estiatorio
room, a—**ena** dhoh**mah**tio
salt—a**lah**tee
ship, the—toh karavee
spoon—kootahli
station, the—oh stathmos
stamps—gramatohseema
sugar—zak**ha**ree
suitcase—vah**lee**tsa
taxi, a—ena tah**ksee**
tea—tsah-ee
telephone, a—**ena** teeleh**f**ono
telegram, a—**ena** teeleh**graf**eema

today—**seem**ehra
ticket, a—**en**a eeseeteerio
toilet, the—ee too-**ah**letta
tomorrow—**ah**vrio
tonight—ah**pohp**see
Tourist Police—Tooristi**kee** astino**mee**a
train, the—toh **tray**no
vinegar—**ksee**-dhee
"**Waiter!**"—Gar**sohn!**"
water—**neh**ro

Part 9
WEIGHTS & MEASURES, NUMBERS & AMOUNTS

WEIGHTS & MEASURES

In Greece, virtually all solids and liquids are sold by kilos and grams, by their weight rather than volume. The single exception is gasoline, which is sold by the liter.

one kilometer—ena heeli**oh**-metro = 0.62 miles (1 mile = 1.61 km.)
   (kilometers—heeli**oh**-metra)

one meter—ena **met**ro = 1.09 yards (1 yard = 0.91 meters)
   (meters—**met**ra)

one gallon—ena galonee = 1 US gallon
   (gallons = galonia)

one liter—ena lee**t**roh = 2 US pints (1 quart = 0.95 liters)
   (liters = **lee**tra)

one kilo—ena kee**lo** = 2.5 lbs. or 1 liter (2 pints)
   (kilos—**kee**la)

one gram—ena gra**ma**rio = 0.04 ounces (1 ounce = 28.3 grams)
   (grams—gra**ma**ria)

NUMBERS AND AMOUNTS

The first number of each group of ten except ten (i.e. one, twenty, thirty, etc.) radically changes its form depending on the gender of the thing being counted, as indicated below. The other numbers change but not so radically. In general, one counts as in English.

CARDINAL NUMBERS

0	mee**dhen**
1	**en**as (m) **mee**a (f) **en**a (n)
2	**dhee**oh
3	**tree**ah
4	**teh**sera
5	**pen**deh
6	**ek**see
7	ef**tah** *or* ep**tah**

8	awktoh
9	enaya
10	**dheka**
11	**en**-dheka
12	**dho**-dheka
13	dheka-**tree**ah
14	dheka-**teh**sera
15	dheka-**pen**deh
16	dheka-**eksee**
17	dheka-eftah
18	dheka-awktoh
19	dheka-enaya
20	**eeko**see
21	**eeko**see **ena** (**meea**) (**enas**)
22	**eeko**see **dheeoh**
30	**tree**ahnda
40	**sarahnda**
50	**peneenda**
60	**ekseenda**
70	ev-**dhomeenda**
80	awk-**dhon**-da
90	**eneenda**
100	**ekatoh**
101	ekaton **ena** (**meea**) (**enas**)
102	ekaton **dheeoh**
112	ekaton **dho**-dheka
200	dheeah-**kosia**
300	trah-**kosia**
400	tetra-**kosia**
500	penda-**kosia**
600	eksa-**kosia**
700	eftah-**kosia**
800	awkta-**kosia**
900	enaya-**kosia**
1000	**hee**lia
2000	**dhee**oh heeliah-**dhess**

10,000	dheka heeliah-dhess
50,000	peneenda heeliah-dhess
100,000	ekaton heeliah-dhess
1999	heelia enaya-kosia eneneenda enaya
1,000,000	ena ekaton-meerio
2,000,000	dheeoh ekatoh-meeria

ORDINALS & FRACTIONS

first	protoh
second	dhefteroh
third	treetoh
fourth	tetartos
tenth	dhekatos

once	meea fora
twice	dheeo foress
three times	treess foress

one-quarter	ena tetartoh
one-half	meeso
three-quarters	treeah tetarta
one-third	ena treetoh
two-thirds	dheeoh treeta

ABOUT THE AUTHOR

TOM STONE first traveled to Greece in 1959 as an assistant stage manager for Jerome Robbins' "Ballets: U.S.A." then on a 17-nation tour for the State Department. He returned in 1967 as a respite from stage managing the Broadway company of "Funny Girl," fell in love with Mykonos, and returned again in 1969 to spend a summer writing the Great American Novel. Needless to say, this didn't happen, but one thing lead to another and he stayed on to live in various parts of Greece almost continuously for the next 24 years.

In the process, he became one of the country's leading lighting designers, taught English at Anatolia College, had his own taverna, and wrote two novels, one of which, *Armstrong*, was published in 1973. He has also written a number of books about Greece, including this volume and a Greek-English/English-Greek Dictionary and Phrasebook also published by Hippocrene Books.

His two children, Samantha and Oliver, were born while he and their mother, the French painter Florence Messager, had a house on the island of Patmos. They subsequently graduated from high school in Thessaloniki, and are currently completing their higher education in the United States.

ILOCANO-ENGLISH/ENGLISH-ILOCANO DICTIONARY AND PHRASEBOOK
174 pages—5 x 8—0-7818-0642-9—#11.95pb—(718)

IRISH-ENGLSIH/ENGLISH-IRISH DICTIONARY AND PHRASEBOOK
160 pages—3 ¾ x 7—1,400 entries/phrases—0-87052-110-1—NA—#7.95pb—(385)

LINGALA-ENGLISH/ENGLISH-LINGALA DICTIONARY AND PHRASEBOOK
120 pages—3 ¾ x 7—0-7818-0456-6—W—#11.95pb—(296)

MALTESE-ENGLISH/ENGLISH-MALTESE DICTIONARY AND PHRASEBOOK
175 pages—3 ¾ x 7—1,500 entries—0-7818-0565-1—W—#11.95pb—(697)

POLISH DICTIONARY AND PHRASEBOOK
252 pages—5 ½ x 8 ½—0-7818-0134-6—W—#11.95pb—(192)
Cassettes—   Vol. I: 0-7818-0340-3—W—$12.95—(492)
**   Vol. II: 0-7818-0384-5—W—$12.95—(486)**

RUSSIAN DICTIONARY AND PHRASEBOOK,
Revised
256 pages—5 ½ x 8 ½—3,000 entries—0-7818-0190-7—W—$9.95pb—(597)

SLOVAK-ENGLISH/ENGLISH-SLOVAK DICTIONARY AND PHRASEBOOK
180 pages—3 ¾ x 7—1,300 entries—0-7818-0663-1—W—$13.95pb—(754)

All prices subject to change without prior notice.
To order Hippocrene Books, contact your local bookstore, call (718) 454-2366, or write to: Hippocrene Books, 171 Madison Ave. New York, NY 10016. Please enclose check or money order adding $5.00 shipping (UPS) for the first book and $.50 for each additional title.